MW00489394

SABER'S EDGE

SABER'S EDGE

A Combat Medic in Ramadi, Iraq

Thomas A. Middleton

UNIVERSITY PRESS OF NEW ENGLAND Hanover & London

To Matt,

From one firefighter to a brother. Thank you for your service to our community. May the Good Lord bless & keep you safe in all of life's travels.

D a Middleton

Published by University Press of New England,
One Court Street, Lebanon, NH 03766
www.upne.com

© 2009 by University Press of New England

Printed in the United States of America
5 4 3 2 1

Library of Congress Cataloging-in-Publication Data
Middleton, Thomas A.

Saber's edge : a combat medic in Ramadi, Iraq / Thomas A.
Middleton
p. cm.
Includes index.
ISBN 978-1-58465-747-7 (cloth : alk. paper)
1. Middleton, Thomas A.   2. Iraq War, 2003—Campaigns—
Iraq—Ramadi.   3. Ramadi (Iraq)—History, Military—21st
century.   4. Iraq War, 2003—Personal narratives, American.
5. United States. Army—Medical personnel—Biography.
6. Iraq War, 2003—Medical care.   7. Burlington (Vt.)—
Biography.   I. Title.
DS79.766.R36M53   2009
956.7044'37—dc22
[B]   2009007656

University Press of New England is a member of the Green Press Initiative. The
paper used in this book meets their minimum requirement for recycled paper

CONTENTS

PROLOGUE

I was resting upstairs on the morning of September 11, 2001. I remember my wife yelling up the stairs that we had been attacked. We watched the television together in horror as the second tower came down. The sound of the firefighters' pass devices of the Fire Department of New York (FDNY) were familiar to me, and they were deafening—the same automated distress devices used by my own fire department—hundreds of them, coming over the television as background noise, the newscasters unaware of their significance, but positively bone chilling to a firefighter like me. I did not know yet how many of my brothers had just died, but I knew it was a lot.

Across America, our nation reeled from the attack. It was a terrible day—but it also brought out the absolute best in people. While the previously little known Osama Bin Laden and his Al Qaeda terrorist network had just caused the greatest loss of life in recent history, the FDNY orchestrated the single largest rescue in the history of the American Fire Service.

Intuitively, I knew that our world had changed—that our nation would ask a lot of our firefighters. But to mete out vengeance? In my lifetime I fought death at every turn. I could accept the distant concept of killing in the cause of a just war, but I could not fathom taking joy in death.

In mourning my brothers, I hoped the terrorists later identified as Al Qaeda would be caught and punished.

I was a firefighter called to war. I served as a combat medic in the worst place on earth. This is my story, but in it are the lives and stories of others. It is with the deepest regard and respect that I remember our actions in theater and the sacrifices that our troops made there.

Sergeant First Class Christopher Chapin
Staff Sergeant Ryan Ostrom
Specialist William Evans
First Lieutenant Mark Dooley
Sergeant Michael Egan
Specialist William Fernandez
Specialist Scott McLaughlin
Staff Sergeant George Pugliese
Staff Sergeant Daniel Arnold
Sergeant Erik Slebodnik
Specialist Lee Wiegand
Specialist Oliver Brown
First Lieutenant Mark Procopio
Sergeant Joshua Johnson
Specialist Christopher Scott Merchant
Sergeant Joseph Proctor
Captain Brian Letendre
Captain Gordon Lewis
May they rest in peace

• • •

SABER'S EDGE

Mobilization

I was working at my desk in the Fire Marshal's Office one afternoon in June 2004 when the phone rang. "Fire Marshal's Office, Middleton," I answered.

Interruptions like this drove me crazy. Working an office job at the firehouse, I no longer felt like a firefighter. I walked past the big red trucks in the morning and listened to the guys talk about their adventures over morning coffee, but I no longer felt like one of them. When I was a line firefighter, I lived their life of derring-do, solving problems by spraying large volumes of water at them . . . now I issued code violations and taught kids to stop, drop, and roll.

I'd been a career firefighter in Burlington, Vermont, for ten years before I transferred to my new job as the assistant fire marshal. I still enjoyed the camaraderie in the firehouse, but I sorely missed the satisfaction of saving lives and the challenge of rushing into a nice hot blaze and knocking it down. Pulling people back from the brink of death or delivering babies into the world were some of the most rewarding things a man could do. Now I had to find satisfaction in testing smoke detectors.

"Sergeant Middleton, the brigade just went on alert." I was about to get back into the lifesaving business. The rumors had been flying for months that my National Guard unit would mobilize, and finally it was happening. I often joked that my unit was so far down the list for mobilization that the Boy Scouts would be called up before they got to us. No one ever anticipated that we would be sent to fight in the worst, most violent place on earth, Ramadi, Iraq.

Although I worked in fire prevention, I was still a firefighter when needed—I just didn't feel like one. It had been three years since I had fought a real fire, a three-alarm blaze that destroyed a historic former

National Guard armory that was now home to a nightclub known as Sha Na Na's. It had been a cold Friday morning in November, and I was at the station, loading up my truck and heading out to an elementary school when the call came in.

"Engines 1, 2, 3, Tower 1, Rescue 1, Car 12, respond to a reported structure fire at Sha Na Na's, 101 Main Street, cross streets are Pine to St Paul, time out 0908, KCB999."

I tossed the last of my stuff in the back of my SUV and pulled out into the rush-hour traffic, heading north for the elementary school, gritting my teeth like a caged beast while my brothers ran for the trucks.

"All responding units, we are receiving multiple calls, reporting flames visible from the roof." The tone in the dispatcher's voice told me this was a real fire.

"To hell with teaching," I thought to myself, as I whipped the truck around behind Engine 2, and stepped on it.

I pulled up at the fire right behind the first arriving units, and got my firefighting gear on. I went to the incident commander with an airpack on my back, hoping to fight fire, but expecting him to ask me to deal with the news media. I waited for a moment with him while the initial reports came over the radio from the first units in the building. I couldn't believe what I heard next.

"Command from Engine 1, we are on the second floor in the office spaces, and people are still working in them. We are sending them out now. The area is clear."

While flames raged above their heads, the office staff was completely unaware. The fire was above the reach of the sprinkler system and there were no smoke detectors in the unoccupied space in the attic. "Command from Engine 1, we poked through the ceiling, and there is heavy fire in the attic. We broke open a sprinkler head, but it is beneath the fire. We're getting soaked and we need to open the roof! Can someone shut down the sprinkler system?"

"Find the sprinkler valve and turn it off, then get up on the roof with a chainsaw and help Tower 1 open the roof," Battalion Chief Michael Richard said to me. "I need a trench cut, or we're going to lose the building!"

Using an axe to break through the glass doors, I went into the basement, where Sha Na Na's was located. The club was known for its great rock 'n roll and its 1950s theme. It held over three hundred people and the popular club had been a big part of Burlington nightlife for a very long time. I had brought my wife here on our first date several years earlier. With a huge fire roaring through the attic two floors above, I was struck by how normal everything was in the club. There was no smoke, no flames, and no water. The only thing betraying the presence of the fire above was the now-activated fire alarm. I went to the sprinkler valve, closed it, and headed out. I could have stopped for a beer and played a game of pool—conditions were that normal.

I went up on the roof and reported in to Captain Leroy Spiller. The wind whipping in through the soffit vents was pushing flames throughout the cavernous spaces, burning the heavy timber roof supports. Cutting a trench was our only chance to save this building, as it would allow the heat and flames to vent up to the atmosphere rather throughout the building. It was a technique I had only used a few times over the years, mostly in my earlier days as a volunteer firefighter back home, fighting barn fires in the North Country.

In this case, the trench cut worked, but the fire had already burned past us, and we had to move down the roof and start over. Intense flames shot out of the huge holes we cut, thick black smoke darkening the sky above us on this bright sunny morning. A huge wall of flame roared over our heads.

We cut again, and then again. Each thirty-foot cut required two to three chainsaws and about twelve firefighters working with pry bars and pike poles. We cut enormous rectangles out of the roof and then pried the sections up and out of the way. Intense heat, smoke, and flames blew out of these new holes. We leaned into them, thrusting with our pike poles to knock out the interior ceiling below us and allow all the heat and fire out from below.

This historic brick and heavy-timber building was solid, and cutting through the roof was no easy task. The gusting wind whipped into the attic space through the vents and fanned the intense flames—adding more oxygen to the fire and blowing out of the trenches we cut. After the first two cuts, Captain Spiller had us move down the roof. We gave up trying to save the parts of the building that were already on fire in order to save the unburned parts, hoping we could get ahead of the fire's advance. We were halfway through this last cut when Battalion Chief Richard suspected the roof was no longer safe to stand on and ordered us off it. Reluctantly, the captain told everyone to start heading down the ladder. One by one our brothers climbed down, while the captain and I drove on, determined to finish this one last cut before our turn on the ladder came. Finally, with flames blowing out of the hole we cut, our faces blackened by the smoke, lungs choking, we finished the last cut and our mission was complete. We headed down the aerial ladder. There on the ground at the bottom, I spotted a photographer I knew from the Associated Press. Our photo made front-page news the next morning.

Our handiwork lit up the sky behind us. It was a spectacular photograph. To the untrained eye, it looked as if we had just lost the building. We knew better. Because we could not get into the attic space to fight the fire, our ventilating the attic allowed the heat and flames to escape into the sky rather than consume the rest of the building. Ideally, we would then find a way to attack the fire from below or at least from one end— but not in this case. The incident commander feared that the roof might collapse, so he ordered everyone out of the building. With no alternative, he ordered a defensive attack—a "surround and drown" tactic, where we used aerial ladders with huge master streams to drown the building from above. The trouble was, each of these master streams flowed a thousand gallons of water per minute, and destroyed everything in their path. The water went in through the newly created vent holes, preventing the fire from escaping, and it forced the fire down into the rest of the building.

The impact of so much water destroyed the interior walls and much of the building, but the basic structure was saved, and it would one day be rebuilt.

• • •

I dreamt about becoming a firefighter since I was five years old, growing up in the small town of Chazy, New York, watching the volunteer firefighters race through town with their lights flashing, stomping flames and saving lives. By the time I was a senior in high school, our volunteer fire department was desperately short of emergency medical technicians (EMTs) and the aging captain of rescue asked me to serve. My first call was late one December night, and it was a barn fire. I was now an EMT, but I didn't yet know a thing about fighting fire. I went to the fire and had a great time spraying water. My first ambulance call was the next morning. I was hooked, and from that moment on I committed to both firefighting and emergency medical service. I remember feeling that saving lives was the single most rewarding thing I had ever done, while knocking down a hot blaze was the biggest sense of accomplishment I had ever experienced. In a way, these twin roles of healer and firefighter foreshadowed my later dual roles as a medic and a soldier.

• • •

I joined the Army Reserve shortly after my seventeenth birthday, wanting to do my patriotic duty in case of war. The prospect of wasting away in an active duty, garrison army never appealed to me, but I felt a duty to serve my country, so developing my nursing skills as a medic in an Army Reserve field hospital was perfect. Seven years later, I was hired as a career firefighter, and I moved to Vermont. I transferred to an armor unit of the National Guard, where I learned about the combat arms side of the Army.

I was blessed to land a job doing what I loved just across the lake from New York in Burlington Vermont. As a young career firefighter with a busy engine company, I thrived on the excitement and challenges of my civilian career. We didn't just train to face danger and save lives, we did it every day. When I wasn't going to college to become a nurse, I loved to spend my weekends in the woods, whether training for war with the National Guard or hunting deer on my own—I was away from the stress of everyday life. I found the perfect combination of tranquility, excitement, and solitude out there. I became an excellent marksman—honing my vestigial predator stalking whitetails in the remote mountains of New York's Adirondack wilderness.

As other Vermont units mobilized before us, I volunteered for many weeks of temporary active duty, working at Camp Johnson, near Burlington, helping with medical screenings. Even though the Fire Marshal's Office was stretched thin in my absence, my brothers never once complained about the added workload my numerous weeklong absences caused them.

Finally, after we had spent months in limbo, the word came down just before Christmas. We were activated January 19, 2005, and we would spend the next eighteen months away from home. After six months of alert status—wondering when the mobilization would happen—the announcement came almost as a relief. At least now we had a known date, and we could begin making concrete plans for our loved ones left behind.

My family took the news as well as anyone could expect. No one wanted to lose a husband or father, even if only for eighteen months. My wife and I had three children together, plus two from her first marriage. She was a strong woman, and steadfast in her patriotism. She had been a single mother of two boys for six years before I came into her life, and she knew how to handle it. She was not looking forward to being alone with our large family, and she was worried about me, but outwardly she was unshakable. It was only in our private moments that her worry would show.

Most of the men in my family had served in the military at one time or another. My father was a World War II Navy veteran, and my uncle began as a naval corpsman before Pearl Harbor, served aboard the USS *New York* in the North Atlantic, and was later a lieutenant during the Korean War. Both students of history and political science in high school, my brother Frank and I enlisted as medics in the Army Reserve during the cold war, never dreaming in a million years that one of us might someday be called up. Both of us left behind the study of politics once we became medics. Frank went on to become a neuroscientist, and I a firefighter. We had grown to despise partisan bickering, but found great satisfaction in helping and accepting others, regardless of their race, gender, or political affiliation. Through our conservative Catholic upbringing, my parents instilled in us a tremendous respect for the sanctity of human life. To view other people primarily through the prism of their political affiliation ran counter to this view.

It was unbearably cold the day we left. Vermont gets very cold in the winter, but in spite of the weather, I think most of our 800,000 residents were there at the ceremony. In spite of the state's liberal leanings and the misgivings that many Vermonters had about the war, everyone, it seemed, supported the troops.

I will never forget the bitter cold wind whipping at my face as I marched single file across the runway at Burlington International Airport, to climb the long stairs to the waiting charter jet—such a stark contrast to the blistering heat and sandstorms that awaited us half a world away.

CAMP SHELBY, MISSISSIPPI

We arrived in sunny Camp Shelby, Mississippi, to begin five and a half long months of training before shipping out to Iraq. It seemed unseasonably warm to us with midwinter temperatures in the forties.

We were blessed with good weather to train in for the most part, except when it rained. Being wet in forty degree temperatures all day long was a lot worse than being out in the snow.

The training was supposed to be the best the Army had to offer. At least they tried to reflect real-world conditions in Iraq and Afghanistan as best they could—in the thick woods of the Mississippi pine belt. Camp Shelby has been a National Guard training center and a mobilization center for deploying National Guard and Reserve troops since the early twentieth century. The majority of the buildings were constructed decades ago, and were in various stages of disrepair. Most of the barracks were made of cinder block and concrete, but at least they were heated and air conditioned, the latrines functioned, and the Mississippi weather was much better to train in than winter in New England. Our forefathers in previous wars had it a lot worse than we did.

Many of the instructors were veterans of the current war, and the Army brought in real Iraqis by the planeload to act as the opposition during our mock battles. It was the best they could do, and to an extent, it did prepare us. However, nothing in Mississippi could fully prepare us for the real thing.

If there is one suggestion that I can make for future units, it is this: train as you will fight. If it is necessary for all the medics to get three weeks more training than the rest of the troops, fine. Mobilize them early and conduct the training before the rest of the troops arrive. Integrate the squad medics into the squad's battle drills so that everyone knows what to expect from Doc, and Doc knows how to shoot, move, and communicate just like everyone else.

In Camp Shelby, our medics were assembled together in one platoon, and we were supposed to train together on medical skills, and then be tasked out as needed to the infantry or armor. In truth, however, most National Guard and Reserve medics seldom get much medical training. As units were activated before us, many of the medics were found to be lacking in the fundamentals. Our medical platoon was a little better than most, or so our instructors told us, as many of our medics were involved with civilian emergency medical services (EMS). Vermont being a rural state, almost every town had a volunteer rescue squad, where many of our medics served their hometowns before serving our nation in this war. After twenty years as a firefighter and provider, I had gone on to become a registered nurse, and worked part time in an emergency department. Two of my fellow medics were also registered nurses, three were civilian paramedics, and our platoon sergeant was an operating room technician. Ironically, though the Army helped me become a nurse, the Army denied me a commission. My sensitivity to latex caused me to fail the physical. Our Vermonters needed combat medics, though, and I answered the call.

Most of the training at Camp Shelby focused on basic combat skills, and built basic individual skills into intense battle drills. The Army expected every soldier to be proficient in the basic soldier skills, but the medics missed three weeks of battle-focused training while we attended a medical refresher course. Later on, we joined the platoons we would go into battle with, but we were not part of the platoons while they got to know each other and learned to function as a group. Unfortunately, no one really thought about how best to employ old Doc.

Unlike the medics of yesteryear, we no longer wore red crosses, and today's medics carry weapons. Historically, the Army placed the medic in the same category as the medical officer—that of noncombatant. History taught us, though, that the enemy did not always respect the Geneva Convention, and in some cases, he would specifically target old Doc. The Geneva Convention provides protection to noncombatant chaplains and to medical officers who clearly identify themselves. It would be unethical for us to wear the red crosses while still carrying a rifle and fighting offensively—we would be dishonestly claiming protection as noncombatants. During previous wars, the combat medic was either unarmed or carried only a pistol. The .45-caliber Colt model 1911 became a hallmark weapon, carried by officers and medics. The pistol was only effective at short range, and was really designed to be used only in defense of one's self or one's patients. It was not accurate enough to knock down targets at longer distance, so there was little chance of a pistol-packing medic leading a charge toward the enemy. During the Vietnam War, many combat medics realized that their enemy did not always respect the covenants of the Geneva Convention and would kill a medic as quickly as an infantryman. Some of the enemy even figured out that if the medic was wounded or killed, the rest of the troops might be less willing to fight— figuring that no one was left to patch up their wounds. Current interpretation of Army doctrine called for each medic to carry one primary weapon (whether a pistol or a rifle) and possibly a secondary weapon as well. The rifle was more valuable most of the time, but the pistol was better in close quarters or when the medic was busy working on a casualty. It was always ready in the holster—even when the medic's hands were busy with other tasks—and it could be drawn, aimed, and fired more quickly when reacting to a surprise attack at short range. Today's medics were prepared to fight when needed, and I was looking forward to it. I am not sure that everyone had quite embraced the concept of soldier-medics yet, but gunfighters we would prove to be.

The first two weeks of Camp Shelby's medical transition course consisted of a civilian basic EMT refresher course. For the soldier-medic who was not active in the local rescue squad, it was a good review of the basic skills practiced in the civilian setting. For the majority of us, however, it was a waste of valuable time and did not do justice to the more advanced skills that would make a difference in the lives of soldiers on the battlefield. For many of us, our clinical skills were quite good in the civilian setting, but we needed battle focus to place our skills in a different context. Sadly, it was only during the final three days of medical training that we finally got some battle focus. At that point, the medical trainers conducted intense simulated battles where we had to treat and evacuate simulated casualties. It was great training, but conducted in isolation, without the actual infantry squads with which we would later fight.

At some point in the late 1980s/early 1990s, the Army Medical Corps realized a weakness in continuing education and embraced a readily available source of external validation for the combat medic—certification as an EMT. Being a basic EMT is good insofar as it helps maintain basic proficiency and familiarity with the current clinical practice in civilian emergency medical services, but the basic EMT does not practice advanced trauma techniques. In the civilian setting, there is a lot more focus on medical emergencies common to the elderly, and except in the inner cities afflicted with gang warfare, there is a lot less penetrating trauma. Advanced trauma skills are reserved for paramedics or emergency physicians—and even they don't practice them frequently.

By contrast, the Army medic typically works with a younger and healthier population of soldiers, where medical emergencies such as heart attacks and strokes are uncommon. On the battlefield, however, advanced trauma skills can be the difference between life and death. The combat medic is trained by the Army in such techniques as needle decompression of a pneumothorax (used for treating a collapsed lung), intraosseous infusions (infusing fluid via bone marrow when unable to start an intravenous line), cricothyrotomy (an emergency surgical airway through an incision in the neck), or field-expedient blood transfusions. While this training is provided in the initial combat medic school at Fort Sam Houston, Texas, these skills are rarely practiced in peacetime, and our level of proficiency suffers as a result.

So much of the training at Camp Shelby seemed geared toward pushing us through that we sarcastically came to refer to the place as "Camp Check the Box." The individual skills stations that took only one small part of soldiering (known as common task training) and beat it into us were the worst. Many of the instructors were so tired of the repetition that their boredom became palpable.

On a positive note, Camp Shelby had mock Iraqi villages and forward operating bases. There were convoy routes and ambushes. The idea was total immersion in the simulated battlefield. The real Iraqi citizens the Army brought in role-played as insurgents, innocent bystanders, and angry mobs. Sometimes they played their roles a little too convincingly. In a few cases, the actors even got into fistfights with our soldiers. That our guys would give in to their taunting speaks to the effectiveness of the simulation.

Unfortunately, our infantry squads trained on infantry tactics without their medics, and we were only added in later as an afterthought. As a result, when the medics were finally assigned to the infantry, the men didn't know what we were capable of or how to integrate us into their tactics.

Personally, I got the most out of the infantry squad lanes. A lane is the Army's way of describing a training event. In this lane, we took all the individual combat skills and practiced them together as teams, assaulting villages full of insurgents, confronting angry mobs, searching and clearing houses, and living as if we were really fighting in Iraq for a week straight. Later on we would take up residence in a mock forward operating base and do much the same thing, but at least with the infantry squad lanes, everyone was infantry—fighting as if our lives depended on it.

I was assigned to play the role of line medic with our maintenance platoon. Ironically, the maintenance guys don't normally get their own medic, as their job is back on the base, fixing the vehicles that the armor and infantry take into battle. However, we were being bombarded with stories from Iraq about how every type of soldier imaginable was being pressed into service as an infantryman. We still did not know if we would even be using our tanks, or if we would all be out there kicking in doors.

All the mechanics took the training very seriously, and I felt pretty good about them if we went into battle together. In the end, though, except for their recovery section (essentially operating tow trucks for tanks), most of them worked in the motor pool in Iraq. With three medics all tagging along for this training, however, I switched to work as an infantryman—just like I would later do in combat.

There were some highlights to the training experience at Camp Shelby that I remember fondly. Nearby, Hattiesburg was a fun place. When we reached a certain point in our training, we were allowed to go out on the town. Most of our guys had a pretty good time in this college town, home to the University of Southern Mississippi and plenty of beautiful southern belles.

In my case, I found relief in more intellectual pursuits. While the Army was doing nothing to hone my trauma nursing skills, I learned that Forrest General Hospital was conducting a trauma nursing course in Hattiesburg (known as the TNCC course). My part-time job as an emergency room (ER) nurse back home required me to maintain TNCC certification. I needed some mental stimulation, so I enrolled in their refresher course. In retrospect, it seems silly to be concerned with maintaining my civilian credentials while prepping for war, but for me it made sense. The training provided by the Army was mind numbing. I needed to be sharp. In addition to the TNCC course, I also completed a distance-learning course in expository writing through Louisiana State University. I bought all of the textbooks I would need to complete other coursework as well. At the time, I did not know how much my role would shift from that of nurse to combat medic with the infantry. I was planning on working in the treatment section at the time, so it made sense to hone my trauma nursing skills. I planned to pursue a second career in nursing, so I worked toward my bachelor's degree. At the time, I still didn't realize that our battalion aid station would not be seeing trauma patients since we would be located on the same forward operating base as a field hospital.

After I got to know the staff at Forrest General Hospital, they let us borrow their facilities to conduct our own training. I put together a group of medics and we taught a combat lifesaver course for our soldiers. With almost all of our soldiers trained as combat lifesavers (combat troops with advanced medical training), our troops were as prepared as we could make them for surviving injuries on the battlefield.

When our task force formed, it became a melting pot of troops from across Vermont. When we later arrived in Ramadi, we became part of the 2nd Brigade Combat Team, 28th Infantry Division of the Pennsylvania National Guard (the 2/28th for short). Two Pennsylvania companies, an infantry company (D/149) from the Kentucky National Guard, a Marine Dam service unit (operating patrol boats on the Euphrates River), and two battalions of Iraqi Army would eventually be attached to our battalion of Vermonters.

Just as it had during other rough times in my life, the church became my refuge. At home, I would almost always attend church, but in times of trouble, my faith seemed to be so much more than just a momentary disconnect, it was a source of spiritual strength that would carry me through. I went to Mass regularly, and it was at Camp Shelby that I became an extraordinary minister of the Eucharist, more commonly called a eucharistic minister or a Catholic representative. In most of the United States, the eucharistic minister's role is limited to helping the priest distribute Holy Communion. There are eucharistic ministers at most of the masses in my home parish and they distribute Holy Communion to part of the congregation. As helpers, they do not replace the priest.

I had been a church organist as a teenager, and served as an altar boy before that. As an adult and a parent, I found a way to get my kids interested in going to church by getting involved with the folk group in our parish. But it was in wartime that the music ministry and my spiritual development really took hold.

The real highlight of my stay in Mississippi was not the training, going out on the town, or even the spiritual growth that I experienced there. It was the strengthening of my marriage with Lisa. In my absence, she was caring for our three young children and holding down a job. I came to appreciate her as never before while we were apart. But she really showed me how much she loved me when on a whim she flew all the way to Mississippi to be with me for a weekend. In all, she made three separate trips, and on Easter weekend, she even brought the children. We had such a great time together on those few precious days together, I would remember them fondly for the next year.

When our training was finally over, we were given ten days of leave before we shipped out. For ten wonderful days, we were reunited as a family, living in the moment and forgetting about the future. We went to the Magic Kingdom at Disney World for a week, and had the time of our lives together. It was a great vacation, and we all cherished the memories we created there.

Eventually it was over, and the time came to ship out for war. There would be no more stalling—this time I was heading for Iraq. My youngest son was only three and he was used to having me around again. He didn't really understand that it was time to say goodbye when they dropped me off at the airport. I still remember him playing blissfully with his trucks while Lisa and I tearfully parted. It was not until I was walking away to the plane that he realized I was leaving for good, and he burst into tears.

SOMEWHERE OVER THE ATLANTIC

Pain. From somewhere in my foggy sleeping brain, something hurt. I didn't want to wake up—slumber was normally a welcome relief—but the ache steadily got worse. Slowly I stirred, foggy eyes struggling to make sense of the seat back in front of me, ears reregistering the constant high-pitched whine of the jet engines. The vague ache materialized into the side of my neck, and I realized I had fallen asleep and my head had fallen over to one side. I must have been tired, because it felt like I had been stuck in this position for an eternity.

Reality slowly returned. My family was nowhere around, so I must not be at home, and no one was cracking jokes, so I must not be at the firehouse. I was flying in a cramped seat, on a very long flight. My foggy eyes looked down and saw an unfamiliar camouflage pattern . . . and I remembered—I was flying to Iraq, and I was once again a soldier, wearing brand-new army combat uniform with a new and still unfamiliar camouflage pattern.

The air on the plane felt stale and heavy, with so many guys all crammed into such a small space. It didn't matter. Nothing much mattered, just the mission before us. We were not put here to have a good time, I reminded myself, but to be tested. God doesn't give us tests that we can't pass, and he must have figured I could handle whatever was going to happen.

I thought back to the fires I raced off to so often in my life. It never mattered how tired or hungry or preoccupied I was. Somehow, when the alarm sounded, we all managed to focus on the job at hand. The aches and pains from before the fire always disappeared, only to be replaced with new ones after the fire. There were the burns, not bad ones, of course, but enough to know it hurt. There was the smoke, burning my eyes and lungs, sometimes vomiting. I didn't mind the aches and pains after the fires, either. They just reminded me how hard we worked to do some good for people—and how, hopefully, I had atoned for some of my sins in the process.

. . . We landed in Kuwait City at around four in the afternoon, local time. The crisp uniform and well-rehearsed speech of the flight attendant felt out of place in this foreign land. She was gracious and kind, escorting us on our journey to who knows where, no doubt aware that some of us would not be coming home alive. I rounded the corner at the head of the cabin and noticed the pins she wore, pledging her support for the troops she ferried. Her words were rehearsed and steady, but her eyes could not lie to us—she knew something.

The stale cabin air vanished; a scalding blast furnace took its place as I got off the plane. Great, I thought, at least now I get to replace the constant wear and tear of this mission with fresh hot misery. I was getting bored with the old pains anyway, and as long as I had to suffer, it might as well be interesting.

Nothing really bothered me that much. It just didn't matter much. We had all become machines to a point, forgetting for a time our roles as husbands, fathers, and regular Joes and assuming the yoke of steady oxen, embarking on a huge task ahead with only the steady pace of the next footfall in mind.

We got our duffel bags off the plane and boarded buses. What freaky little islands these buses were. Outside, the white-hot fury of the desert sun baked us while a million tiny chisels borne by the wind carved our features into resolute masks. Inside these impeccably clean, air-conditioned buses, comfort reigned supreme . . . the steady drone of the big diesel engine a welcome change from the high-pitched whine of the jet engines.

We had been travelling for over twenty-four hours when our buses somehow found an isolated compound out in the desert. Camp Buehring was about as far from anywhere as you could get. The temporary buildings and cargo containers there seemed only brief tenants in a vast timeless desert. The sand blew unimpeded through the razor wire. Our boots sank into the sand as we walked, while sweat became our only relief.

A halo encircled each light in the night sky. The constant sand flying through the air obscured them like streetlights in a Vermont snowstorm, giving a false sense of civilized safety here amidst the sand. . . .

At dawn we traveled for live fire training to the remote Udari Firing Range. Set apart only by the presence of small wooden target frames staked into the sand at regular intervals, this area of desert sand looked much like the rest.

Perhaps they knew we were coming, or perhaps our fire drew them, but much to our surprise, several Bedouin nomads appeared out of nowhere. Seemingly lifted from the pages of a history book, they walked out of the desert in their traditional robes and watched us shoot our weapons.

In our world back home, our live fire ranges were high-security places, with very strict discipline and tightly controlled access. There was no way anyone could approach our firing line. Back in the United States, we picked up every one of our empty shell casings and turned them in. Out here, these nomads were apparently so poor they were willing to sit around in the hot sun all day in order to pick up our brass when we were done shooting.

While it was possible they were Iraqi spies, realistically, they were not a threat, sitting there unarmed while we carried enough weapons and ammunition to take down a small country. Our military superiority was obvious, but somehow I knew that they would be here long after we left.

• • •

These remote transitory outposts were not happy places. Many of the troops were combat-support troops from a wide variety of units who were thrust into ill-fitting roles as provisional MPs or makeshift infantry. The trouble was, they had practically no enemy contact, and often the units to which they were attached did not take care of them. For the troops deployed here, Camp Buehring became their prison. The troops stationed here were separated from their families and subject to the desert conditions like the rest of us. Unfortunately for them, they never got the chance to take their frustrations out on the enemy. In retrospect, I am glad I was sent to Ramadi. Dealing with the challenges that these combat-support troops faced would have driven me nuts. To their credit, most of these men and women suffered quietly and did everything they could to help us out.

A lot of the combat veterans who saw action in Ramadi scoffed at the thought of troops who never saw combat suffering from PTSD. I, for one, felt empathy for them. They didn't ask to be assigned to the rear areas or placed into the ill-fitting roles for which they were poorly prepared. Troops who were really medics, cooks, and clerks found themselves pulling guard duty in desolate misery, facing an empty desert from which their enemy never materialized. All the while, they were confined to base and forbidden to visit the very cities in Kuwait they protected. It is no wonder they grew disillusioned.

Into the Fiery Sands of War

Our days in Kuwait drew to a close and we prepared for our unit's first combat mission since the South Pacific islands campaign of World War II. Most of our troops flew into Iraq in a cargo plane, and then transferred to helicopters for the final leg of the journey. I tend to get airsick and I actually like driving, so I volunteered to go on the convoy. Our medical platoon used an up-armored five-ton truck that we outfitted as a mass casualty ambulance. My good friend Lt. Gunn rode shotgun while I drove. The lieutenant was a physician's assistant and a former marine. Big as an ox, and usually munching a wad of chew, he was perfect for this mission. Since we were technically an ambulance, we didn't have a .50-caliber machine gun on our roof like most of the other vehicles, so we got to close our gunner's hatch and enjoy the air conditioning. As we prepared to move out, we loaded ammunition into our magazines. Just before our convoy headed out for Iraq, I paused for a moment as I chambered the first round. I wondered if I would have to use it, and still naively hoped I could go home without firing a shot.

Most of our medics stayed behind in Kuwait when we pulled out. It was strange that a third of our platoon was prepping for battle while the rest were still playing cards and watching DVDs. They would fly in later that week in a relatively safe C-130. The quiet acceptance that I had felt all along was fading just a little. I knew that being nervous was natural, and I just had to drive the truck. I called home and said good-bye to my wife without revealing that we were heading into Iraq and harm's way. Intuitively, she knew that could have been our last conversation. I did not fear death, but I could feel the pain it would cause my family. I could not bear the thought of her having to tell the kids if the worst should happen.

The first thing that struck me on the Iraqi side of the border was all the bombed-out houses with families living in them. The area was a vast, desolate wasteland, struggling in the throes of recovery from the effects of two wars. I couldn't fathom what would possess these families to live here, except that perhaps they had nowhere else to go. There were homes with the roofs blown off, entire families living in tattered make-shift tents. During the first Gulf War, Saddam's Iraqi Army fled Kuwait through this area. The allied onslaught pummeled them as they retreated. Thousands of Iraqi soldiers, tanks, and other vehicles fled through this area and our aircraft destroyed them. All these years later, the remnants of old Soviet-made Iraqi tanks still rusted away in the desert.

Amidst the battered ruins they called homes, surrounded by a dry, barren wasteland in which no crops could grow, children blissfully played. There in the middle of it all, undaunted, were the most adorable Iraqi children, racing out to greet us. I took pictures of many of them, and waved to them all. They were so happy to see us, with huge smiles on their faces and cheerful waves. I wanted so much to give them food or water or hugs in return for the warmth they gladly shared with us. I had been apprehensive about entering Iraq until then, but after seeing those happy children, I felt very much at ease. Children are amazing. They truly are a gift from God.

FIRST CONTACT

We drove on a divided highway through the night, and by morning we had made it halfway across the country. We pulled into Camp Scania, not far from Baghdad, and we stopped to rest. I thought this was to be another short rest halt while we fueled up, and didn't know that we were going to be here all day. My back ached, so I left the lieutenant in the cab with the air conditioning on, and I climbed into the back of our truck to stretch out. The cool of the fresh morning air was exquisite . . . and soon both of us were fast asleep.

I woke up six hours later, roasting in the hot sun, soaked in sweat and feeling terrible. We went to chow and I forced down some dinner and as much Gatorade as I could, but it didn't help much. Nightfall came and I asked Lt. Gunn to take over the driving. I just couldn't do it anymore. I sat there in the darkened cab, riding down Route Mobile (a main high-way across Iraq) with an IV in my arm. Eventually I started to feel a little better, but I was so incredibly tired, I just wanted to sleep. I drifted off and slept fitfully, wondering how much use I would be to a casualty in

The children in Ramadi were incredibly resilient in the face of constant dangers. (Photo by Sgt Brandon Allmond)

my condition. Every bump we hit crept into my sleeping mind. This was not rest—it was torture.

"BOOM!!!!!"

"Holy crap!!" Lieutenant hollered, "Did you see that?" The lieutenant hollered again, "We just got hit, dude! That was an IED at three o'clock! One hundred yards!"

"Say what?" I asked—annoyed that something woke me up.

"KaBOOM!!!" another brilliant flash of light, this one right in front of us—the desert seemed to leap into the air and descend upon us like a filthy burning avalanche. The road disappeared in front of us. Shrapnel, rocks, and dirt pounded our truck—the blast wave slammed into us—a gravel-laden tidal wave, cresting and breaking upon us. Our thick steel armor smashed the wave apart. Lieutenant stomped on the accelerator, charging blind through the clouds of dust, rocks, and shrapnel.

"Contact! IED, contact! IED," someone screamed over the radio. We were OK, but the humvee in front of us had a gunner standing in the hatch, and Sgt. Norris Pedulla riding in the back seat. One of B Troop's medics, Pedulla was a soldier's soldier. As passionate in caring for his men as he was ferocious in pursuit of the enemy, he had been Regular Army for several years and done a tour in Bosnia, and he and I were now heading into Ramadi together.

"Charlie Mike! Charlie Mike!" someone else hollered, meaning drive through it, and continue mission. It sounded like Sgt. Pedulla—maybe they were OK.

Eventually the vehicle in front of us came into view, intact, and reported no casualties. I looked over at the lieutenant, and he looked like a caged bull, ready to explode with fury. I took a deep breath and settled back into my seat. No one was hurt, and we weren't stopping. A few minutes later I found myself drifting back to sleep when Lieutenant looked over, incredulous, and asked how I could possibly sleep after an attack. It really wasn't a big deal. I didn't get out of my seat, so it didn't really feel like an attack.

RAMADI

Just before dawn we arrived at FOB Ramadi, exhausted from our trip. Slipping in under the cover of darkness, we could see very little of our surroundings . . . just a left turn across the median, off Route Mobile, and through the heavily defended "Trooper Gate."

There was a dirt berm surrounding the FOB, about twenty feet tall, and the dirt road into the FOB drove up and over the berm. There were concrete barriers, which formed a serpentine route, designed to slow down an oncoming VBIED (vehicle-borne improvised explosive device). Atop the outer dirt berm was the first guard post, consisting of towers on each side of the roadway, manned with .50-caliber machine guns. They were called "Trooper Recon." There was no barrier at the outer gate, but an attacker would have to drive through heavy fire from Trooper Recon to get past the berm. Just inside the berm was a very large parking area in which a convoy could coil up and wait for clearance through the inner gate. No one wanted to leave incoming convoys outside the gate as targets while the vehicles were first searched, then allowed through the inner Trooper Gate, one at a time. A huge armored vehicle blocked the only way into the FOB, and it acted as a gate. The gate guards would drive the track backwards out of the way to allow vehicles to pass, then drive it back across the opening between the concrete barriers afterwards.

A quick breakfast, and soon we were fast asleep in temporary quarters. The plywood shacks were known as SWA (South West Asia) huts. They were small and air conditioned—holding only six to eight men in

The US flag and Vermont battle flags wave over our headquarters at Fob Ramadi. The unit crests for each of the companies attached to our BN are attached. (Photo by SSG Sonny Durenleau)

each one—and they were a big step up from the huge tents we had had in Kuwait. The plywood did not offer much protection against shrapnel, though, so they were surrounded by huge "Hesco" barriers—essentially ten-foot high, two-foot thick cardboard boxes filled with dirt and wrapped in chain link fence.

We awoke later that day, still stiff and sore from the long ride. The base was dirty and dusty and hot, but it did not seem quite as hot as Kuwait. Maybe we were just getting used to it. Right after chow we shuffled off to our first intelligence briefing, welcoming us to our little corner of hell.

In the introductory briefing, we learned that there were two mortars fired at us during our trip here, and there were actually four IEDs. Two of the IEDs didn't detonate. The third IED was found and disabled before it could hurt anyone, and the fourth IED blast hit our convoy. Fortunately the mortars missed their target. I was grateful, because some of the IEDs were 155 mm artillery rounds, capable of destroying a tank. If one of them had hit a humvee, it would have been fatal. The mortars did not hit anything, but I do recall hearing two explosions and wondering what they were. We figured it was friendly artillery fire at the time, and no one paid much attention to them.

The briefing introduced us to our FOB—an old detention camp for Iranians captured during the Iran/Iraq War. We learned that Saddam used this place to torture and kill thousands, and that at one point U.S. forces had discovered a mass grave here. Main Supply Route (MSR) Mobile passed just to the north of the city of Ramadi. Our battalion's area of operations would be split by our FOB, and would include the areas to our north, south, and west. The Marines were responsible for the area directly across the Euphrates to our east—downtown Ramadi—while we were responsible for the MSR itself and points north. To the north, northeast, and northwest of our FOB was a mixed area of rural villages and farms. Most of the land there was irrigated and fertile—within a few kilometers of the Euphrates—but there were some isolated hamlets that rose out of nowhere in the middle of the desert.

The other way out of FOB Ramadi was called Ogden Gate, and it opened out onto a four-lane divided urban boulevard that we called Route Michigan. A left turn on Michigan led to a bridge over the Euphrates and downtown Ramadi. Across the road and to the right lay the Tameem District of Ramadi. A neighborhood directly across Route Michigan from our FOB had been military housing for Saddam's elite Republican Guard. When we invaded in 2003, the Iraqi Army didn't stand and fight, they just returned home in civilian clothes, taking their weapons with them. These men would later form the heart of the insurgency in our area.

Ramadi at the time was a violent and nasty place, with terrorists, insurgents, and people who didn't like us everywhere. Some were foreign-born terrorists who killed without regard and sought to achieve their goals through fear. Others were insurgents who simply resented our presence and fought against us. Local insurgents did not normally kill Iraqis. Before the 2003 invasion, Saddam Hussein's government employed many of the Sunnis in and around Ramadi. Things had fallen apart since then. There had been no garbage collection in years, so the trash just piled

An Iraqi farmhouse near the Euphrates River and MSR Mobile. With irrigation ditches and the ability to grow their own food, many families out in the countryside were far better off than their counterparts in the City. (Photo by author)

up beside the roads. Although there were municipal water and sewer pipes, most of the plumbing had not worked in years and raw sewage flowed through the streets. In the past, most of the men in Al Anbar Province were employed by Saddam's government in various civilian capacities. In order to have a government job, they had to join Saddam's Baath Party. When the U.S. interim government implemented a policy of de-Baathification and disbanded the Iraqi Army, the soldiers and government employees, who were accustomed to a higher standard of living, soon found themselves unemployed, broke, and hungry. With too much time on their hands and an interim U.S. government in power in Iraq, many of these discontented men took up arms and became hardcore insurgents. When they learned that they could earn $100 for killing an American, many of them tried to do so out of desperation to feed their families, not necessarily out of a desire to further radical Islam. We learned that the majority of the people in Al Anbar Province seemed indifferent to our presence and apathetic about their own predicament, but were willing to look the other way when the insurgents caused trouble.

This problem confounded itself when the insurgents destroyed much of their own industrial infrastructure, putting even more of the population out of work. The insurgents used legitimate businesses and factories to hide snipers and store weapons, often resulting in U.S. forces closing down those businesses. The U.S. Army's 1/9th Infantry Brigade Combat Team, 2nd Infantry Division, had seen a lot of casualties here, and the 1/9th predicted there would be a lot more in the coming year.

It was more humid here than in Kuwait, probably because the Euphrates River and Lake Habbaniyah were nearby. We saw photos of the irrigation ditches along both sides of the Euphrates, which supported crops and orchards and sustained the population. Beyond the relatively narrow strips of cropland on each side of the river, however, was just hot dry desert with villages here and there. The homes were mostly made of concrete—or something like it—and many of the roads were barely visible under the blowing, drifting sand.

Looking at satellite photos of the area, we saw how Ramadi straddled the Euphrates, with downtown on one side and the Tameem District on the other. To the west, Iraq's Great Western Desert stretched all the way out to Jordan.

The city of Ramadi was the capital of Al Anbar Province, and home to about 400,000 people. The Tameem District of Ramadi was considered the poorest, filthiest, and most violent part of the city. It was an L-shaped residential area of about 40,000 residents, wrapping its "L" around an industrial area adjacent to the campus of Al Anbar University. A set of abandoned railroad tracks passed along the top of a low ridgeline to the southeast, and the main road through town was Route Michigan, which stretched from the bridge to downtown Ramadi on the east through an arch at the western end of town. Route Michigan extended out into the Great Western Desert, paralleling MSR Mobile, which lay a few kilometers away, on the north side of our FOB and the city of Ramadi. Along the southern perimeter of our base was a part of the Tameem District known as 5K. It formed one leg of the "L" while the residential area that made up the other part was simply called "Tameem."

It was during this introductory briefing that I realized we had nowhere near enough combat power to effectively control all the territory assigned to us. Our first priority was to keep open our main supply route—MSR Mobile. Our second priority was to defeat the insurgency in our area of operations and try to restore law and order to a lawless land.

We would live in temporary housing for two weeks. The permanent quarters were assigned based on the length of one's tour. Our unit would be here for a year, so we rated concrete buildings. We moved into them as soon as the unit we were replacing moved out. The unit from the 1/9th infantry had deployed here after a year-long tour in Korea. They would finally be going home to Fort Collins, Colorado after this. They lost sixteen people from their battalion, and their brigade as a whole lost forty-eight in Al Anbar Province. The Marines based here did seven-month tours, so they lived in the less-protected SWA huts the whole time.

We finished our briefing and Lt. Gunn and I took a walk to check out the base. The chapel, PX, phone center, and barber shop were all next door to one another on the far side of the FOB, while the dining and laundry facilities were closer to our quarters.

That weekend, I attended Mass at Memorial Chapel. Unfortunately, both of the priests at this FOB were rotating home with their units, and our own priest was re-assigned to Al Asad Air Force Base. Eventually we learned that a Navy priest assigned to nearby Camp Blue Diamond would travel here periodically and conduct Mass.

Like many military bases, FOB Ramadi was an amazing melting pot of different faiths. During my time in Ramadi, I met chaplains who were Roman Catholic, Russian Orthodox, Jewish, Mormon, and at least a dozen different Protestant denominations. We were not always able to attend services in our own faith, so we learned to embrace the commonalities found in other Christian denominations.

Faced with the challenge of imminent death on a daily basis, many of our troops became more interested in their respective faiths. Even those who did not regularly participate in some type of worship service were very tolerant of those who did, and did what they could to support us.

The dining facility was surprisingly good. We stood in line waiting for chow inside somewhat sheltered buildings. After sweating in line for a while, we reached the last step, the hand-wash station. It was not optional. We lived with dirt, sweat, and oppressive heat. Washing our hands with real soap and warm water was even more welcome because we then stepped through the glass doors at the end of the tunnel and into immaculately clean, air-conditioned glorious splendor. The contrast was stark. Outside was a dark, sweaty bomb shelter into which hundreds of foul-smelling hungry troops were crowded. Inside awaited lobster, scallops, sirloin steaks, fresh fruits, and a cornucopia of exquisite deserts . . . all prepared by a dedicated crew of civilians brought in from such places as the Philippines, India, and Pakistan. They cooked the stock fare very well, following their recipes precisely. Once we got to know them, they would occasionally share the more elaborately spiced and flavored authentic dishes from their own countries that they prepared for themselves.

The civilians in the dining facility (known as a DFAC for short) were a terrific group of people. I got to know many of them during the special Mass that our priest held for them in the DFAC every Monday night. I made a point to bring them liturgical music, and I would fill in and conduct a prayer service, bringing them the Holy Eucharist when the priest could not make it to our FOB for a Mass.

The rest of our platoon arrived several days later, in the middle of the night via helicopter. They arrived just in time to begin the left-seat/right-seat rides. The term "left-seat/right-seat rides" describes our method of transferring responsibility for the battle space from one unit to the next. The two units split our vehicle crews in half at first. We rode along as passengers under the 1/9th Infantry's command for a week, then we brought them with us under our command for the second week. After two weeks we were on our own and they shipped out for home. We settled into our combat operations quickly, and hardly noticed that there were no fast-food joints at our FOB.

We were an armored battalion. As such, we trained to fight our battles using M-1 tanks. Normally, an armored battalion has one headquarters company and four tank companies. We quickly transformed into a mixture of one part armor and two parts infantry. The tankers (Charlie Company, 1/172 Armor, based in Morrisville, Vermont—augmented by tankers from Alpha Company out of Newport, Vermont, and some from B Troop 1/104th Cavalry split up and became part of other companies. A Company, 3/172 Mountain Infantry out of Jericho, Vermont, and B Troop, 104th Cavalry each gave up a platoon of infantry to Charlie Company. The medics who operated the battalion aid station and staffed the medical evacuation section remained assigned to the headquarters company, while the medics who rode into battle with the tanks and infantry were attached out to the line units as needed.

My first introduction to tanks was in the summer of 1993, when our entire 86th Brigade deployed to the Canadian Forces Base at Gagetown, New Brunswick. We spent a month in the field, engaged in continuous war games. I had transferred to the Vermont Army National Guard from the U.S. Army Reserve's 310th Field Hospital out of Malone, New York, knowing nothing about tanks or how the armor fought battles. It was quite an introduction. The tankers prided themselves on maximum speed and violence—and their swagger matched the speed and lethality of their weapon systems. Encased in seventy tons of armor, they carried an air of invincibility. What a refreshing change from the stale pallor of a predominantly middle-aged field hospital medical staff full on noncombatants. I was accustomed to a leadership of medical professionals, and an NCO corps of aging, party-going baby boomers. While highly competent at their medical mission, a less tactical group of soldiers could not be found. The cruel battlefield logic of the cold war, and the theory of mutually assured destruction resulted in a military culture in which no one ever expected to have another conventional ground war. The field hospital was the Army's successor to the M*A*S*H* units made famous in the TV series of the same name, and that unit's laid-back, party-going hippie culture was very similar.

In my introduction to combat arms, we raced around the huge maneuver areas at CFB Gagetown, free at last from the fences and narrow roads of our U.S. bases. The tankers thrived on the experience, able to open up the throttles on their tanks and maneuver the way the tank was meant to perform. I was the company medic for the Morrisville-based Charlie Company. An isolated mountain village, Morrisville was primarily a farming town, with enduring strength passed down through the generations. These men treasured their old-school Vermont values, toughened by generations of farming and hard work, and they carried their unique Yankee accent like a badge of honor given to them by their forebears. They seemed like a people frozen in time, with the keen marksmanship of a man who hunts to put meat on the table and sinewy muscles toned by a lifetime of hard work on the farm.

In the armor, there was usually only one medic and a single M-113 medical evacuation vehicle per company. I got to know the men of Charlie Company well that summer, and some of those old-school Vermonters—great guys like Bum Hale, Gabe Bullard, and Kevin Brown—were still serving together with the same unit twelve years later in the desert battlefields of Iraq.

With the end of the cold war and the Army's emphasis on a lighter, more maneuverable force, much of the army was getting away from tank warfare and going back to the light infantry of yesteryear. On this urban battlefield, we found that a mixture of the two was ideal. Each hybrid company used the tanks mostly as stationary observation posts and QRF (quick reaction forces). The infantry rode in up-armored humvees and had to dismount to get into the fight. Our troops rarely moved in platoon-sized elements, but instead sent three tanks to man observation posts while only two humvees—between six and ten men—patrolled the sector. The tankers were very good at engaging targets at long distance, but they were not well suited to baking in the sun while stationary in the open desert, with only a narrow angle of vision. When we were minimally staffed, we rolled with only three men in each humvee. Leaving a gunner in the truck, this left us with only four dismounted soldiers to kick in doors and storm buildings. By contrast, the Marines on the other side of the river never traveled with less than nineteen dismounts.

Our medical platoon had only twenty-six medics when we arrived. An armor battalion was supposed to have thirty enlisted medics and three officers, with one medic assigned to each tank company. We quickly learned that each infantry platoon needed a medic and we stretched our guys to the limit meeting this requirement. We kept only a minimal crew at the aid station, and most of the evac medics moved out to the line units. This left us shorthanded, so we pulled a lot of extra duty. The remaining evac medics merged into the treatment section, and staffed both the aid station and a forward aid station out at observation post 4 (OP 4).

A few days later I rolled down MSR Mobile for the first time riding high in the gunner's hatch of an M-113 armored personnel carrier. What a view it was. Immediately outside the dusty gate to our FOB, we climbed onto the highway and the traffic fell away in both directions. The locals were well trained to keep their distance from our vehicles, and we had the road to ourselves. We looked to the north and saw verdant pastures and wealthy homes. This was nothing like the wide-open desert we passed through in southern Iraqi daylight far to the southeast. We had driven through here on our convoy into Ramadi, but it was in the dark of night, and we could see only the vehicle in front of us through the dim green circular view of the night-vision equipment.

I was struck by how ordinary everything looked. There were farms, bridges, crops, orchards, four-lane highways, and regular families going about their daily lives. I gazed in awe as we crossed the Euphrates River.

It was a rich moment, riding high in my gunner's hatch across this ancient and historic river of Babylon—a scene cut straight out of the Bible. I was struck at how small and shallow it seemed. By contrast, America had a thousand streams bigger than this—but this was the desert, and this river was all they had. It irrigated fertile croplands and orchards on both sides of the river, extending a thin and tenuous lifeline into an otherwise desolate wasteland rife with the stench of decay. We pulled into the fortified position, OP 4, alongside our security element—a giant tank recovery vehicle known as an M-88. There was also a tank, positioned atop a four-lane highway overpass, while we parked at the base of the bridge protected on one side by the bridge embankment and on the other side by ten-foot-tall concrete barriers known as "Texas" barriers. These were like Jersey barriers, only much bigger.

We could see and shoot over the top of the Texas barriers. The areas immediately in front and behind the 88 and 113 were open, but no one could approach from those directions unseen. The tank provided "overwatch," while the 113 and 88 responded whenever we took casualties out on the north side of the base.

During the left-seat/right-seat rides, I had scored a lot of ammunition from the 1/9 guys. I distributed it to many of our medics, and I finally had a full combat load. Some of our medics were rolling out the gate with only two or three magazines. We learned that OP 4 took hostile fire all the time, and yet we still struggled getting equipment and supplies. At least there was plenty of food and water. I got the impression that if our medics actually fired at the enemy, we would just boggle the supply people's minds. They couldn't even get us our basic combat load, let alone resupply us after a mission. Of course, if we didn't actually fire our weapons at the enemy, then I guess we wouldn't run out of ammo, would we?

The enemy had no night-vision goggles, rifle scopes, or even binoculars, so their harassing small-arms fire wasn't accurate. Our predecessors explained to us that our biggest advantage was our ability to engage targets accurately both day and night. They told us we were not to leave the FOB without binoculars or night-vision goggles. So one day as we prepared to leave on a mission, I ran over to supply, and found it padlocked. I went next door to three other companies' supply rooms, and no one would help us. I finally found SSgt. Crocket, the battalion supply guy.

At first he balked at the thought of issuing us equipment, and he insisted that we go through our own company supply clerk. I told him I was heading out on a mission in a few minutes, our medics were being shot at constantly, and we were sitting ducks without night-vision goggles or binoculars.

He just looked at me. I gave up and I started walking away, when he called me back. I guess it took a minute for the full impact of my words to sink in. We were not in Vermont anymore, asking him to order equipment that we might need next summer. We were headed into combat in a few minutes, and in need of the equipment he had in storage. He suddenly remembered where the binoculars and night-vision goggles were. He went and dug out three pairs of each. I had what I needed in no time. It's amazing what can happen when the bullets fly and the bullshit stops.

I went to Mass that night, and thanked God for keeping our medics safe. Before my next mission, I prayed the act of contrition and a decade of the Rosary. I felt at peace going out the gate after that. Afterwards, I made it a point to pray before missions.

The Autumn of Innocence

Our greatest difficulty in Iraq was discerning the enemy combatants from the ordinary civilians. Aside from the members of Al Qaeda in Iraq and their affiliated terrorist cells, most Iraqis were just ordinary people who wanted to go about their daily lives. Under Saddam, the favored Sunni minority that populated Ramadi was able to do just that, while much of the Shiite majority was excluded from educational opportunities and decent jobs. In Ramadi, at least there was a municipal government that provided basic services such as police and fire protection, electricity, and clean running water.

When we took over Iraq from Saddam and his ilk, many Iraqis initially welcomed us as liberators. Our failure was in firing everyone involved in the key infrastructure—and then not replacing their functions. We didn't dispatch sufficient troops, and didn't consider the impact of so many unemployed, disillusioned soldiers and government officials.

The Iraqis' problems began with the municipal electrical service. It was offline more than it was online. The alternative power was supplied by huge diesel generators that supplied power to a whole village through undersized makeshift electrical wires. In some neighborhoods, thousands of these individual wires crisscrossed the roadways—often sagging to only a few feet off the ground.

With unpredictable electricity, the pumps did not consistently supply what was left of the municipal water system. Families had to make do with a feeble stream of water piped into a small elevated tank, often placed on the roof, which would boost the pressure through gravity.

Flush toilets were a rare commodity. Many families relied on a small trench out in the yard, surrounded by a makeshift shed. In many cases, the same outhouse had the water tank on the roof and was also the

An Iraqi merchant slaughters a goat in the street. Combined with the desert heat, it made for a lovely ambience. (Photo by SGT Brandon Allmond)

shower stall, providing the only cleanliness in the presence of raw sewage and flies.

Unable to power their refrigerators, the Iraqis obtained most of their meat supply by killing an animal shortly before cooking it. It was common to see markets selling live chickens and other animals, and a pool of blood running down the street—entrails left there to rot in the sun. The merchants would kill the animals at the time of sale. The stench from these markets was unbelievable. Although there was edible and freshly killed food available, the rotting entrails and blood festered on the sidewalks in the blistering heat. It was not an appetizing experience for our western sensibilities.

The livestock itself was a sight to behold. Donkeys, wild dogs, and herds of emaciated goats roamed through the city, foraging through garbage for something to eat. These same animals became food for whoever caught them. Sickly looking dairy cows were around, but they were nothing like the large healthy herds we had in Vermont. Many families kept chickens and a cow or two and would subsist on the eggs and milk they provided. There were no large farms that I saw.

The western winds blew across the Great Western Desert in Al Anbar Province, gathering sand in their powerful gusts. The sand and dust blew into everything, obscuring our vision and cutting into our skin like a thousand tiny razors. Being in Iraq felt like standing in front of a sandblaster inside of a blast furnace, inhaling dust and sand with every breath. Our constant physical misery was compounded by injuries, death, and the dehumanization brought on by the horrors of war.

With radical Islam considering martyrdom a sure way of getting into heaven, suicide bombings became a common tactic of our enemies. Perhaps it was their powerful faith that led them to employ such drastic measures, but I suspect it was mixed with desperation.

Whatever the cause, we faced a significant threat from VBIEDs. To counter this threat and prevent the placement of IEDs along the roadways, our predecessors developed a system of observation posts that guarded our main supply routes at regular intervals. The concept was to keep the most important routes under constant scrutiny in order to engage and destroy VBIEDs and people who placed IEDs.

The best place to conduct surveillance of a four-lane highway was an overpass. In addition to offering a great vantage point, these overpasses were key access points, through which everyone hoping to cross the highway must travel. Coalition forces took over almost every bridge over MSR Mobile, including several in our area of operations.

Beneath many of these overpasses, the local people would often create their own crossroads, cutting through the guardrails and driving across the desert up onto the highway, through the median, and down the other side. Some of these improvised routes were quite dangerous, allowing vehicles to emerge unexpectedly from blind areas, and became the scene of frequent, horrific traffic accidents. The Iraqis felt that these accidents were all our fault.

OP 4 AND THE FORWARD AID STATION

As the 1/9th Infantry medics introduced us to our OP, they explained its history. Through their sheiks, the Iraqis convinced our preceding unit to establish a forward aid station at the base of one such overpass that we referred to as observation post 4. The mission for this forward aid station (FAS) was twofold, to provide quick reaction medical support to our units north of the FOB and to provide an immediate response to the Iraqis who were constantly crashing into one another where their improvised road crossed the highway. The M-88 crew functioned as the security escort for the ambulance, and the ambulance crew returned the favor during recovery missions.

Our security escorts from the tank recovery section took their jobs very seriously. I never worried about anything while we rode with them. I remember being the gunner on our medic track one afternoon as we returned from OP 4. I was armed only with my M-16 rifle, and I raised my rifle to wave a car off. Before I could blink, the 88 came around to our right, and there was Jade Phillips on the gun, backing me up. It felt good to know that Jade and his crew would not hesitate to protect us.

I hardly knew them at the time, but we were there for each other. Jade Phillips and his 88 crew were escorting the 113 back to the base one afternoon after picking up a casualty. The 88 pulled across the highway in a blocking maneuver to allow the 113 to cross in front of the oncoming traffic and enter the FOB. Dozens of cars stopped on the highway, keeping their distance. One car passed several other idling vehicles doing seventy to eighty miles per hour, and as it approached, it dodged around several other stopped vehicles. Jade fired directly into the vehicle with about a half a magazine, and the car swerved off the road and came to a stop. Threat gone, the 88 crew continued their mission. Like so many other times in my own experience, the tactical situation did not always allow them to render aid. Jade never learned whether he killed anyone that day, and the unknown was probably worse than reality.

About a week later we pulled into OP 4 for a day shift. It was a bright sunny day, with a slight breeze blowing. Brent Reader and I stood up in the crew hatch, casually glancing around from time to time while Jade Phillips kept watch atop the 88 next to us.

Brent was an Abenaki Indian from the Swanton/Highgate area of northwestern Vermont. He spoke eleven languages and taught Abenaki tribal history at the University of Vermont. The son of a combat medic veteran of the Vietnam War, he joined the National Guard after September 11.

We heard small-arms fire and IED blasts and mortar and artillery fire all day long in the hot August sun. Still, we had an enjoyable visit, and had a great time swapping stories of the North Country. One of his parents was from the Mohawk tribe near where I grew up, and the other was from the Abenaki tribe in Highgate. We covered a lot of historical and philosophical ground in our discussions, from Aristotle to Saddam Hussein to the siege at Oka, Quebec.

We were standing there talking when we slowly realized there was an old taxi cutting across a field and heading straight for us. We were on the alert for VBIEDs. Our procedure was to wave the driver off, fire a warning shot in his direction, and if he did not stop at that point, kill him.

I held the taxi driver in my sights for several moments as he drew closer, but he did not appear to have hostile intentions. Atop the 88, Jade also noticed the car and called to his TC (track commander) on the headset. "Do what you have to do!" he was told. Glancing sideways at us, he realized we were also aiming at the car and waving our arms. Ever respectful of rank, Jade deferred to me without a word between us. The driver was basically taking his time as he pulled up onto the highway less than fifty meters in front of us. He was too close, and I was about to fire. I aimed for a place in the dirt. Would Jade and Brent realize these were warning shots? Or would they take my cue and just annihilate this guy? At the last possible moment he turned left and headed down the highway, never even noticing that we had two M-16s and a .50-caliber machine gun trained on him the whole time.

After the taxi drove away, Reader and I went back to our discussions of whatever we were talking about. It was not until perhaps fifteen or twenty minutes later that we stopped and thought about what just happened. I mentioned to Reader that today was the first time I had ever drawn a bead on a man, and that we almost killed him. Reader paused too, as the impact sank in.

When we got back to the FOB, there was a mortar attack north of our building. There were several attacks during the day, and our counter battery fire was heavy and almost constant.

The 1/9th Infantry had used a twenty-four-hour rotation out at OP 4. They were a lot younger than we were. We quickly changed our schedule to a twelve-hour, day/night rotation. The days were unbearably hot inside the parked armored vehicles, baking in the desert sun day after day. One of the guys actually brought a meat thermometer out there and measured temperatures of 160 degrees. We roasted out there during a twelve-hour day shift. To stay any longer was just torture.

I had never really done well in extreme heat. I had now been a heat casualty more than once, first as a firefighter, and now as a soldier in this war zone. I quickly figured out that I was built for the night shift. Unlike a lot of the guys, I had no trouble sleeping in my air-conditioned room during the day, and I tolerated the heat a whole lot better at night. I was not scheduled exclusively for nights, but I traded willingly with any medic who was willing to swap.

The crazy Suburbans. The insane ways the Iraqi's transported cargo was a source of constant amusement. (Photo by SGT Brent Reader)

At least at the end of our night shift, we got to watch the races. Every night in Al Anbar, a curfew went into effect. Every morning before daybreak, a rush of vehicles hit the roads, all of them jostling for the pole position. The first time I saw the races, I almost died laughing. It was during the right-seat/left-seat rides, and I was out on the OP, scanning the morning horizon with one of the medics from the 1/9th Infantry.

"Here they come!" he called out.

"Here who comes?" I asked, thinking we were about to be attacked.

"The Suburbans!" he shouted exuberantly, jumping up and down with excitement. "You gotta see this!"

I jumped up through the crew hatch and looked down the highway. A wall-to-wall nonstop fleet of Chevy Suburbans four across flowed over the top of High Water Bridge, swarming down the bridge like a bunch of fire ants on crack. It was bizarre enough to see such a sight, but their cargo was even stranger. Each truck was piled high with dozens of huge orange plastic water tanks, strapped on with all manner of straps, nets, and ropes. They were piled up on top of the Suburbans by the dozens, three times as high as each truck, and twice as wide. The long sweeping gradual curves of the highway were barely perceptible, but they almost made the top-heavy circus trucks topple over. Clearly, we were not in Kansas anymore.

"What in the world?" I asked, incredulously.

"They do this every morning!" he explained, "and they race each other from Syria all the way to Baghdad! Every once in a while they topple right over!"

Some people enjoy football. Some enjoy baseball. I have never understood the attraction of NASCAR, but to each his own. For this battle-hardened and half-crazed sunbaked medic, watching the Suburbans was as good as it got. Apparently this highway we watched all day and all night was the main trade route between Jordan, Syria, and Iraq. The water tanks the Suburbans imported were used on top of almost every house in Iraq, providing a reservoir for domestic water, and boosting the pressure in their faucets through gravity.

"Oh just wait 'till you see the buses!" He smiled, gleefully.

I couldn't imagine anything more ridiculous than the barrel-carrying Suburbans racing down the highway at over ninety miles an hour, jostling for position four across on the two-lane road. But then came the buses.

"Here they come! Oh, check it out!" my wacky friend was about to explode.

After what seemed like hundreds of fast-moving Suburbans leading the way, the traffic gave way to the slower moving buses. Ancient city buses that looked like they jumped out of a time capsule came lumbering along. Every one of them sagged in the rear like a station wagon carrying a ton of bricks. I couldn't imagine the weight these huge vehicles must be carrying. Many of them had huge piles of cargo strapped to the roof, but all of them were clearly overloaded. They swayed side to side like a herd of elephants heading for water.

"What could they possibly be carrying?" I asked, mouth hanging open.

"Potato chips!" He answered with glee.

"What?" I seriously considered taking his temperature at this point. "Potato chips?!?"

"Yeah, we got really curious one time, so we pulled one over. I don't know how he managed to drive. Every square inch of his bus was filled with them. There was barely any room for the driver!"

"Was he carrying anything else?"

"Nope, not a thing. It was crazy . . . that whole bus was packed with nothing but potato chips."

Not only had we left Kansas, we landed in the twilight zone.

• • •

Overall, it wasn't bad duty, except for the sense that we were sitting ducks for the enemy. The insurgents knew exactly where we were, exactly how we parked our vehicles, and the hour we changed shifts. They had virtually free reign of the buildings around us, as we never patrolled them. OP 4 was located near the edge of three different units' battle space. The B Troop rovers patrolled the area to our west. To our east were the C Company rovers. No one patrolled the area to our north, and the area to our south only saw periodic foot patrols by the Marines at Camp Blue Diamond. There was no twenty-four-hour presence to our south, and even when the Marines were in sector, they were on foot, with limited mobility, and could not respond to emergencies. Even if they had used vehicles, we still had no direct radio contact with them, and had to relay messages through several layers of the chain of command.

It was a recipe for disaster. We observed the same buildings day in and day out—some vacant, some occupied—but we were never permitted to go in and search them. The enemy was free to use any one of the buildings as a vantage point to attack us, and the 1/9th Infantry medics warned us that they did so constantly. From the 1/9th medics we learned about the constant sniper activity, the frequent rocket propelled grenade (RPG) attacks, and the occasional VBIED that would charge this position. They also told us about the families who lived in each house. From them we learned which families loved us and which ones hated us.

I hated being a sitting duck. I wanted so much to get out there after the bad guys, but we were not there to conduct offensive operations. We were supposed to stick to defending ourselves and providing an emergency response when the units we supported took casualties. We settled for conducting thorough surveillance and calling in the rovers whenever we became suspicious.

Many of the other troops were similarly constrained to manning observation posts. Keeping our main supply route open was, our leadership stressed to us, our most important mission. It was emasculating to be so constrained. Considered noncombatants, we did not pursue the insurgents who targeted us. Instead we spent twenty-four hours a day in full view of the enemy, waiting to get shot at.

Over time, I could see the changes in some of the men who worked in these defensive positions. By October, anxiety and paranoia were common. They knew the enemy could observe them and line up a shot at his leisure, and the constant vigilance took its toll. How liberating it was to break free of our static position at OP 4 and head out on the offensive— to become the hunter rather than the hunted. It was an opportunity to make a difference in this war, and I relished it.

I carried the hard-learned lessons from the OP with us—keep moving. The enemy had very few snipers, and by remaining in motion, we denied them the opportunity to line up a shot. Charlie Company's OPs along the highway received a lot of small-arms fire. The company commander knew that his primary mission was keeping the highway open. With barely enough troops to do so, he was not willing to allow his roving patrol to leave the highway much. For the most part, they did as they were told, and only mounted offensive operations after the end of their regular shifts, when another platoon took over the highway.

One night in September, the frustrations that I shared with the men of Charlie Company were particularly evident. I was in the medic track at OP 4 when we spotted suspicious activity on the upper floors of an abandoned building across the highway from our position. We called up to the tank on top of the overpass above us, and they too saw the same suspicious activity. OP 4 is located on edge of B Troop's sector, where it meets Charlie Company's area.

We radioed for the B Troop rovers to investigate, but they were tied up on another mission. We thought we were watching enemy forces set up for an attack on our position, and we did not want to remain idle while they carried out their attack. We asked for Charlie Company's rovers to respond. They came to our position, and were willing to stay with us for added security, but with their directive from their commander being not to leave the highway, they were unwilling to go into the building in question as it was out of their area of responsibility and they had very little manpower.

Within half an hour, the B Troop rovers arrived and worked out a plan. The B Troop guys assaulted the building while the C Company rovers established a cordon around the target. No insurgents were found, and we never did figure out what it was that we were seeing up there through our night-vision equipment.

With Charlie Company's primary focus being to prevent the enemy from setting IEDs in their sector, they did something the rest of the battalion almost never did. They split their rovers, and each patrolled the highway alone. While one humvee headed east, the other went west, each patrolling the same circuit, but in opposite directions. Their objective was to maintain constant observation of as much highway as possible.

It's amazing how quickly fate can intrude on routine. One afternoon, a three-man crew in one of their lone humvees pulled over a suspicious minivan full of military-aged males. Two of the crew got out and approached the minivan armed only with pistols. Inside the van were eight enemy insurgents armed to the teeth and itching for a fight. As our soldier opened the sliding door on the passenger side of the van, one of the insurgents inside turned and fired his AK-47 at him. The soldier pulled his pistol and shot the men inside the back of the van. His partner dropped to the ground in front of the vehicle and began firing through the windshield. From atop the humvee behind the minivan, the roof gunner on the humvee had a .50-caliber machine gun trained on the vehicle, but he did not have a clear shot because his men were in the way. One of the gunmen in the backseat turned and fired at the gunner. Once his men were clear, the gunner fired one hundred rounds from the .50-caliber into the van and kept firing until the weapon was empty. While he reloaded, the weapon was hit by bullets fired from an enemy AK-47 and disabled. The big .50-cal rounds had punctured the van, though, causing it to catch fire. The gunner grabbed his M-4 carbine, and along with the two dismounts firing their pistols, kept firing into the vehicle until the enemy stopped firing. The ensuing fire consumed the vehicle and the enemy bodies in it. Outnumbered eight to three, our men prevailed, killing eight and receiving only minor shrapnel wounds in return. Although they prevailed, the scars from that engagement ran deep in the hearts of our men. Before that routine traffic stop went bad, they did not perceive much of a threat from the insurgents. They thought of their sector as a lonely stretch of highway, empty except for the vehicles driving through it on their way to somewhere else. Now, they realized, they were just as much a target as their counterparts in Tameem.

JOE LEWIS

On the far side of Ramadi, meanwhile, the men of Alpha Company, 3rd Battalion, 172nd Infantry were in one hell of a fight. Their area of operations was formerly military housing for Saddam's Republican Guard, numerous factories and warehouses, and Al Anbar University. The Tameem District was also the most impoverished slum in Ramadi, with raw sewage flowing in the streets, mounds of garbage that stretched on for miles, and more die-hard insurgents than anyone could imagine. Every house, every doorway, every roofline was a potential hiding spot for an IED triggerman, a sniper, or an RPG team. Whenever we dismounted in Tameem, we kept moving, turning constantly to observe all around us and to avoid giving the enemy a clear shot at the weak points in our armor. The need for this constant movement and vigilance was punctuated one day in September, when one young Philadelphia police officer from B Troop was carried into our aid station with a gunshot wound in his thigh from an enemy sniper.

Joe Lewis was a South Philly cop, and a wise guy like I never met before. It was late September and he was standing next to his humvee near Route Michigan when a bullet struck the scope on his rifle, breaking it apart and driving pieces of shrapnel into his thigh. Always a trooper, however, he stayed in the fight, calling in reinforcements over the radio while his doc, Bill Gates, cut his pants open and bandaged his leg. Gates got in the driver's seat and drove Lewis back to the FOB to the battalion aid station where the medics tried to carry him in. Joe insisted on getting off the stretcher and having a smoke. There he stood, pants shredded, smoking away, with that wry grin of his. Someone asked him how he felt.

"I'm fucking pissed," Joe replied. "The bastards shot me and ruined a perfectly good pair of pants."

He was persuaded to come into the aid station where the rest of his clothes were cut away, pissing him off even more. To our relief, there were no other wounds. The bullet had struck the scope on Joe's rifle and fragmented from there, creating many small fragment wounds on his thigh.

Joe refused to be evacuated back to the United States; instead, he wanted to recover in Ramadi with his unit. Each day he would hobble down to the battalion aid station and have his wounds cleaned and redressed. We all got to know Joe while we worked on his wounds each day. Usually we would send him to our nearby shower where the water would help to deep-clean the wounds before we applied a new dressing.

On one such morning, I met Joe stepping out of the shower as I was stepping in. With both of us completely naked, it was a little awkward.

I said to him, "You know, Joe, you are a lucky guy. How many other patients get to go back and tell their buddies they got to take a shower with their nurse?"

DEATH COMES

We finished our night shift on OP 4 one Thursday morning, waved at our relief crew, and headed back to the FOB. On the relieving 88, Spec. Scott (Scooter) McLaughlin manned their gun. Always smiling, Scott never had a cross word for anyone. He was a dedicated husband and father who thought constantly about his family and his land back home.

Always a social butterfly, Brent Reader climbed out of the medic track and into the 88 to share a cigarette with them. Reader's partner on this mission was a nonsmoker, and Reader loved to laugh with Scooter and the guys. The topic with Scooter was always the same. Together they dreamt of getting back home to their wives and children—sharing funny stories about the kids.

Brent finished his cigarette and went back to the 113. He settled into the book he was reading and started to get drowsy in the morning heat.

A single shot rang out. "I'm hit!" he heard Scooter call out. Scrambling to his feet, Reader was out the hatch and into the 88 in a flash. Scooter crumpled to the floor, blood pouring out of his chest. The color drained from his cheeks. He looked down at his chest and his eyes grew wide. He looked up at Reader, unable to speak now, only his eyes imploring Reader to do something.

Reader tore open Scooter's body armor. The round caught him above the body armor and slammed into his upper chest. Reader slapped a dressing on it and pushed down as hard as he could, trying desperately to stop the blood flow. The other guys grabbed Scooter and slid him out the hatch and onto a litter. The 113 roared to life as they loaded Scooter in the back, Reader's hand clamped down on his chest.

They were at the hospital in record time, and the surgeons whisked Scooter directly into the operating room. The bullet had torn through the great vessels above the heart and collapsed both lungs. The surgeons did everything they could, but Scooter was gone.

That night we gave up staffing OP 4 with our medic track and 88. Fewer troops were getting wounded in that area, so there was less need for the ambulance. With Scooter's death, our commanders brought the 88 and 113 inside the perimeter. In addition, Forsaken Stronghold and another observation post nearby had established a strong presence in that area.

It was during one of those first nights back inside the gate that we actually got to know the guys in the recovery section better, including Jade Phillips, who would later join with Glen Woods and me in forming a band and providing a musical ministry for the troops. We had worked side by side out on OP 4, but we mostly stayed buttoned up inside our respective armored vehicles, and didn't get to know one another much. Inside the gate, the medics in the steady-state operations section and the recovery crewmen created a home for ourselves. Twelve-hour shifts standing by in case of casualties or disabled vehicles were the norm. It was a working environment a lot like the firehouses I had worked in back home, getting pretty good at video games and watching a lot of DVD movies.

It was a tough week, with the loss of five soldiers from our battalion, one from another, and another who was stationed at another FOB near Habbaniyah. The days were filled with mourning and recovery, both physical and spiritual. I was assigned to the midnight shift out on the OP. Mercifully, I was not there when SPC McLaughlin was killed. The men took it hard, but were strong. The two mechanics who were with him when he died took the loss of their friend especially hard, but they really impressed me with their outward resiliency. I could only imagine the depths of their inner pain.

The night after Scooter died, the regular 88 crew had the night off. In their place stood SSgt. Bates and SSgt. Griffin, two old friends from the St. Albans Armory whom I had not spent much time with in recent years. Along with Sgt. Benard (AKA Booger) and my partner, SSgt. Dorn, we had a wonderful evening inside the entrance to our FOB (the outer perimeter gate). I brewed a fresh pot of Green Mountain Coffee that I had just received from my sister Holly, and brought it out in a thermos. The coffee was spiked with the tales of hunting camp, ice fishing, and past summer camps, and we all got happily drunk on foggy reminiscence. It was five in the morning before anyone looked at his watch.

The next night was much the same, this time with Spec. Goodrow, Spec. Phillips and SFC Martin. Again, we regaled one another with tall tales and laughter all night long. We made us crazy tall tales like "The Magic Shaman and His Golden Conex" and laughed all night long. Goody and Phillips in particular were especially close to McLaughlin, and neither had heard of our mystical shaman. They were rolling on the floor beside themselves in stitches. It was a privilege to help these guys ease the pain of their loss with laughter. Spec. McLaughlin always had a smile on his face, and I am sure he was laughing with us.

ECP 3 AND THE BRADLEY CREW

After spending a week working nights on the ambulance at Trooper Gate, I was awakened early the following afternoon for a mission brief. It was the first week of October and someone hatched a bold plan to travel through the entire district of Tameem, to a railroad bridge used by the insurgents, to build an entry control point (ECP) to be staffed by the Iraqi Army (ISF). With Ramadi being the most violent city on earth, and Tameem being the worst part of Ramadi, I was not looking forward to the job. I was fortunate to be partnered with Joe Nelson, an old friend from way back. Joe and I manned a 113 set up as a forward aid station at the construction site, while Sgt. McCloud and PFC Reader manned another 113 set up for evac.

The mission did not start well. As we were leaving Ogden Gate, one of the massive trucks overloaded with concrete barriers rolled over, seriously injuring the driver and blocking over half the convoy inside the gate. Reader and McCloud treated and transported the casualties back to the FOB in their 113, while we continued on to our destination.

The engineers with us did what they could with the materials that made it through, but the loss of half our convoy really set us back and made us stretch our mission from two nights to three. During our first night out there, we definitely possessed the advantage of surprise. The people of Tameem were staring at us in utter disbelief as we convoyed back to the FOB. The units before us had given up on this part of town, and the insurgents knew it. They were shocked to find us building a fortification in the furthest corner of their world, stopping the flow of arms across the Euphrates River into Ramadi. At that point, however, our element of surprise was gone.

While we slept back at the FOB that day, mortars were fired into our newly created position. Thankfully, it was empty. We did not have a good feeling that night when we rolled out there. Our departure was delayed due to enemy action in Tameem. We finally arrived and began working at around 0100. Well into daylight, we finally left around 0900. On our way out of the entry control point, an IED detonated behind our last vehicle. There was very little damage and no one was injured. We didn't give it a second thought, and we drove through the dirt-poor streets of Tameem, once again enduring the expressionless stares of the local people. While we knew that many of them harbored deep hatred for us, it was impossible to read most of them. Only one young boy gave us a thumbs up. Most just stared blankly. We got back to our barracks, relieved that nothing had gone too wrong yet, and slept soundly that day.

We awoke on the third evening and gathered on the upper deck of the Support Platoon barracks for a briefing. We had just begun talking about the night's mission when we heard an explosion and saw a column of smoke rising from the far side of Tameem. We would later learn that a Bradley Fighting Vehicle near our ECP had just blown up, and that five members of the Pennsylvania National Guard lost their lives. These men were members of Bravo Company, 109th Infantry and were attached to the 1/172nd. Their deaths brought Task Force Saber's death toll to eleven.

That night we traveled back through the darkened streets of Tameem once again, more on edge than ever. Our lead element reached a point in the road near our destination where a huge hole opened up in the road, rendering it impassable. The IED that detonated at the end of our last shift behind our last vehicle caused it, unbeknownst to us. One of our engineers retrieved a bucket loader from the construction site, and filled the hole for us, re-creating the road. He noticed that the loader was not handling right. Upon further investigation, he discovered one tire blown to shreds and the fuel tank punctured by shrapnel. A mortar had hit close to the bucket loader that afternoon while we slept, and almost destroyed it. While our convoy stalled in Tameem, the hair began to stand up on the back of my neck. I was fairly well protected in the driver's hatch of my 113, but as we scanned for targets, I spotted a figure moving in the shadows only twenty meters away. A man had turned on a light and silhouetted himself in his window, staring out at our convoy. He had no idea that I had drawn a bead on him with my pistol, just waiting for a weapon to appear. None did, and eventually we moved on.

We drove past the still smoldering wreckage of our Bradley, the bodies of five men still inside. We arrived at the site to find fresh damage from an RPG. Our men worked all night building the fortified ECP and on into the next day to finish the job. We all knew we had been very lucky thus far, and understood the risks if we had to come back for a fourth night of construction. Early that morning, small-arms fire broke out, and we all scurried for cover. I climbed into the gunner's hatch of the 113 and scanned for targets, finding none. The Iraqi Security Forces (ISF) had only been in their new tower less than an hour, and were already facing their first enemy attack. They returned fire with their machine guns, but we doubt they had targets to aim at. We waited until the shooting died down and went back to work, exposed by daylight to the enemy's fire.

We finished our work by 1100, and headed out. As we were leaving, small-arms fire broke out once again. We buttoned up our collars and just left. I could not help but feel like we were abandoning our Iraqi allies when they really needed us to stay.

Later that day I awoke to learn that the ISF soldiers on that ECP (now labeled ECP 3) had come under heavy attack, and three of them were wounded. Our medic tracks were nowhere around, and our QRF ambulance had to respond from the FOB, all the way across Tameem to pick up the casualties, and return. The difficulty with this position is that there was only one way in and one way out. It was backed into a corner of the river, with no other escape route. It would not take the enemy long to figure out that our 113 responded whenever there were casualties, and to target us with a trap.

When we got back to the FOB, I just took my mind off the war. I got a package from Mom and Dad with an Adirondack Life calendar in it. The cover photo featured Lake Lila Beach, and the memories it spurred brought a sense of peace to my troubled mind. I wrote them a very nice thank-you note, and was successful in keeping my mind off the war all day long. It could be worse—lots worse.

Not long after we finished constructing ECP 3, our battalion mustered up all the forces we could, including Marines and ISF soldiers, and we conducted a massive cordon and search of all of Tameem. Several top bad guys were arrested, and a lot of bomb-making materials were confiscated. They kicked in every door in the town, and made everyone aware that a new marshal was in town.

As much as I wanted a piece of the action, I was relegated to the sidelines on that mission. Someone had to work elsewhere, and much to my chagrin, I was assigned to the forward aid station on the midnight shift. My partner and I were there at the aid station, asleep, but available if things really turned ugly. Fortunately, they did not, and we slept well.

Throughout my tour in combat, I found that the best way to retain my sanity was to take my mind off my troubles in my down time, and think about something else. When faced with stressful situations like combat, the human body reacts well for a short period of time. Our adrenal glands kick in, pumping us full of adrenaline, and blood flow is shunted away from the digestive system and channeled to the skeletal muscles in preparation for fight or flight.

Remaining in a hypervigilant state for a long time, though, is a losing proposition. The muscle cells burn up their energy stores, and the digestive system is not functioning to replace the lost nutrients. The effects of constant adrenaline, vigilance, and fear flowing through the human mind are not good. It is absolutely essential to stand down periodically. It was in denying rest and supplies to the Iraqi Army prior to the start of the Gulf War in 1991 that our Air Force was successful in softening them up for our ground invasion. By the time our forces entered Iraq and Kuwait, the exhausted, dehydrated, and undernourished Iraqi forces largely gave up their will to fight. In retrospect, given the caliber of Iraqi forces I worked with in 2005 and 2006, they might not have ever had much stamina in the first place.

While assigned to the main battalion aid station (BAS) our medics were on duty, twenty-four hours a day for five consecutive days. When the aid station duty ended, we went on QRF duty for the next five days, listening to the radio all night long, and getting dispatched to emergency evac missions. The QRF, of course, was expected to help out at the aid station when needed, to maintain an instant response capability, and to generally get by with very little sleep. From the QRF duty, we rotated out to the FAS, first at OP 4, then later at Trooper Recon, where we spent twelve-hour shifts standing by. At least on the FAS duty, we were not expected to remain constantly vigilant during our down time, and we could sleep when the mission allowed. It was not uncommon to go days on end with little to no sleep. While everyone recognized the need to make sacrifices for the mission, these extraordinary demands on our people served no useful purpose, and could easily have been avoided. There was enough anguish and death in the world around us without our own people making things worse for us. My optimistic efforts at boosting morale were seriously challenged. I was not really despairing, but I had had enough.

I never liked the confinement of our aid station. I was a lot happier with the atmosphere in the line companies. The guys were serious about their work, but their attitude was decidedly informal when they were off duty. They never worried much about being caught relaxing; they were expected to relax.

With near total exhaustion a constant companion, I had to scale back somewhere. The only part of my miserable existence I had any control over was my participation in the chapel. Although I loved providing music for the civilian Mass at the DFAC I needed to rest. As long as there was a priest present, I reduced my participation to one Mass at the Memorial Chapel and one Christian interfaith service at Saber Chapel. It was a lot less draining, and it enabled me to spend more time rehearsing. The extra time off really helped. I remember one Monday evening after church, I even watched the New England Patriots beat the Atlanta Falcons. The Patriots won by 3 points when Adam Vinatieri came through with a field goal.

It was almost like being home, except for the mortar attack in the first quarter, and the counter battery fire going out through the second quarter and half time. At least everything calmed down by the second half. I was reflecting on how normal and American it felt to watch football and drink fake beer with the guys, here in this remote outpost in the middle of a war. Every now and again, a tank would rumble by, but other than that, it was easy to forget the war for a while. After the game I called home and had a nice chat with my kids—a nice day, and to top it all off, a head cold I'd been suffering from was getting better.

My brother John is a school music teacher in Massachusetts. He and his students did some fund raising for us and sent us some musical instruments for our chapel. I played the congo drums they sent every week, and our music was a comfort to soldiers, sailors, and marines from across the FOB. In return, John asked me if I would write a few words for his students, to be read during an assembly on Veterans Day. It was extremely difficult to hold my angry desire for revenge at bay and to cling to the values and goals I spoke of in the following passage:

Dear John—

I heard there was snow in Vermont yesterday, a full-blown winter storm in my beloved Green Mountains.

I think about snow here . . . longingly. The kind of snow that falls slowly all day long, showing us where the deer went and when they went there.

The kind of snow that packs well, enabling swarms of gleeful children to roll it into snowmen.

The kind of snow that blankets the town with a fresh quiet innocence, mounts halos on the streetlamps and muffles your footsteps.

I think often of home, and the families there who suffer quietly without us . . . wives struggling to raise our children alone, children missing their big strong Daddies.

It is for our families that we are here. For as long as we are willing to make this sacrifice voluntarily, our sons and daughters will not face a draft.

As long as we are here, our communities will not see the horrors of war delivered to American shores.

As long as we are here, the people of Iraq benefit from the protection of a powerful Army while they set up their fledgling democracy.

And as long as we are here, the values that we embody as a nation shine forth like a torch in the night, keeping darkness at bay.

I pray that the people we have come here to protect will someday become a peaceful nation, prosperous and free.

Taking the Fight to the Enemy

Some men reacted to enemy attacks with fear. I got angry. I wanted to take the fight to the enemy. One night while working the overnight shift with SSG. Bert Severin, I let him know how I felt. Severin was the squad leader for the line medics assigned to A Company and B Troop. A mountain infantry medic from Jericho, Vermont, he moved with the light step of a cat stalking its prey. I made a point of standing guard, even though we didn't have to, and I told SSG. Severin how frustrated and angry I was—just sitting there waiting for the enemy to take one of us out. Meanwhile, SSG. Severin had been trying to figure out a way to give his medics a little time off. He remembered our conversation and brought it to the platoon sergeant. I soon transferred to the line, where I became a relief medic. I went from one platoon to the next, giving the other medics a day off. It was a great assignment. I got to see the battalion's entire battle space, and got to work with almost every platoon in the battalion. I was in a unique position to see how different leaders dealt with similar situations in a variety of settings. On Mondays and Tuesdays I rode out with a dismounted infantry platoon made up of our own Scout Platoon from Vermont and a platoon of combat engineers from the Rhode Island National Guard. We patrolled the palm groves and croplands where turtledoves landed in the spectacular greenery and insurgents infiltrated the farmers' fields laying out ambushes and launching mortars at our FOB. On Wednesdays and Thursdays, I patrolled with Vermont's Alpha Company in the streets of Tameem, and on Fridays I patrolled the highways with Philadelphia's B troop, 104th Cavalry. In Tameem, and to a lesser extent in the villages northwest of the FOB that B Troop patrolled, every building and every direction was a potential hiding spot for a sniper. Every pile of roadside trash was a potential IED. Anti-tank mines and

RPGs were the norm there, and we were usually in contact with the enemy every day. It was a miracle that more of us did not die in Tameem. Dozens of our men were wounded there, and a lot of our guys were hurt badly enough that they were sent home.

Sometimes I stayed with the same platoon for several weeks while their medic went on leave. For the most part, though, I walked alone. I made many casual acquaintances in the troops I worked with, but only a few close friends. It was a lonely existence, but this was a blessing in many ways. I felt their losses less when our men were killed or maimed. I remember reading about troops in Vietnam, and how they would avoid friends so they would not suffer as much when their buddies died. I guess it worked for me, too. Overall, though, our Green Mountain Boys done good. We didn't lose very many, and we gave one hell of a lot worse than we got.

BOOGER, BECHTEL, AND B TROOP

In early October, I went out on my first patrol with B Troop's Lt. Watts and his platoon. We blew up suspected IEDs, burned dead animal carcasses, and searched cars. However, the highlights of the day involved a puppy and a suspect.

Patrolling through a village south of OP 2, Spec. Bechtel and I found a puppy scared and hiding in some trash. Although it was illegal, Bechtel and the boys adopted her, and the boys from B troop had a new member in their family. We rode out to OP 1, where there was an isolated position surrounded by wide-open desert. It is a relatively safe place to take a break and hide, and the men there were happy to keep the puppy for a while. It was tremendous to see these battle-hardened men crack open their scarred shells and melt into little boys, gleefully playing with their new friend.

We soon returned to patrolling, and found a car positioned only a few hundred meters north of OP Thumper, the scene of a horrific ambush that left several of our men severely wounded a few months earlier. The car appeared disabled, with its hood up and the driver standing out in front. This is a common ploy used by the insurgents to get within sight of their objective. We stopped, questioned the man, and began to search his car. When asked by our interpreter if he had guns in the car, he answered yes he did. Spec. Bechtel thought he meant they were in the trunk and took the man to the rear of the car to have him open the trunk. The man kept pointing to the front of the car, and Bechtel took this as

Pausing in a ditch with the Scouts' Lt. Armstrong. Irrigation ditches like this one enabled the Iraqis to grow crops near the river in the absence of rain. (Photo by author)

hesitancy to open the trunk. So, he insisted the man open the trunk, and the man grew more agitated, gesturing to the front of the car. I was on the driver's side of the vehicle while they talked, and had just begun to peer into the windows. I spotted the stock of an AK-47 on the front seat just about time the suspect decided to reach for it. The driver's door was open, and I immediately dropped to a knee and aimed my rifle at him, commanding him to stop. Thankfully he did. We detained the man, but he was later released when it was learned that he was not an insurgent, but rather a security guard working for a powerful sheik in the area—and he really did have car trouble. I started spending one day a week riding with Lt. Watts, while Bechtel drove. It was always an adventure.

TOUR OF DUTY

—B Company, 109th Infantry (Mechanized), based in Scranton, Pennsylvania, patrolled a rural area sandwiched between the highway and the Euphrates River. A few kilometers south was a main east—west secondary road known as Route Duster. This road was known to be filled with

B Troop secretly adopted this puppy. With her keen senses of hearing and smell, no one snuck up on our guys at OP1. In Iraq, dogs are generally not viewed as pets, but rather as unclean scavengers. (Photo by author)

IEDs and had claimed the lives of many U.S. servicemen, including two medics and a physician's assistant from the 1/9th Infantry. This road seemed to be one of the main roads used by the insurgents. Along Route Duster was an unused mosque. Intelligence reported that the imam was killed several years ago, and there were no local residents who reported going to services there. In spite of its lack of any religious activity, the place seemed to be a beehive of activity every day and night of the week. Wires were spotted leading into the mosque from a nearby internet café. We learned that it was actually a command center for the insurgents.

The guys from B Company, 109th Infantry, sprang from the hard-scrabble coal-miners of western Pennsylvania. They were tough and well suited to their mission. Like all of our companies, they were made into a hybrid unit, augmented by our own Scout Platoon and a platoon of combat engineers from the Rhode Island National Guard's 876th Engineers under the command of a platoon sergeant named SFC Esposito. A cook by trade, Espo found himself thrust into the role of infantryman, leading combat engineers into battle.

Unlike the majority of our battalion's area, this sector was largely rural, well-irrigated farmland, and the majority of our patrols there were conducted on foot by platoon-sized elements, and backed up by the lighter, more maneuverable Bradley Fighting Vehicles, rather than by tanks. The Bradley is equipped with a 70 mm main gun and has similar optical systems to our M-1 Abrams Main Battle Tank. The Bradley is also an armored personnel carrier, with a drop-down ramp in the back for quick dismounts but with the added advantage of a 70 mm gun for fire support.

ANDROSOV, BOCHICHIO, AND THE ROUTE DUSTER MOSQUE

One of our Vermont medics, SPC Aleksey Androsov, was attached to Espo's platoon of combat engineers from the Rhode Island National Guard. They went out on a dismounted patrol one morning, bringing along our battalion surgeon, LTC Bochichio—a board-certified anesthesiologist who normally worked at the Pentagon specializing in weapons of mass destruction. Like many Army physicians, he deployed on a ninety-day tour with us in the middle of the worst place on earth.

SPC Androsov was the son of a retired Soviet diplomat assigned to the UN, and he grew up splitting his time between his Russian home and New York City. He was a cadet at Vermont's Norwich University, studying biology, when he was called to active duty. Aleksey disliked carrying a weapon, but he did so reluctantly when ordered to. A devout Russian Orthodox, for whom I had a lot of respect, he and I both struggled to discern right from wrong in this complex battlefield. While I overcame my reservations about using weapons, Aleksey insisted that he would fire only to protect himself or his patients. The Pentagon-based anesthesiologist and the Russian-born combat medic soon found themselves pinned down in a sheik's house, under intense enemy fire.

It was September 2005, and in an effort to build goodwill, LTC Bochichio arranged for the delivery of a generator and some medical supplies to an Iraqi clinic near Route Duster. They were unaware that the previous day, other U.S. forces accidentally killed the son of a sheik near the clinic. Before going to the clinic, Espo's platoon went to the home of the local sheik to tell him about the delivery and seek his favor. It was not his son that was killed, but rather the son of a sheik from an adjacent village. The sheik who lost his son gathered his men and struck out in search of vengeance against any U.S. forces they could find.

Carrying a generator and medical supplies, Espo's platoon escorted LTC Bochichio and SPC Androsov to the home of the sheik who controlled the area around the clinic. Some of the men took up positions on the sheik's roof, where they were spotted by the other sheik's insurgents. SFC Esposito and his platoon were inside the sheik's compound discussing their delivery when a large element of between fifty to sixty of the other sheik's men attacked. There were only eighteen U.S. soldiers present, and when Espo's radio operator attempted to call for reinforcements, the radio malfunctioned. Under heavy attack, cut off and unable to radio for help, Espo's men fired flares into the air to signal their 113s on Route Mobile (approximately two kilometers away). The 113 crews spotted the flares and were unable to raise Espo's patrol on the radio. They figured out something bad was happening, and they immediately set out across the difficult terrain to help.

The combat engineers from the Rhode Island National Guard spread out on the sheik's roof, engaging the insurgents and defending the compound. The insurgents soon figured out that there were not many U.S. soldiers present, and they encircled the trapped patrol in the compound. LTC Bochichio and SPC Androsov took up positions at the door with their 9 mm pistols drawn, periodically checking the guys on the roof for casualties. The situation was getting desperate, and our guys were down to the last of their ammunition.

After what seemed like an eternity, the 113s arrived and opened fire on the insurgents with their .50-cal machine guns and M-19 automatic grenade launcher. There was only a driver and a gunner in each truck, and no one available to carry ammo into the building.

LTC Bochichio set up the 113 for casualties while Androsov ran back and forth, grabbing as much ammo as he could, and running it up to the guys on the roof. Many of the insurgents were killed, and those who survived retreated. Many of the insurgents sought cover in the local mosque, while others ran down Route Duster to get away.

B company's commander was in the area with his executive officer. Each commanded a Bradley Fighting Vehicle. The Bradleys engaged the mosque with their 70 mm main guns, along with the .50-cal and M-19s from the 113s. Our forces are prohibited from attacking mosques, unless the enemy used it as a base of fire from which to attack. Our forces proceeded to destroy the building, and the Captain's Bradley gave chase to the retreating insurgents down Route Duster. An IED hit the commander's Bradley and disabled it. There were minor injuries, but no one was seriously hurt. The Mobile Wrench M-88 that came to tow the Captain's Bradley was also hit by an IED, but it was still able to complete the mission.

It was a close call for our guys, and had it not been for the courageous actions of everyone involved, they might have been wiped out.

True to his Hippocratic oath to first do no harm, our physician did not fire at the insurgents, but he braved a lot of enemy fire to deliver ammunition to our troops who did. For their bravery that day, several soldiers, including SPC Androsov, were awarded the Army Commendation Medal for Valor.

Route Duster became a priority for B Company, 109th Infantry. It was too dangerous to actually drive there, so our favorite way to get there was with a dismounted patrol from several kilometers away. By approaching unseen from the north, we were able to get within sight of the road and observe the enemy planting IEDs. A favorite tactic was to take over a house with a good view, and remain there for a day or so, hoping to get lucky. Often we did.

Later on in our deployment, our forces discovered an enormous weapons cache buried beneath the crops planted between Route Duster and the Euphrates River. There were hundreds of fifty-five gallon drums buried in the field, and each one was chock full of weapons and explosives. I later learned that a high-ranking officer from Saddam Hussein's Republican Guard owned much of the land in the area, and he had a huge compound in the orchards there. We suspected he was heavily involved in the insurgency, but the extent of his involvement was not immediately apparent.

LIKE VIETNAM, ONLY DRIER

Every Monday I relieved SPC Androsov and walked the dusty paths with his platoon among the reeds and orchards near the Euphrates River. It was September 2005, but it could have been 1968 half a world away. I thought back to the scenes of Vietnam that I remembered from the hit TV show *Tour of Duty*. I would even hum along to the sixties music featured in the show, like the Rolling Stones and Credence Clearwater Revival. Walking along with a platoon in reed beds and palm groves is a very different experience from roving in squad-sized elements mounted in humvees through urban neighborhoods or wide-open desert.

The most notable difference between the city and the country in Al Anbar Province for me was the stench. The cities and villages had no functioning municipal sewers or trash services. Sewage was dumped in the streets, and trash was put out to rot. In Ramadi, the stench was powerful. By contrast, the farm country and rural homes were much cleaner. They were still impoverished, and had only intermittent electrical service, but at least they were not overwhelmed with filth.

There were other, more subtle differences as well. Being on foot all day long was a lot of work. In 120 degree heat, drinking adequate water and maintaining a proper electrolyte balance was a challenge. All of the soldiers carried body armor and at least seven magazines full of ammunition. Medics carried all that, plus the additional burden of a rucksack aid bag. At one point, I weighed myself with all my stuff, and I weighed in at over 350 pounds. Keeping up with soldiers twenty years younger and fifty pounds lighter than me was not easy, but with sheer determination somehow I managed to keep up.

I enjoyed the workout and the challenges, though, and I looked forward to those days. The fresh air was a nice change. The enemy was out there, and we were frequently in contact, but many of the ordinary civilians in these areas really just wanted to live their agrarian lives and be left alone. While they would shelter the insurgents if they had to, they did not seem unhappy to have us around maintaining the peace. B Company, 109th Infantry, had their hands full in this area, but they managed to defeat or chase out the insurgents for the most part. A choice had to be made between a vehicle-mounted approach like that used by other companies, or dismounted patrols. B Company did not maintain observation posts the way the other companies did, so there was no twenty-four-hour presence in their area. The trade-off, however, was that when they hit the field, their entire combat power was able to maneuver. Their tactics proved to be effective.

I went out on my first two missions as a relief medic with the Scout Platoon. I had a bond with them, as I have known them for many years, drilling in the same armory in Swanton. My first mission went out at 0800, and was a seven-hour foot patrol south of the highway. We went sneaking through the woods and tall grass (unusual for Iraq) and infiltrated a village unnoticed. We searched a house, found nothing, and continued on. After we moved out, the last man in the formation spotted the eighteen-year-old male in the house making a cell phone call. Lieutenant Armstrong ordered him detained. A more thorough search of the house revealed IED-making materials. We detained him and left the area to go north to our vehicles.

When we had almost reached our tracks, an IED exploded within six feet of two of our soldiers. They were uninjured, thankfully, because the charge had been hastily placed, and most of the blast was directed away from them.

I went out again several hours later, on a night mission. As was my custom, I prayed part of the Rosary on the way out. It was an interesting patrol, sneaking around this village at night with night-vision goggles on, peering into every hiding place.

At one point, we heard a huge explosion, rather like a launch of an artillery round. Then we heard the unmistakable sound of incoming. We quickly dove off the road into the ditches on both sides. I thought for sure we were dead. Many Iraqis do not have sewers, but dump everything into the ditches. The stench was horrible. I had sometimes heard that at the moment of death people's life will flash before them, or they will pray or think of their families. I did nothing of the sort. I turned, sniffed the air, and thought, "Great! I am going to die in a sewer!"

BULL SHOOTING
Danger came in an unexpected form while we were out on a dismounted patrol in the farms and palm groves south of OP 5. We had two platoons but just one medic. I was in the middle, between the two platoons, and we were making our way through a farm and on past a rather irate bull. The bull was chained to a stake in the ground, and our guys were spread out in ten-meter intervals, crossing the barnyard in a column of two. It was clearly evident who the country boys were, as they

weren't the least bit bothered by the bull. The city guys, though, were clearly scared of him, as he snorted and jumped around at us, looking from one soldier to the next, and raring at us. I had just made it past him, when I heard one of our guys scream behind me. I turned to see that the bull had broken loose from his stake and was charging straight at one of the guys. The soldier ran and jumped over a ditch, grabbing a tree trunk on the far side, and getting out of the bull's way. The bull did not slow down for the ditch, and went in feet first, slamming his head against the far bank. SGT Davidson, fearing for his buddy's life, tried to distract the bull, so he would not gore the other soldier, clinging to the tree, just out of reach on the far side of the ditch. Sure enough, the bull turned on Davidson, clambering back up out of the ditch and running straight at him, horns down, ready to tear him in half. The slightly embellished version of what happened next was the front-page story of a "newspaper" that mysteriously appeared all over the FOB the next day. The "reporter" took some liberties and the bull became a lovesick cow.

THE BRAVO BULLSHOOTER

SGT Davidson Narrowly Escapes With His Life,
Almost Killed Saving Life of Soldier

Dateline Ramadi; It was a beautiful fall morning in the serene orchards and pastures South of OP 5. The breeze was blowing, and the leaves were falling as the men of B Company, 109 Infantry patrolled through the area. "A Beautiful Day to Die," thought SGT Davidson, as he stepped around a cow patty and shrugged off the feeling of impending doom that nagged at his soul.

Passing through a cow pen, two calves were quietly munching hay. Most of the patrol made it past their irate mother, chained to a stake in the yard, but not SGT Cardinale. The mad cow snorted and scuffed her hooves as most of the patrol walked by, but something in the way he mooooooved, stirred this forlorn bovine into action. In an instant, she broke free from her chain and was on him in an instant. "I could tell she was upset. Maybe she thought I was the deadbeat bull that left her with these two calves, but I swear it was not me!!" SGT Cardinale said afterward.

The cow rushed at SGT Cardinale, tossing him aside like a used Kleenex, he landed across a creek. "Thank God the creek was now between us, because she stumbled and fell trying to chase me across it."

Rushing to his buddy's aid, SGT Davidson came out of nowhere. In the proud traditions of Rodeo Clowns everywhere, he distracted the love lorn bovine from the object of her affections.

The Cow turned and charged right at SGT Davidson, and he stumbled backward in the face of her advance. Tripping and falling, only a few feet remained between him and the great horned demon, the hot breath from her giant cow nostrils steaming before her like the very flames of hell. SGT Davidson tells us what happened next.

". . . Out of options now, and in fear for my life, I fired at her. She reared up and continued at me. I fired again, and again, and again. Finally, she lay at my feet, struggling to breathe. I fired again at the fallen cow, and finally her demons left her."

"Clearly it was a good shoot," said SFC Esperanza, "We are authorized to use deadly force to save our lives, or to stop a rape. Clearly this cow intended to rape SGT Cardinale and kill SGT Davidson. Iraq is better off without the likes of this unholy beast."

• • •

CHARLIE'S HIGHWAY

After my introduction to this area with the Scout Platoon, I filled in occasionally with Charlie Company doing roving patrol out on the highway. The guys were suspicious of an abandoned house south of one of their observation posts, and planned to search it and make sure it was indeed vacant. The house offered a perfect vantage point for snipers to fire at one of our observation posts, and like most houses in Iraq, it was made of concrete and stone, so it offered protection from our counterfire.

Generally speaking, the Charlie Company rovers did not leave the highway much, so this was a new experience for all of us. It was broad daylight, and there was not much concealment from the house as we approached. We pulled our vehicles over on the side of the highway out of view, and tried to maximize the use of natural concealment as we approached from the front and the rear. There were only five men along on this mission, and they planned to use four men in a stack to assault the front door, just like we trained to do in Camp Shelby. This left me to cover the back door alone.

We approached the front yard of the house, staying low behind the earthen embankments of the irrigation canal one hundred meters or so from the front. From here I spotted a similar berm running right along the back of the house.

I set out alone to find a vantage point from which to guard the rear door, and they waited a few minutes for me to get into position. I crept along, bent over double at the waist to stay out of view, thinking of how beautiful this area was. It was my first exposure to operating in this thickly vegetated area, and I could not help but think of Vietnam. In my mind, the lyrics to "Paint It Black" played over and over, and I reflected on how crazy this was to be working alone. I was not terribly concerned, though, because I figured the house was empty and this was largely a training exercise.

When I reached the intersection of the two irrigation canals, I poked my head up over the canal, and realized that the other canal would take me to within ten feet of the back door. Reasonably certain the house was empty, I got low in the canal, up to my knees in the clear water, and crept up to the house. I scanned from inside the canal and found no movement in the house, but could see that our guys in the front were still a long way off.

On a whim, I got ambitious and leapt out of the canal, charging silently across the remaining ten feet to stop with my back against the wall of the house. I crept along to the first window, and popped my head up, scanning the room with my rifle ready . . . the room was empty.

I went on to the next window and the next window and found the entire house empty.

Smug now, I waited until our guys rushed across the front yard, watching from around the corner as they crossed the last twenty meters of open ground. "The house is clear," I said calmly from around the corner.

"What the f . . .?" they exclaimed

"Yeah, I cleared it from the back yard, there's nobody in there." I smiled, coming around the corner into their view.

It would not be the only time that I left the infantry guys shaking their heads and wondering about this crazy medic in their midst. I was not content to sit out the fighting while our guys did all the work. As far as I was concerned, I was a team player. I fought with the memory of 343 brother firefighters, and over 2,000 civilians murdered by Al Qaeda on September 11. A growing number of my fellow Guardsmen made the ultimate sacrifice as well.

Life by the Sword

During my first night on patrol in the Tameem District of Ramadi with Alpha Company, I got a taste of things to come. It was an afternoon/evening shift in mid-October, and I rolled out in the late afternoon riding with Joe Lewis to conduct some random house searches.

We searched homes at random to keep the enemy off balance. Although it sounds overbearing, in reality we conducted most of these random searches politely. Normally we knocked on the doors and we were courteous with the families. We didn't mistreat people, and we didn't break their stuff or destroy their homes.

I always carried a bag of candy in my pocket for the kids, so that after we finished the search, we could let them know we were not monsters. In my mind, it was always a good idea to befriend the children. They had not yet spent a lifetime learning to hate us, and someday they would be the leaders in this country. It was worth the effort to set an example of being professional, ethical, and even kind. It was only when we suspected insurgents were hiding in a given house or when we stumbled across evidence of insurgents that we became more aggressive and thorough.

When Joe was finally able to resume patrols back with his unit, he would frequently have his medic check his bandages, sometimes while on patrol. The first day I rode out with Joe and his platoon was one such day. We had a great time getting acquainted, with Joe telling all the guys what a great medic I was, and how I would do anything for you. I told them about how I grew frustrated working in the rear and had asked to come out with the infantry for a change. They liked me right away.

So out of the blue, Joe picked out a house and said, "Let's search that one!" Apparently this would be a random house search, since no one else saw a problem.

Receiving small arms fire, our guys take cover behind the
CROW truck. (Photo by SGT Brandon Allmond)

We lined up in a stack by the door, gave it the boot, and charged in,
sweeping every room with our weapons. We put the family in one room
for one guy to guard, and some of our guys proceeded to do a detailed
house search, while Joe and I stood in the foyer. Grabbing a nearby bed-
room, Joe called me in, shut the door behind us, and dropped his pants.
"My leg is really hurting, Doc, can you do something with it?"

Incredulous, I stared at him. "Did we storm this house just so you
could drag me in here and drop your pants?" I asked. "Yeah, pretty
much . . . it really hurts doc!"

Shaking my head in disbelief, I opened up my aid bag and knelt down
in front of Joe to change his bandage and give him a shot for pain. As
luck would have it, that's the position we were in when one of the guys
opened up the door behind me, and just stopped in shock. But that was
Joe, always kidding around, and not the least bit bashful.

In the early evening hours, just after nightfall, we knocked on the door
of a house in 5K. As is the Arab custom, the man of the house met us at the
door, wished us the Peace of Allah, and invited us in. It is their custom that
one must invite visitors in and offer food, drink, shelter, and protection.

The family had just finished their evening meal of rice and lamb, and some of the children were watching something in Arabic on television. Their selections were generally limited to news programs, music videos, and a limited selection of old western movies dubbed into their language.

Right away I sensed that something was different about this family. Unlike the majority of Iraqis, this man was over six feet tall and had bright red hair and a pale reddish complexion. Except for his traditional robes he looked very western, and could have passed me on the streets in any American city without a second glance. I wondered if he was actually an American spy, trying in vain to look like an Iraqi.

The man seemed to have no comprehension of English, however, and through our interpreter we learned that he was the illegitimate son of an Iraqi woman and a British soldier stationed here decades ago. Although he looked western, he seemed to have no other ties to the west. He had served in the Iraqi Army when he was younger, and seemed hostile and irritated by our presence in his home.

He denied any knowledge of insurgent activity in his neighborhood, and told us he operated a market nearby. His home was modest but clean, and his quality furnishings indicated to us that his market was successful. He had a comfortable home, several children, and a successful business, and I wondered if perhaps we were barking up the wrong tree in searching this guy's home.

One of our guys, however, found an AK-47, several magazines, and two rifle grenade adapters in the house. The rifle grenade adapters were used to fit a rocket onto the barrel of an AK-47. The rocket was launched when a blank round was fired through the rifle. It was not very accurate, but it was deadly and easily concealed. It was permissible and very common for almost every household to possess an AK-47. They were allowed to keep one magazine to use for home defense. The weapons could not be carried outside the home, and no other weapons or ammunition (pistols, RPGs, grenades, or extra magazines) were allowed. Possession of prohibited munitions was sufficient grounds to send someone to prison as an insurgent.

The red-headed man claimed ignorance about the extra magazines and claimed the rifle grenade adapters were leftover from his days in the Army and he had forgotten that he even had them. Our squad leader didn't believe him, so he decided to bring him back to the FOB for further questioning. Our policy was that he must be handcuffed and blindfolded during the ride in. We could not allow a potential insurgent to see the details of our base defenses. We had a "detainee kit" buried somewhere in the trunk of the humvee, underneath lots of other stuff. We led the prisoner out to the vehicle without handcuffs or blindfolds, and had him wait there while our driver looked for the kit in the dark.

The rest of us spread out to pull 360 degree security—each of us scanning for threats. It seemed like it took forever to locate the handcuffs in the dark. We were attracting a lot of attention, and it was time to leave the area before the insurgents had time to launch an attack. I learned that they would watch our movements through town and wait for us to stop, then attack with small-arms fire or RPGs.

Through the greenish glow of my night-vision monocle I scanned the empty street in front of me. Between the haze of the monocle and the dusty sand blowing around, the misty night air looked like a foggy night back home. There were a few empty vehicles parked here and there, but no pedestrians anywhere. Suddenly three men appeared at the end of the block. They walked casually out into the middle of the intersection, two of them carrying rifles and the third man carrying an RPG launcher. They froze like deer in the headlights—surprised to find an American patrol parked in the middle of their neighborhood, dismounted soldiers all around.

I whipped my rifle up and took aim, while shouting a warning to our guys. Before I even brought the rifle to my shoulder, they were gone, running down the side street out of our view. I had no doubt they intended to set up an ambush or circle back to attack from another direction.

We grabbed our prisoner and threw him into the back seat. Someone had finally found a pair of the disposable plastic "zip-cuffs" handcuffs we carried, and he was struggling to assemble them and put them on when I shouted my warning. I climbed in with the prisoner, aimed my pistol at him, and we took off. We did not want to allow the three-man RPG team time to set up an attack. Our red-headed prisoner cooperated—he understood perfectly well the universal language of a muzzle pressed into his rib cage. We managed to get him handcuffed and blindfolded while our driver "un-assed" the area (got us out of there fast).

I couldn't believe it took so long to get the handcuffs out and put them on in the dark. Essentially the zip-cuffs are like two large plastic cable ties. They come as one long black plastic piece, and both ends must be brought around and inserted through the locking device in the center, forming two loops for the prisoner's wrists. This is not easy to do in the dark, looking through a single night-vision monocle. The sight picture is good, but with only one eye in use, the monocle does not provide any depth perception. Once the cuffs are tightened around the prisoner's wrists, they can not be loosened. The only way to take them off is to cut them away.

We rode back to the FOB in silence, the prisoner gritting his teeth and fuming at his predicament. He did not say a word, but clearly he was bristling. I could not help but imagine the life this fifty-plus-year-old man had to endure growing up as an ashamed illegitimate son of a British soldier and an Iraqi woman of ill repute. His pale skin and red hair must have marked him as a constant target. Perhaps he had little contact with the western world after he was fathered. Perhaps he knew no better life than this. It was a little disconcerting. I was expecting the enemy I had never met to look like an Iraqi. This character was unsettling; it felt like I was pointing a weapon at an ally—a British subject.

After almost enduring an RPG attack thanks to the clumsy zip-cuffs, I got in touch with a police officer friend back in Vermont. He mailed me several brand-new pairs of top-quality Smith and Wesson police handcuffs. I carried two pairs and distributed the rest to my buddies.

In time, I used my new cuffs a lot. They were very quick to put on, were re-usable, and had a double-lock safety feature that prevented the prisoner from tightening them further—facilitating an escape by convincing a guard to remove them. The metal handcuffs were also less prone to injure the prisoner—eliminating the need for medical treatment and grounds for the prisoner to claim he was abused.

There were deeper reasons for me to deal humanely with the prisoners we took, however. I was methodical, dispassionate, and professional about searching them. Displaying these traits was an indirect way of leading our men by example. We also realized that most of our prisoners would eventually be released. Being humane to them did not fuel their negative stereotypes of us, and it did not cement their hatred of us to the point that they would carry out a lifelong vendetta. Hopefully these men would one day lead peaceful and productive lives in a safe and secure nation. On a personal level, however, I was curious about the Iraqi people. Providing humane treatment to the prisoners or medical care to their wounded gave me an opportunity to see for myself the human face of this invisible enemy we fought. Most of them were unremarkable—but in the eyes of some, I found fiery daggers of molten bloodlust, forged in hatred and fueled by death —evil incarnate—as if Satan himself was among us.

DEATH BY THE SWORD:
TWO MARINE AVIATORS AND LT. MARK PROCOPIO

I came to love working with Alpha Company under the command of Major Jason Pelletier. True to the name of their task force, Alpha Company was an aggressive bunch, who lived by the sword and took the saber's edge to the enemy's throat. After months of frustration in the defensive role, this was exactly where I wanted to be, and I preferred working with Alpha Company over any other. I patrolled Tameem three days a week with three different platoons from Alpha Company, and I spent a month filling in with SFC Eric Duncan and Blue Platoon when their regular medic went home on leave.

I rode out one morning with Red Platoon, under the leadership of SSG Scott Mattheson—a huge man well versed in the history and lore of the American desert southwest. SSG Mattheson spoke with a southern drawl and carried himself with the strength of a mustang. He likened the streets of Tameem to the old days in the wild, wild west. Out here, the sheriff upheld the law with the end of a gun. It was that simple.

On the far side of Ramadi, a team of four insurgents hid in the thick underbrush. As a Marine Corps Apache helicopter flew overhead, they stood and fired a surface-to-air missile. The two marine pilots aboard the Apache were killed in the crash. Nearby, an unmanned aerial vehicle (UAV) transmitted images of the engagement to our TOC (tactical operations center), where our people tracked the movements of the four insurgents.

Back in the TOC, the battle captain noted the location of the crash site and radioed Charlie Company to dispatch their rovers.

The UAV operator saw the four-man missile team run from their hiding place to a white truck nearby. They fled into the city of Ramadi, attempting to hide in plain sight by losing themselves in heavy traffic. Although there were a lot of white trucks, just like this one on the streets, the UAV operator tracked them, and the TOC described their vehicle to our patrols over the radio. They were headed straight toward us.

Out on MSR Mobile, Lt. Mark Procopio saw the helicopter go down south of his position near Route Duster. He responded immediately, without waiting to be sent. His two-vehicle patrol raced across the open desert, avoiding roads filled with IEDs. But buried in the dirt near a bridge they had to cross was a shaped-charge mine. The explosion tore through the humvee floor, killing Lt. Procopio instantly. Miraculously, the other soldiers in the humvee were not injured. One of them, SPC John Sue, a former paramedic and Navy corpsman, tried desperately to save his lieutenant, but to no avail. By the time our 113 ambulance arrived, he was gone.

Our other patrol spotted the target vehicle as it approached a key intersection. In no time, the four insurgents found themselves spread out on the pavement at gunpoint.

Alone in my thoughts and oblivious to the world around, I rode in the back seat of Alpha Company's rovers in Tameem, contemplating life and escaping through the tunes in my MP3 player. I did not hear the radio traffic when it told us about a BOLO (be on the lookout for) alert for a white bongo truck with four military-aged males in it.

We arrived moments after the first team took the men out of their truck. We took over guarding the prisoners, while the other team searched the vehicle. I searched and handcuffed them, then headed back to my truck.

As I crossed the street, another white bongo truck loaded with crates came at us, weaving around the parked cars and accelerating toward our position. I waved my weapon at him, and then pointed it at him. He did not seem to notice. I raised my weapon and fired one tracer round across his front and into the dirt, then switched it to burst and raised it at the windshield. Fortunately he stopped, turned around, and fled the area. I did not yet know for sure that the men we captured were indeed the men who killed the two marines. The truck I fired at was identical with this one. I reflected on my first shots fired in anger. I could have just as easily taken the driver out. Should I have?

It was not until two years later that I met up with SSgt. Mattheson (now a commissioned officer) and he told me the whole story. He knew all along that the four men we captured were responsible for the death of Lt. Procopio and the two marines, but I didn't. The truck I fired on was just a bystander, but our prisoners had American blood on their hands. We had all done the right thing. The guilty were captured and brought to justice while the innocent were not harmed.

I remember reading years ago in a book about the Vietnam War that eventually men in combat learn to accept their own mortality. The book described a period of great fear followed by the realization that death is a certainty. The last stage of this process was described as a state in which the soldier knows he will not make it home alive, but goes on, figuring that he might as well do the most he can while he is here. I have reflected on that passage many times in my career as a firefighter, when death seemed near. In this conflict, I made a conscious effort to accelerate the acceptance process in my mind.

No one can really lie to himself, but we can make a concerted effort to control our outlook on life. I found that I was pretty good at keeping up a positive outlook, secure in my faith that we were doing good here, that I was at peace with God, and that should I die here He would look after my family. I was not eager to die, for I had many years of fatherhood to look forward to. I did not have such a sense of ownership of this war that I felt compelled to give my life in its cause. I am, however, a committed patriot and altruist. I believe that what we came here to do is a just cause. I further believe that as much as I have a duty to provide for my family, I am also obligated to answer our nation's call in time of war, and I have done so. I served to the fullest, never holding back hoping for the extra element of safety, but always alert in battle and mindful of the dangers.

SOLDIERING IN DISSOLUTION

I always try to keep an upbeat attitude. Partly this is for my own benefit, as I am mindful not to fall victim to a downward spiral of despair. However, this is also for the benefit of the troops around me who have it worse than I do. I find that a smile and a kind word can really help. On a daily basis, I am no longer concerned with defeating the insurgency, but am content to bring relief to just one person at a time.

One afternoon in October, while riding along with Alpha Company. in the Streets of Tameem, I got reacquainted with an old friend. He joined the Army National Guard after September 11. A principled man, he felt it was his duty to help protect his country. He became a voice of reason in the squad he led, treating all Iraqis with dignity and respect, keeping the hot-tempered youth around him in check. A patriot, but also a liberal, he did not envision coming to Iraq in a conflict he felt was motivated more by greed for oil than concern for national security. Feeling disillusioned and deeply betrayed, he fought now to keep his soul intact and his buddies alive, spiteful of the president and the defense secretary who had sent us here to conduct a "half-assed war." His sentiment was tactical and straightforward. If we were to defeat these insurgents, we should do so at once, with overwhelming force. There should be a division here rather than a brigade. We agreed that to attempt to secure a city of fifty thousand people with one patrol and four dismounts was ludicrous. I told him about an idea I had, identifying the core values that our military embodies, and passing them on to the next generation of schoolchildren back home. He was keenly interested in this thought, and wanted to help.

Later that afternoon, we rolled through the streets of an area we called "2 Bravo," patrolling the most dangerous part of Tameem looking for insurgents. We talked about how ludicrous this was, to cruise around deep in enemy territory, waiting for them to attack us so that we could fight back. We agreed that we should be stopping those who inflicted terror on innocent civilians, but with a massive offensive, after which we would establish a safe environment for everyone. Using only two vehicles and six men acting as bait was a crazy way to find the bad guys. It was a recipe for failure, and a futile attempt to provide security for the Iraqi civilians.

We rounded the corner onto Route Jones, the main street dividing Tameem. "BOOM!!!" As if on cue, an IED exploded right next to us, engulfing us in a cloud of thick smoke and showering our truck with shrapnel and rocks.

"Get us out of here!!" the squad leader screamed. He was closest to the blast—I couldn't tell if he was hit. I stomped on the accelerator, racing out of the kill zone. Looking behind us, our squad leader scanned for our second truck. An eternity later, the other humvee raced out of the cloud of smoke.

A quick check confirmed that everyone was OK. The IED was a mortar round buried in the dirt beside the road. Evidently, it was buried too deep, and we were spared the worst of the blast. After our shift ended, I checked out the shrapnel damage to our truck. It was just pure luck that our gunner was not killed.

Although I disagreed with his view of the war, I felt great sympathy for men like our squad leader. It was difficult enough for me to suffer through this conflict, but I didn't have an issue with our mission. To me, killing in the cause of a just war is not a sin—shocking and brutal, yes, but not a

An IED explodes near our patrol. In this case, it did
little damage. (Photo by SGT Brandon Allmond)

sin. The soldiers who genuinely believed that we were not fighting a just
war, or the atheist soldiers who did not believe in an afterlife—for these
men the present was all they had . . . so sad . . . no future, a civilian life
they might never return to, and just this dismal wartime reality around
them.

GUNFIGHTERS

We rolled out of Ogden Gate one afternoon for an evening shift. I settled into the backseat of SFC Duncan's humvee as we rolled down MSR
Michigan, headed for OP 293, a key observation post on the western edge
of Tameem. Traffic fell away in front of us for the most part—they knew
better than to come close to our humvees. Our driver dodged around
potholes, otherwise known as IED craters, while our gunner waved his
arms and shouted at other drivers. From time to time he fired a few
warning shots, getting the attention of the errant drivers who failed to
notice our presence and get out of the way.

I mused about the similarities between clearing traffic with a weapon
atop a humvee versus clearing traffic with a siren and light bar on a fire

engine back home. Both were effective, but for some reason very few people ignored the warning shots in Ramadi like the occasional driver ignored the lights and sirens back home.

There was not much going on that afternoon, and SFC Duncan shared his thoughts on combat as we patrolled. There were so many ways for the enemy to attack us. The key to our surviving the enemy's attacks and then defeating the enemy was to identify and kill the enemy before he killed you.

Survival in this violent urban battle space depended on what he described as a "combat mind-set." This required a "can do" attitude and a clear and open mind that was alert, analytical, and aggressive. The key to survival in this complex urban battlefield was to identify the enemy's tactics, interrupt them, and then defeat him. There is no second-place finisher in a gunfight.

The combat mind-set began with conquering one's own fear of dying. Some soldiers simply resigned themselves to their inevitable deaths. Others accepted becoming "evil for a while" and hoped that a merciful God would consider their sacrifices along with their sins. I was initially taken aback at the thought of our troops becoming "evil for a while," but in time I learned they were not suspending the rules of engagement or ignoring their moral compass. For all the tough talk, "evil for a while" actually referred to their concern for collateral harm to noncombatants while engaging the enemy. We tried hard to minimize collateral damage, but sometimes it could not be helped.

Our young gunner summarized SFC Duncan's philosophy in simple terms. He learned everything he could about the enemy tactics before he went out the gate. While on patrol, he was constantly alert for any component of the enemy's known tactics. When he identified hostile intent, he engaged the target rapidly, decisively, and with sufficient force to eliminate the threat.

Often, the enemy broke up his actions into many steps in order to better conceal his true intention. A common tactic was to position an observer somewhere, and equip him with a means to observe and communicate sightings of our movements to others who waited to attack us. In other cases, several people would actually drop off different parts of IEDs on the roadside. Each one would merely slow his pace a little, drop something and move on. The last man would stoop and throw them together in only a few quick seconds. The completed IED could then be remotely detonated, or it could be rigged such that the victim caused the detonation. The key to countering the significant threat that IEDs posed was recognizing any part of an enemy tactic and taking decisive action to stop it.

SFC Duncan described the combat decision-making process as the OODA cycle. The acronym stood for observe, orient, decide, act. First we observe something, then orient toward it, decide if it is a threat, and finally act upon our decision. (The OODA cycle was first described by Col. John Boyd, a U.S. Air Force fighter pilot who fought in the Korean War. These concepts were later given concrete form by SFC Duncan when he and CPT Chad Dearborn coauthored a training manual on close-quarters combat, entitled *Gunfighter*.)

I stared out at Tameem as we drove through it, reflecting on and internalizing these lessons. For me, conquering my own fear began with reconciliation with God. I made it a habit to pray on our way out the gate. I felt at ease in combat, secure in the faith that I would be OK if I should be killed.

FORSAKEN STRONGHOLD

In view of the amount of enemy activity taking place near Route Duster and the agricultural areas near it, the decision was made to construct a stronghold there with a permanent presence. The occupation of the stronghold would primarily be a mission for the Iraqi Army, but with U.S. advisors along. Our troops would also be responsible for the majority of the construction work.

With the 876th Engineers already responsible for their own sector to our east, and one of their platoons already detailed to our battalion, the mission to construct the stronghold fell largely to the combat engineer platoon I filled in with, along with our own HHC Support Platoon.

The house that we took over as a base while we built the stronghold offered a great view of the road, but little in the way of amenities. Our Support Platoon braved countless hours traveling to and from this stronghold delivering building materials. Our recovery section (the same guys who provided security for our medic track at the gate to our FOB) spent weeks on end setting up Texas barriers with their 88 recovery vehicle, not only around this stronghold but also throughout our entire area.

The only good way in or out of this stronghold involved a thirty-minute trip across the dirt farming areas, on a series of what we called

Several Iraqi soldiers pose near their campfire
with the author. (Photo provided by the author)

the canal roads. It was dangerous and time consuming, and the troops
working at the stronghold knew they would be waiting a long time for
reinforcements when the enemy attacked.

My part in creating the stronghold was to go along as the medic with
the same platoon of engineers. It was interesting to see the same guys I
had patrolled with now shed their body armor and weapons and become
builders once again. Within this one platoon were representatives of
most of the building trades, including carpentry, masonry, and plumbing. The only thing they lacked was an electrician. I was an assistant fire
marshal, but I lacked any particular skills in construction, so I volunteered to run wires, worked with the similarly unskilled Iraqi soldiers,
and hauled sandbags to reinforce the windows. It was hard work, but I
enjoyed it. It gave me insight into the character of the Iraqi troops we
hope to someday turn this country over to.

Many of the Iraqi troops truly wanted to make a difference, and actually worked hard, but a sizable number of them did not care about the
construction of this fort they would later inhabit and depend upon for
their very lives. Some of them were so lazy they would do no work unless

threatened. There seemed to be a general lack of motivation and discipline in the Iraqi forces. Our communication was limited by the lack of an interpreter, but we were able to communicate sufficiently through pantomime and the small amount of Arabic I knew. I would have liked to speak more with these guys, and learn about their backgrounds, but the language barrier was steep.

A few weeks after the stronghold was completed, I returned to the area with a different platoon from the 109th Infantry. We had established an observation post atop a nearby house, and I spent some time up on the roof, keeping watch over the road. My hours there were uneventful, but I had some really neat experiences. From this vantage point, I came to appreciate the tremendous natural beauty of the area, with tall palm trees, verdant pastures, and frequent visits by turtledoves. The Garden of Eden was supposed to be somewhere near here, all those years ago before the area became a desert. The irrigation ditches along the Euphrates here had restored fertile soil from the desert sands. The peaceful doves that would land on our combat outposts would belie the war we fought and offer us hope for eventual peace.

Directly across the road from the stronghold, our units found an enormous weapons cache. The insurgents had planted vast armaments and explosives beneath the rich moist croplands there near the river, and would launch mortar attacks and other activities from there. They could travel in and out of the area unarmed, pick up their weapons and bombs when they got there, and cause us a lot of headaches. It was a great day when our guys found this cache, and it took several days and hundreds of trips by truck to get everything out.

A lot of our men were hurt, and several were killed in bringing this part of the country under control. The 109th infantry did it the hard way, with sheer grit and determination.

The Streets of Tameem

The streets of Tameem were a deadly and unforgiving place. Just venturing out there was putting your life in extreme danger. A slum with about fifty thousand inhabitants, it was rife with snipers, IEDs, and RPG teams. Every rooftop, every doorway, every corner potentially held a deadly ambush. The insurgency was alive and well here, and those who did not come here to attack us were driving through on their way to attack the Marines on the other side of the river.

Many of the streets were narrow, with three- and four-story buildings built very close to the roadways. The roofs and upper windows offered vantage points for snipers and RPG teams. In other areas, courtyard walls surrounded small yards and offered the insurgents a vantage point from which to fire on our patrols. IED triggermen could hide anywhere and never be discovered. Raw sewage flowed unchecked through the garbage-strewn streets. The intensity of the stench was heightened further for us by our edgy tension.

The insurgents had a wide variety of weapon systems to use against us, from AK-47s, RPGs, mortars, and IEDs to less common sniper rifles and explosively formed projectiles capable of penetrating several inches of heavy armor and disabling a tank. It seemed as if every house had a parapet wall around the roof and a concrete or stone wall around the yard. Few of the windows had glass in them. The architecture gave the enemy an infinite number of places to hide while they triggered IEDs or shot at us. The insurgents used their plentiful cover to attack our patrols almost every day. At the beginning of each shift, we would sweep the main roads for IEDs and usually find several. Fortunately, we became quite adept at spotting them, and most of them were disarmed before they could explode. A cordon would be set up around the bomb

SSG Jeff Murtha covers an approach to his concealed
position in Tameem (Photo by SGT Brandon Allmond)

and the emergency explosives ordinance team would come out and deal
with them. Most bombs were blown up in place, and a few were disabled
and brought back to be studied.

The best way to locate the insurgents here was either to collect information on their whereabouts through informants and target their homes,
or through random house and vehicle searches. It was common for us to

bang on someone's door at any hour, enter, and search their home. This tactic had been in use for so long that the locals came to tolerate it. Usually at the end of the house search when we did not find anything, we would try to visit with the family good-naturedly, ask them about their neighborhoods and the enemy activity there, and make friends with their children. There was an added advantage to speaking with people privately, in the shelter of their own home: they were free to speak freely with us and not be seen doing it. In fact, by randomly searching all sorts of homes, we were able to conceal the identities of our actual informants.

The zip-lock bag full of candy in my pocket was handy for communicating to the children that we were not bad guys coming to take them away. We wanted very much for the children to know that they could trust us and should not attack us. Their parents may have hated us, but ten years from now these children would have to decide whether to become insurgents or perhaps to live peacefully. Often I would be presented with sick or injured children to heal during our tours. It was great to see that the parents trusted us to help their kids, and great to have a chance to help them.

In some cases, we quietly took families under our wing. We could not be too obvious, or they would be killed by the insurgents, but we did what we could. SSG Jeff Murtha of Blue Platoon was one of our toughest squad leaders. He and his driver, Sgt. Brandon Allmond, were especially touched by a mentally retarded Iraqi teenager named Abu Jassim. Like most families in Tameem, Abu and his family struggled to survive. They were poor, but they were friendly to everyone who visited their home—including SSG Murtha and his crew. The guys would stop by to visit Abu and his family from time to time, and were always welcomed.

I was touched by the kindness shown on both sides. SSG Murtha fooled almost everyone with his tough exterior, but he tipped his hand when he and the guys all chipped in and bought Abu Jassim a CD player for Christmas. I don't think Abu understood the significance of the holiday, but he loved music. The CD player meant so much to him, and we would see him walking the streets listening to it all the time.

We would focus our efforts on the main routes around Tameem and try to keep at least these roads free of IEDs. To this end, we had three observation posts that we manned, two with armored tanks or Bradley Fighting Vehicles and one with humvees. The armored vehicles were

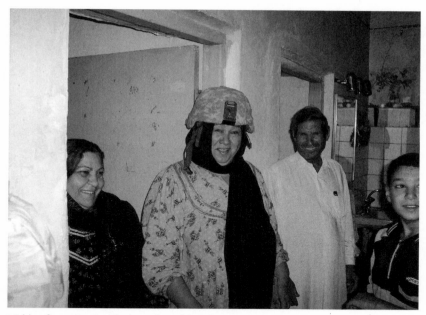

Hidden from view inside the safety of their home, many families were friendly. (Photo by SGT Brandon Allmond)

equipped with ten-power night-vision scopes and with thermal scopes (a heat-sensing optical system used to see at night). They could use their entire weapons array very effectively with these optics, and often did.

ROUTE JONES—THE MECCA OF DEATH

Route Jones was a four-lane boulevard with a median, running through the main part of town. On one side were factories, warehouses, and Al Anbar University; on the other side was a large residential area that presented most of our problems. There were old rusting playgrounds near the edge of the road, and mountains of trash everywhere. Herds of goats, stray donkeys, and thousands of people crossed Route Jones every day on their way to work or school, and the trash on the roadsides made a great place to hide IEDs. The insurgents would mingle in with the crowd on foot, and several of them would each carry a part of an IED. One would have the triggering device, one the explosive charge, still another wires to connect them all. The last guy would be the one to assemble all the elements and leave it to blow us up as we passed. These terrorists didn't usually stop moving long enough for us to catch them.

Despite the constant small arms fire and IEDs, children continued to play on the old rusting swing sets alongside Route Jones. (Photo by author)

We were constantly vigilant for the tell-tale signs of an IED: freshly turned dirt, antennas or command wires, or garbage left right next to the road. We often traced the command wires back to the insurgents' hiding place, and we used electronic jamming to interfere with the radio signals used to detonate IEDs. In spite of these efforts, our troops were blown up countless times on Route Jones. We found the best way to defeat them was to declare the entire street a free-fire zone. The word went out: you may cross this road, but do not stop or bend over for any reason or we will kill you. Not only were our gunners effective with the massive firepower of their main guns, but using the high-powered aiming systems on the tanks for their .30- and .50-caliber weapons they could observe and kill very effectively from almost two kilometers away with a single shot. The tactic was very effective. Once people started seeing insurgents dropping dead while they set their bombs, people quit doing it.

One of the first insurgents I saw gunned down on Route Jones died in a most interesting way. He was kneeling down in the median setting a charge. When he died, he remained in the perfect prayer position, arms outstretched toward Mecca in front of him. Perhaps Allah was kinder to him than we were. Although I would normally treat enemy wounded as our own, I would only do it when the tactical situation permitted it. In this case, being in the median on Route Jones was like being one of the pigeons in a sideshow shooting gallery. All that was missing was the bell that would ring when one of our vehicles would get small-arms fire. I looked through a set of high-powered binoculars at the dead man, from a hundred meters away. "Yep, he's dead."

When the insurgents began to catch on that they were not killing very many of us with IEDs and small-arms fire, they began to change their tactics. They started using more victim-detonated IEDs, VBIEDs, RPGs, and complex attacks using IEDs to stop our vehicles and then secondary attacks using small arms and RPGs to attack our dismounted troops.

Our best defense against this varying array of enemy tactics was constant vigilance for any part of an enemy tactic in use against us. We learned that the enemy did not have to stand up and shoot at us to have hostile intent with lethal results. One man might conduct tactical overwatch of our position, reporting our movements to others who set up the attack. Another man might conceal an IED or an RPG, while yet another was the triggerman. Any of these actions became justification for the use of lethal force.

PROFESSOR JONES

We were out on our first patrol of the day one November morning, sweeping the main roads for IEDs. We went down Route Jones and turned around in an intersection. One of our guys spotted a suspicious rice bag in the median, with freshly turned dirt nearby. It was in a key intersection where hundreds, perhaps thousands, of Iraqis were soon to pass, on their way to work or school. We set up a security cordon with our two vehicles and called for emergency ordinance disposal (EOD) team and the QRF. It was the beginning of the rush hour, and traffic was heavy. Some of the guys talked about just leaving the IED and letting it blow up on someone else. We would not do it, of course, but the people who lived in this neighborhood were the heart of the insurgency. How ironic that they might blow themselves up trying to kill us. Even more ironic was that we might be blown up trying to prevent them from being killed while they supported those who set the bombs.

We shut down traffic in all four directions, but with only two vehicles, and a busy four-lane boulevard intersection, this was no easy feat. Our .50-cal gunners were young, nervous, and outnumbered. We all dismounted and assumed positions blocking the many avenues of approach to prevent the cars and pedestrians from getting near the bomb. Within minutes, dozens of cars and hundreds of pissed-off Iraqi civilians gathered, many carrying books on their way to class at the university. Horns honking and drivers yelling and shaking their fists at us in anger, these people had to get to work and could not understand that we were tying up traffic to save them from getting blown up. It was extremely frustrating that our only means of communication was the end of a gun. The Iraqis must have assumed we were just setting up a random traffic stop to harass them. I heard one of our gunners yell to the squad leader, telling him the hajis were too close and things were getting out of control.

The squad leader was tense and frustrated. We had no interpreter with us that morning, and our command of Arabic was limited to commands such as "Stop!" or "Put your hands up!" Our only other Arabic words were the traditional Muslim greetings, "Assalamu Alaikum" for "May the Peace of Allah be with you," or "Marhaba," the less-formal, secular form of "hello."

I faced the cross street alone while the other three dismounts spread out to form a perimeter. We were stretched thin and the Iraqis could clearly see it. Their rumblings and shouting grew angrier and louder by the minute while we stood guard, helpless to explain the danger they faced crossing the road; our only means of saving them from death was to kill them. We could not kill all of them, and I was certain that if we killed the first few we would certainly be overrun, our weapons turned against us, and our bodies desecrated. I thought calmly about how to communicate with them. I searched the crowds for the leaders, figuring we could either communicate with them or shoot them if the crowd advanced. I wore a face of iron. If these bastards were going to take us out, I was taking as many of them with me as possible.

I studied these apparent leaders . . . a handful of young men pacing back and forth impatiently, whipping others into excitement. Mob mentality was setting in and we were losing control. I looked around for an older man, more patient, higher in the pecking order than the young bucks. Surveying the first several cars, I looked for men whose life experience and common sense could prevail over the young bucks itching for a fight.

While my gunner's voice grew more and more tense by the moment, I lowered my rifle, walked up to a very nice Mercedes and bowed deeply with my hand over my heart—rifle at my side. "Assalamu Alaikum," I said respectfully to the well-dressed middle-aged driver. "May the Peace of Allah be with you." Clearly this man had a good job in a place with air conditioning, most likely as a professor at Al Anbar University.

"Allekum am S' Allah," he responded, the traditional Islamic reply meaning "And may the Peace of Allah be with you also." The traditional Muslim duty to feed, clothe, and protect strangers who present themselves at one's door, give them whatever they required, a tradition born of life in the parched desert sun where a traveler's life depended on the generosity of strangers, was one of the things I admired most about the Arabs and Islam.

Although an armed American soldier speaking through the window of a car door of his Mercedes in the middle of a riot was a far stretch from a nomad asking for water, the ancient tradition still held sway.

"Pardon me sir," I asked him in my most formal English, "but do you perchance speak English?"

"Yes, of course." He replied, with a quizzical, suspicious look, as if surprised by my proper manners.

"Thanks be to God!" I exclaimed joyously, raising both arms to heaven the way the Muslims did in prayer, and smiling broadly at the good fortune that blessed us.

"Please sir, I must ask for your help." And with that I filled him in on our situation, explaining that there was a bomb in the street, that we did not want any harm to come to the innocent people we were sent here to protect, and that the people must stay back for their own safety. Nodding deeply with understanding as I spoke, the man replied,

"Yes, of course I will help you," he said, and he got out of his car. "Shukran" I said to him, "Thank you," and I bowed deeply. He returned the formal gesture and turned and spoke with the crowd before us.

He gestured over several adult men in the crowd for a huddle. They all nodded in understanding then spread out into the crowd. I watched as they circulated, the crowd's tensions evaporating as they spoke.

Our EOD team arrived and made a terrific show of detonating the IED in place, showing the doubtful Iraqis what might have happened to them had we not helped them.

SACRIFICIAL LAMBS

Many of the Iraqis seemed apathetic toward death, a people who learned to survive by hiding in the sands and fighting only when it suited them. They had little sense of the personal empowerment that comes with democracy and a healthy economy. While we treasured children and vested our hopes for the future in them, after so many years of war, the enemy we faced seemed to consider their own children as cannon fodder.

Throughout my stay in Iraq, I came to know children there to represent many things: hope, happiness, resiliency—but sometimes they were also a threat. There was one family in particular who turned my stomach in the way they used their kids against us.

One of our units observed a possible IED, partially concealed in a pile of dirt alongside a roadway in Tameem. As was our custom, a few rounds were fired at it—to either detonate it or clear away the debris and make it easier to identify. In this case, nothing blew up, but the rounds cleared away enough dirt to reveal the IED. Instead of charging in, however, we took a different approach and maintained our distance, observing the IED through the sights of a Bradley Fighting Vehicle some distance away while the humvee patrol that I was part of left the area. Our ruse worked. Within a short time, the bombers assumed we had not spotted their IED, and they sent their young boys out to rebury the bomb. Our Bradley saw the adult men come out in front of a house and direct the boys, and saw the boys go back into the home after they were done.

After our EOD team disabled the IED, we paid the family a visit. Inside the home, we found several adult males and all of the boys. We took the men back to the FOB, and we were not terribly gentle with them. It turned our stomachs to see how these cowards would use their children as cannon fodder, sending them out to do their dirty work while they hid in safety.

Most of the time, though, the kids just wanted to be kids. They would play outside right alongside the roads filled with IEDs. Soccer games flourished amidst the garbage piles and sewage in the streets. As much as some Iraqi adults used their kids to fight us, most Iraqis would not intentionally target their own children. We didn't see many IEDs set in residential areas, and they would bring their kids inside when they planned an attack.

RITTENBURG'S SNIPER AT OGDEN GATE

One afternoon, SSG Murtha and his gunner, SPC Charles Rittenburg, were called back to the front gate to provide security to a resupply convoy heading to ECP 3. The guys liked heading back to the gate, because it meant some time inside of the wire where they could relax for a minute.

Rittenburg was originally a tank gunner. He was assigned to SSG Murtha's squad as a gunner in a CROW truck. The CROW truck featured a remote control .50-caliber machine gun mounted on the roof, with a powerful aiming system. A single round from the CROW could drive a tack from a mile away.

While waiting for the Headquarters Company HHC convoy they took the opportunity to drop their body armor and remove their helmets as they got out of the vehicles. They were making small talk when they heard the snap of an incoming round and someone called out "SNIPER!" Unbeknownst to them, apparently the 222 Field Artillerymen (Utah National Guard) who were manning the gate had been plagued by an unskilled sniper who liked periodically to take potshots at people inside of the gate. This time the sniper took a shot at one of our tank commanders, hitting the top of the turret just inches below him. Even before the word "sniper" was uttered everyone ran to the cover of the vehicles. Rittenburg jumped into the gunner's seat of the CROW vehicle, instinctively grabbing the controls.

Every time that he rolled into the FOB, he disengaged the elevation tracking of his CROW's weapon, causing the machine gun to point nearly vertical while he was still able to control the optics and scan the horizon. Unfortunately for this particular sniper, when Rittenburg left his truck, the .50-cal mounted in the CROW may have been pointing at the sky but his optics just happened to be trained at the sniper's position. When Rittenburg jumped into his seat and grabbed the control stick, the weapon automatically realigned to the optics.

Even before he heard the .50-cal locked back into place, Rittenburg observed a middle-aged man push himself up from a prone position and pick up his rifle. For a fraction of a second he was distracted by two gate guards running up a flight of stairs to a guard tower as he yelled to his truck commander (SSG Murtha) that he had the sniper. Even before Rittenburg had the words out of his mouth, Murtha told him to engage. As the would-be assassin made his way between two water reservoirs on the roof, Rittenburg's first two rounds took the legs out from under him, throwing him backwards and the following rounds kicked up an odd mixture of blood and cement chips.

Apparently the gate guards had been taking rounds from this guy for

SPC Charles Rittenburg on the controls of his
CROW system. (Photo by SGT Brandon Allmond)

over a week without ever returning fire. Because he was stupid or ignorant enough to engage a member of Blue Platoon, and because of a good
measure of luck, he was removed from the playing field.

WARNING SHOT RICOCHET

Once a month, most of the companies rotated their platoons from
one shift to another, so that no one got stuck all the time working in
the blistering heat of the day or grew complacent in the lonely boredom of the night. In Alpha Company, they changed shifts by having
the platoons work two twelve-hour days, back to back. I spent two such
twelve-hour days in Tameem in early December, and they were jam-
packed with enemy contact. We had an RPG fired at us, experienced a
coordinated small-arms attack, and then hit two IEDs. Afterwards, our
posture became more aggressive in the neighborhoods the attacks came
from. None of our people were hit, but one of our humvees was badly
damaged.

One afternoon, we found a black market gasoline dealer selling gas
out of two fifty-five gallon drums in his pickup. Normally we don't mind

SSG Murtha surveys a market in Tameem. Commerce was alive and well in Ramadi, even in the midst of war. (Photo by SGT Brandon Allmond)

free trade, but that is how many insurgents got their fuel, as we had observation posts monitoring the regular gas stations. Much of the insurgency was funded by these technically illegal sales.

There were at least fifty vehicles—taxis, family cars, and trucks of all sizes crammed into this intersection with open stall markets all around. We rolled up with two humvees with .50-caliber machine guns on each roof, and five dismounts. Our squad leader gave the crowd what for, trying to disperse them and figure out who owned the truck. No one was cooperating, so he flipped the drums over and dumped out all the gas.

An eighteen-wheeler tried to work its way past all the stopped cars and enter our perimeter. I was pulling security in that sector, but I did not think it was necessary to fire. My squad leader did, and he fired two warning shots with his M-4. One of his warning shots ricocheted and hit the driver in the head.

We didn't even realize he was hit at first, but in a moment he slumped over the wheel. The crowds still did not disperse, and we had to form a three-man wedge to get to the guy. I opened the door to the truck, and while the other two guys watched my back, I opened the driver's door, pulled him out and onto my shoulders in a fireman's carry, and carried him across the street into a market stall for cover and began working on him. I expected him to be dead, but he wasn't. He was unconscious, but breathing well and had a good strong regular pulse. One of our guys stayed at the patient's feet and provided me with security, while the others tried to regain control of the scene and arrange our vehicles for transport. Small-arms fire was everywhere. I was having visions of Mogadishu, Somalia, in the movie *Black Hawk Down*.

I bandaged his head and started an IV, and we moved him to the stretcher and into the humvee, only to discover the stretcher was so long that the doors could not close. (The only way to fit him in was across the backseat.) Remember the small-arms fire and IEDs everywhere?

I stood backwards behind the passenger seat with the litter against my knees, hunched over inches from the guy's face. That's when we started rolling down this bumpy road and the patient started to seize and turn blue. His jaw clamped shut, and he started to display decorticat posturing (a seizure-like activity with clamped jaw and hands and feet rotated inward, it's an ominous indicator of increased intracranial pressure and impending death). He needed an airway fast, and I was about to open his throat for a cricothyrotomy, when I got another idea. Bouncing around in the back of a swerving hummer on a road full of potholes, I wasn't crazy about using a scalpel. Instead, I tried inserting an endotracheal tube through his nose. It worked like a charm, the patient started breathing easier, his skin color pinked up and he stopped seizing. Still, it was a very long fifteen minutes to the hospital on the FOB.

It wasn't his day to die yet. They flew the guy to Baghdad, but they were unable to save him. He was taken off life support and passed away six days later.

So we got even more aggressive in our tactics for the rest of the day, and took down house after house, searching out Irhabee (the Arabic word for terrorist) with a vengeance. The insurgents were alive and well, but this innocent trucker was going to die. It was like the wild, wild west out there.

Faith and the Just War

It is said that what does not kill you makes you stronger. The insurgents tried hard to kill me, but they failed. In their wake, they left a bitter and determined soldier who fought aggressively against them.

The experience of killing the enemies of our nation was not the difficult one that I imagined it would be. Before I headed into combat, I used to think about how it might feel to take someone's life. When it happened, I didn't really feel much of anything. While there were home-grown insurgents who attacked us out of frustration or resentment, they were not the same terrorists who attacked us on 9/11. In another situation, these people would likely lead peaceful lives. There were others, however, who were not the least bit interested in making peace. The more radical Islamists would stop at nothing to spread their brand of hatred, and they would never change their ways. My conclusion was that they needed to die. How was I to square this with my belief in the sanctity of life?

Shortly after we arrived in Ramadi, our only priest, Father Kaminski, was transferred to a remote Air Force base out near the Syrian border. With no priest assigned to our FOB, a Navy Reserve chaplain named Father Waldemar Killian—stationed at nearby Camp Blue Diamond—traveled to our FOB for Mass. Father Killian was an interesting guy. He was of Polish descent, with an Irish last name, and he ministered to a parish in Chicago. Father had grown up in Poland under the old communist regime, and somehow found his way to the Vatican under Pope John Paul II. He was a very humble man, down to earth and pious. He cared little for the bureaucracy, but ministered to the troops with all his heart.

It was to Fr. Killian that I turned when I first began to question my own actions and the act of killing in a just war. The popular media back home had been characterizing this war as something other than honorable, and it really bothered me that Pope John Paul II himself was questioning what we were doing here.

Fr. Killian was just the guy to speak with. He knew the church's teachings about killing in a just war, and he gave me a copy of them. Father Killian and I discussed each of the four conditions for moral legitimacy, and whether each was met in this war:

> The damage inflicted by the aggressor on the nation or community of nations must be lasting, grave, and certain.

The damage inflicted on Iran, Kuwait, and the Kurds in Northern Iraq by Saddam Hussein was irrefutable and, in my opinion, would have continued. Saddam refused to comply with the restrictions placed on him by the United Nations Security Council. Clearly, Saddam possessed chemical weapons. After all, he used them on his own people and on the Iranians in the Iran/Iraq war. While Saddam deliberately tried to convince the world that he possessed nuclear weapons, he may not have. In either case, the world leaders at the United Nations, the United States Congress, and the president of the United States all agreed that military force was required. In my view, therefore, this requirement was met.

> All other means of putting an end to it must have been shown to be impractical or ineffective.

Can a decade of failed attempts to contain Saddam be considered adequate for this requirement? I believe so. Saddam did not respect the no-fly zone, and he carried out atrocities against the Kurds.

> There must be serious prospects for success.

In Iraq, Saddam's military was no match for our forces. While a successful invasion was never really in doubt, a legitimate argument can be made that there was inadequate planning for establishing peace in Iraq afterwards. Hindsight, however, is 20/20. At the time the decision was made to invade Iraq, was there a serious prospect for success? I believe so. The lasting peace has been elusive, but it is not beyond our grasp. It will take patience and sacrifice, but it is attainable. (The stunning turnaround in Al Anbar Province is an example of what can happen in the rest of Iraq.)

The use of arms must not produce evils and disorders greater than the evil to be eliminated. The power of modern means of destruction weighs very heavily in evaluating this condition.

While some have attempted to portray our military actions in Iraq as having produced a greater evil than that of Saddam and his Baath Party, I can only offer my first-hand eye-witness testimony that our military conducts itself honorably and within the rules of war. While my writings in this book document some of the temptations I faced, the presence of temptation does not mean succumbing to it.

Finally, the question arises of who should rightly possess the responsibility or moral authority to commit forces and initiate a just war. The guidance provided by the church simply states that:

> this responsibility for evaluating these criteria for moral legitimacy belongs to the prudential judgement of those who have responsibility for the common good.

It is clear that in his role as the commander in chief, the president of the United States has such a responsibility. It is often forgotten, however, that the United States Congress must also participate in the decision to go to war. No one person alone may declare war.

Is the United Nations such an authority that by its very existence it may legitimately represent the consensus of the human race? In those rare instances when the UN is able to endorse the use of force, one might argue that its approval constitutes moral legitimacy. In his writings, Pope John Paul II seems to share this perspective.

But what about those instances when the UN is unable to reach a decision? What about those instances when a majority of the human race may agree on a given course of action, but such consensus is vetoed by a permanent member of the Security Council? Does the lack of a UN endorsement doom a given action to immorality? I don't believe so.

Father Killian reiterated that in the Catholic Church, the pope is considered infallible on matters of faith. Father believed that at least initially, the pope may not have had access to the intelligence information needed in order to accurately judge the moral legitimacy of this war. Father pointed out the change in tone of the pope's writings before he met with President Bush and afterwards. It was Father's belief that the president probably shared inside information with the pope that helped him conclude that what we did in Iraq was justifiable.

Eventually Fr. Killian's tour was over. He returned home to his parish in Chicago, where he picked up the pieces and got back to ministering there. We continued to correspond for a while, and he and I both continue to pray for our troops.

For a long time after Fr. Killian left, we had no regular priest. We would depend on the generosity of whichever priests stopped by in their travels. We would generally have Mass every two or three weeks, and I would provide the liturgy of the Word and sometimes a communion service when we had no priest. It was during this time without a priest that our Catholic Congregation in Ramadi became even stronger. We had no one but each other to rely on for support, and we carried on celebrating the liturgy of the Word each week. When a priest would visit, I would ask him to consecrate extra hosts, and we kept them locked in our tabernacle. With the sanctified hosts, I led Communion services in addition to the liturgy of the Word.

AND ON THE SEVENTH DAY, FAITH CRESTED

As my life in combat became a routine, I came to observe a strange phenomenon. For us, this was a nine-to-five war. We left the FOB and went on patrol for eight hours, enduring enemy attacks and finding IEDs around every corner. It was 130 degrees and very draining wearing full body armor, patrolling the areas, and searching houses all day while carrying an extra hundred pounds of gear and ammunition. We fought skirmishes all the time, and took random small-arms and RPG attacks every day. We got blown up, shot at, worn down, and severely challenged by everything around us: the heat, the insurgency, the desert sand, and the urban filth.

At the end of every shift, though, we rolled back to the FOB, unloaded our weapons, took showers, ate well, and slept like kings in air-conditioned comfort. I did not mind going out and doing battle. It was the mission our nation sent us here to do. The key to staying healthy for me was taking my mind off the war when I was not fighting it, to stand down from the combat mind-set. When we got back from our missions, I would lock up my rifle in my room and seldom carry a weapon around the FOB. Whenever anyone would ask, I would politely inform them that I was a medic. Most people still assumed that meant I was not supposed to carry a weapon. I only began carrying my pistol around after I was ordered to do so.

Although I spent one day a week with God, the power of faith was a constant presence. I did not carry a weapon around the FOB, but I cloaked myself in the spiritual armor of God. Being the floating medic, I had a certain amount of flexibility in scheduling my own day off each week. Invariably, my day off was whenever the visiting priest could come to our FOB for Mass. At first, our Sabbath came on Monday evenings, then later moved to Sunday afternoons. Every Sunday morning I joined my best friends for a Christian interfaith service in our own battalion's Saber Chapel. VT battalion's Protestant chaplain held a nondenominational service for members of many Christian faiths. In his services, we connected with many Vermonters from our own unit, as well as many troops from other units who either lived on our end of the base or found our chaplain's style something they enjoyed.

A side benefit in having our own chapel—really just an air-conditioned tent with flourescent lights and a floor of pallets and plywood—was that our chaplain and his assistant, Sgt. Glen Woods, had a place to call home. We were able to find refuge in Saber Chapel anytime we liked. It was seldom used for other purposes, so we could go there and rehearse our music or pray whenever the spirit moved us.

The larger Memorial Chapel was all the way across the base, and was used almost every evening for different activities. There were three to four services every Sunday, including Christian interfaith, gospel, Mormon, Catholic, and even an occasional Jewish or Eastern Orthodox service. The building was made of stone and concrete, with attractively finished wood-grain paneling on the interior. It had homemade wooden pews, a homemade tabernacle, two pulpits, and a beautiful altar mounted conveniently on wheels. An enormous wooden cross was hung on the wall above and behind the altar—such a welcome touchstone for Christians surrounded by radical Islamists who considered us infidels and were bent on our destruction.

The Muslim call-to-prayer schedule is dictated by the moon cycles. Thus, it varies a little bit each day, generally occurring before dawn, mid-morning, noon, dinnertime, and in the late evening. The custom was for the imam to climb the minaret tower above the mosque and sing the prayers to the faithful. In modern times, the imams were relieved of this duty by automated loudspeakers mounted in the towers, set to broadcast their message at the correct times. Our really knowledgeable soldiers were able to discern the normal prayer calls from the terrorist

Our homemade tabernacle, where we kept the Blessed
Sacrament in the Memorial Chapel. My mother sent us the
statue of St. Joseph, next to the tabernacle. (Photo by author)

messages that the imams delivered. The mosques were considered off-
limits by our forces, and the enemy knew it. They took full advantage of
this protection to hide weapons, hold meetings, and communicate with
one another.

Knowing that the purpose of the loudspeaker's prayer call was not always to praise Allah, we grew wary of these times. Often, following a particularly riveting sermon, the population launched attacks on U.S. forces. Frequently our interpreters would tell us that these loudspeakers were not giving sermons at all, but were in fact a means by which the insurgents communicated—sending thinly veiled commands to their troops hidden as Arabic songs meant to sound like prayers. Some of our guys learned the actual prayer music enough to know when the imams in the mosques deviated from them. We did not always know when they were calling for an action against us, but we learned enough to know that when an off-schedule prayer call went out, we should be alert for an attack.

MY FAITH

Some of my fellow soldiers would wonder how a religious medic with strong moral principles could be so comfortable with killing another. After all, I was supposed to save lives, not take them. How could I profess a faith that seemed incompatible with my actions? Some of them failed to grasp the distinctions between murder and combat.

Arriving at this point was a journey for me. The journey began when I was a teenager and first decided to join the Army. I had an abstract concept of the true cost of the freedom we all enjoy as Americans. Although I would later come to make my own sacrifices in battle, I knew that our way of life was paid for with the blood of patriots. I was taught and I fully accepted that in the defense of lives and liberty, evil men must die.

When the call came some twenty years later and I would have to saddle up for war, I was mentally prepared. In my mind, I had already concluded this war as just. Many others disagreed, but for me it was straightforward: our nation was attacked, and we had to react.

I am Catholic. From a very early age, we were taught the difference between right and wrong, and the implications of making the wrong decisions in life. I accepted the abstract precepts I was taught, largely without question. Oh, sure, I think the church can be a little stodgy at times, and could use fresh air and sunlight, but my underlying faith in the one true God was a given.

Like many Catholics, I was spoiled. It is easy to attend Mass every week, receive the sacraments, and leave the faith at the church door. Very few of us will be tossed into a den of lions or swallowed by a whale, but all of us will be tested in this life.

Although he looks like a preacher spreading the word, this is actually one of Charlie Company's tankers loading ammo into a tank. (Photo by SFC Dave Swan)

During the difficult times in my life, I would always find my way into a church. The familiar rituals and prayers would always provide comfort. During my time in Iraq, however, my faith would be tested like never before. The prayers and rituals of Mass were not always available. Sometimes I would be the only celebrant, called upon to deliver the Holy Eucharist to others in a Communion service when a priest could not make it to our base. The Mass was not there, but God was present in the form of the bread and wine consecrated into the body and blood of Christ by the priest on his last visit.

During those lean evenings in a foreign land, alone with Christ and a very small group of fellow soldiers, we found the grace of the Holy Spirit. The strength that we received from our shared faith helped us all to somehow persevere.

MUSIC

I served as an organist in my teen years, and later played percussion and sang bass in our parish folk group. The members of our folk group back home were very supportive of our music ministry in Ramadi. I frequently e-mailed with members of the group, who helped me pick out songs. They sent us sheet music, and even took up a collection and sent me some AT&T phone cards so I could keep in touch with my family.

When we were activated and we had no musicians for Mass at Camp Shelby, naturally I came forward to help. Later on in Ramadi, Glenn Woods, Jade Phillips, and Courtney Allen joined me to form a musical group. We called ourselves "Heavenly Crest" after the toothbrushes I pressed into service as makeshift drumsticks during our first Mass together in Ramadi. The praise music they introduced me to was so uplifting and joyous, one could not help but sing praises when these joyful noises filled our chapel. Between the interfaith service on Sunday, the Catholic service on Monday, and a rehearsal at least one night each week, our faith was a daily source of comfort and guidance, no longer confined to the seventh day, but on the seventh day it crested.

The members of our band grew to be close friends during our service in the chapel together. Our friendship was a constant source of strength for all of us, and Jade and Glen and I, in particular, relied upon each other for counsel. It was after one of our chapel services that I wrote the following passage in my journal, describing each of us and the bonds that we shared.

FRIENDS

There are honorable men here whom I have fought battles alongside, whom I don't really consider friends. There are Iraqis who have tried to kill us at every turn, with bombs, rockets and rifle fire—enemies who at least show the courage of their convictions.

Through it all, our fellowship has carried us—Glen, Jade, and me. Walking very different paths through this Euphrates Valley, we all escape together in our faith, music and friendship.

Glen, the staid Chaplain's Assistant—quietly supporting the men, carrying us all in his counsel,

Jade, at 26 the impetuous youngster among us—tough, irreverent and generous all at once—with an inner spirit that soars through the heavens with the power of his tenor song,

and me, the warrior, medic and Eucharistic minister—as likely to be blasting irhabi as to be fixing him afterward—firing, healing and praying, often all at once.

Kindred souls, really, bound together in faith, friendship, and music.

One of the chaplain's assistants from another unit organized a monthly night of fellowship, and all were welcome. It was a great way to break down barriers between soldiers of different faiths, different units, and different branches of service. Our female vocalist, Sgt. Courtney Allen, agreed to sing there one night, and she asked me to accompany her on the piano. She did a great job, and the crowd loved it. Her song "I Want to Know You" was a gospel favorite, sung in the style of a folk ballad, and I added lots of arpeggios in the lower octaves that complemented her clear alto voice wonderfully. After months of chapel services with nothing but Glen Woods's baritone, Jade Phillips's tenor, and my own bass voice, it was such a delight to have a female vocalist with us. This was Courtney's night to shine, and she did really well.

Fortunately we went first, because later on the musical flavor changed to a supercharged jazz, and that would have been hard to follow. There was an unbelievable jazz guitarist named SSG Leger who played jazz with a New Orleans soul and a fiery energy that defied the laws of physics. Another soldier jumped in with a mean harmonica that would have chased the devil out of Georgia, while another soldier brought out his saxophone. Lots of different guitarists jumped in, taking turns trying to keep up with SSG Leger. Like several drummers, I took a turn beating

Not only were we blessed with plenty of fake beer, but our faith and friendship carried us through the trials of war. Left to right are the author, SPC Jade Phillips, and SGT Glen Woods. (Photo by SGT Courtney Allen)

the skins, and everyone had an absolute blast. I got out my digital camera and recorded some of the improvisations, later giving them names like "8 Bar Monica" and "Chapel Sax Jive" and playing them back on my headphones out on patrol. The music blew me away.

God's call to become an extraordinary minister of the Eucharist was—quite literally—posted on Camp Shelby's mess hall walls: "Catholic Representatives needed." I had always been involved in the music, though never with the Eucharist, but I was willing to help.

INSERTING OUR PRIEST

We started hearing rumors that another priest was coming. He was delayed for some bureaucratic reason or other, but eventually found his way to Ramadi. On the day he was supposed to arrive and celebrate his first Mass with us, Naval Reserve Chaplain Father Michael Deusterhaus found himself pinned down in Camp Blue Diamond, just across the Euphrates River from our FOB. Father Deusterhaus was a gregarious and energetic man on his second deployment to Iraq. He was not

Navy Chaplain Father Michael Deusterhause with his marine
bodyguard, CPL Zach Boss and the author at Camp Blue Diamond's
Follow Me Chapel. (Photo by Chaplain Peter Lawson)

someone who would let a minor thing like a gunfight get between him
and providing the sacraments to the troops who needed them.

Father paced like a trapped bull in the TOC at Camp Blue Diamond.
He waited impatiently for the firefight to stop, but on and on it went. The
only two bridges across the Euphrates were involved in the fighting, so
Father was trapped.

"Oh, come on, are you telling me there is only one way to cross that
river?" he asked the battle captain in the TOC.

"Well, yes Father, there are only two bridges, right next to each other,
and they are under fire. We can't send you out there."

"But I have a chapel full of troops at FOB Ramadi who are waiting for
Mass. I have to get to them."

One of the staff officers in the TOC was a devout Catholic, and over-
heard this conversation. He knew of another way.

"I know of a small boat, Father, hidden in the reeds. If you don't mind
crossing the river in it, we can get you to FOB Ramadi."

And so they went. Father and his marine bodyguard got into their

The civilians who worked in the dining facility built this manger scene in celebration of Christmas. Left to right are CPL Zach Boss, SGT Glen Woods, SGT Courtney Allen and the author. (Photo provided by author)

body armor. Corporal Boss was a communications specialist, and had never been in combat, but like every marine, he took his duty to protect the priest very seriously.

"I may not be Catholic, Father, but I'll be dammed if a priest gets killed on my watch!"

The gunfire raged above them as our forces tried to encircle a band of insurgents near the river's edge. Their tiny boat slipped across this biblical river of Babylon unnoticed; their faith crested the waves on this, this sabbath that they kept. Father jumped into a waiting humvee on our side of the river, and dashed off to the chapel, just in time to begin Mass.

CHRISTMAS IN RAMADI

Christmas was a joyous occasion at FOB Ramadi. Stripped of all the usual trappings and dropped into a war, we focused on the true meaning of Christmas. My friends in the band and I spent the day bringing cheer to our fellow soldiers, and in doing so, found happiness.

We went caroling around the FOB, visiting all the barracks. We stopped in at the hospital here, and cheered up the medics on duty. We went over to the Field Artillery, made up largely of Mormons from the Utah National Guard, and sang for them. They were most appreciative, and their first sergeant called them all out of the barracks for us. Their guns stood silent as we stood with candlelights in the darkness, singing "Silent Night." So, no, I did not despair at Christmas, I found ways to celebrate, shoulder to shoulder with my brothers in arms.

BREAKING BREAD TOGETHER

Just as with the troops they supported, the civilians who worked on our FOB came to tolerate one another's religions peacefully and to embrace the core values we all shared. At Christmastime, the Muslim civilians in the DFAC even went out of their way to decorate with enormous homemade Christian symbols. They even made a creche depicting the baby Jesus in the manger. I was surprised to learn that Muslims recognize Jesus, but they consider him a prophet.

Perhaps the most telling example of religious detente was the night during the Muslim festival of Eid, at the end of their holy month of Ramadan, when the military arranged for a civilian Iraqi imam to come to the DFAC to hold a service. By coincidence, the imam came the same evening as the priest. Both faiths held services at the same time, in opposite ends of the same huge dining room. What a contrast from the intolerance and hatred we saw outside our FOB walls in Iraq. In our DFAC, we all prayed together in the same room. In the towns and villages outside our walls, it was considered sacrilege for a non-Muslim to enter a mosque.

It was not home, but there were enough homey elements here for us to feel at ease at the end of our shift in combat and returned to this slice of Americana. How different an experience from the wars of our forefathers.

Haji Gets Blown Up

I rediscovered that slightly edgy feel I used to get during a busy shift on the ambulance, situationally aware, tactical, and on my game. Having resolved my moral questions, I came to embrace this combat mind-set. It was a good feeling, but I would also be just as content to ride around in the hummer all day doing nothing.

One morning in early December, while I was on patrol with B Troop out on MSR mobile, we stopped at the main gate and were visiting with the medics assigned to Voodoo Mobile when we heard a huge explosion. Our other humvee was inside the FOB getting an interpreter, and so we responded alone. Our OPs were reporting that a suicide bomber had detonated a car bomb on the highway and that U.S. humvees were hit.

We rolled out to find none of the marines were hurt, but an Iraqi by-stander was killed. The blast flipped an eighteen-wheeler with a tandem trailer on its side, but the truck shielded the marines from the blast. They were extraordinarily lucky. We found them forming a security cordon around the blast site, from a long way out. Initially we had no radio communications with them, as they were on a different frequency, so it heightened our concerns for them and we had to physically run over to them to make sure they were OK. I positioned our vehicle to block traffic from our end, and Sgt. Sorrento and I got out, I grabbed my aid bag and my rifle, and we ran in. We did not know what to expect, and we thought the truck driver was likely to be badly injured. He had already been removed by civilian bystanders and was being taken to a local civilian hospital by a private vehicle. We could not determine for sure if he was dead or just wounded, because the bystanders spoke only Arabic and we didn't.

After checking the vehicle, Sorrento and I ran the rest of the four hundred meters to the marine vehicle damaged in the blast. We found five marines inside who were not injured, and they helped maintain the security cordon. When our lieutenant arrived, he took command of the scene, and we took our place on the perimeter. I spotted the bomber's hand lying in the road, and retrieved it for identification purposes. The marines discovered the bomber's testicles in the back of their humvees. Radical Islam holds that if you die a martyr, Allah will provide you with seventy-two virgins in heaven. We all got a huge laugh at the prospect of the suicide bomber going to reap his supposed reward of seventy-two virgins, only to find he had no balls. If that isn't hell, I don't know what is.

Shortly after the bombing, we got a call from one of our observation posts a few miles away. They were receiving sniper fire, so we rolled out there in a hurry to support them, and the marines took over the cordon. We went through the town in a big way, searching for the gunmen, but found no one. A few hours later they called us back there, for sniper fire from a different direction. We searched more houses, but still came up empty.

THE FIREHOUSE BOMBER

Positioned out in the open, right up next to the edge of Route Jones, was an Iraqi fire station. There were shops across the street and houses built right up against the back of the station, and some of the fire officers lived in them. The houses provided an ideal safe passageway, allowing firefighters and insurgents alike to approach the edge of Route Jones undetected by our observation posts. The station and some of the small shops near it had commanding views of the open areas nearby, and offered an excellent place for a triggerman to hide. While the firefighters were supposedly neutral in this conflict, we suspected they were insurgents themselves or allowed the insurgents to use their building as a vantage point.

Many of the IEDs on Route Jones were placed suspiciously close to the firehouse and the shops across the street. Some days IEDs were placed directly in front of an auto-repair shop. When enough of their bombs detonated we had had it. Clearly, the insurgents could not have placed the IED without the shopkeeper knowing about it, and the attacks continued, despite repeated warnings. Our guys finally stopped and told the shop owner that if any more IEDs were placed near his shop, we would destroy it. Sure enough, another IED went off and some of our guys got hurt. The tanks stationed on each end of Route Jones responded, and blew the place apart with their main gun rounds.

The firefighters saw this attack and were shocked. Neutral no more, they opened up on our forces with their one AK-47. It wasn't long before they ran out of ammunition and we paid them a visit, demanding the officer in charge. The captain appeared, and our squad leader made a point of dressing him down in front of his firefighters.

I looked at this ragtag gang, hanging around the station in ill-fitting bunker gear. They wore firefighting coats in spite of the heat, and rubber boots around the station all day. The gear had never seen a fire. I doubted that any of these guys were really firefighters.

We got nothing out of the captain, so we arrested him. I asked for the job of applying the handcuffs and taking him in. While I did so, I spoke with him through our interpreter. I told him I was a firefighter also, and that I would treat him with dignity out of respect for our profession. He said he was honored to meet me and wished it was under better circumstances.

Several weeks later, another insurgent blew himself up near the fire station on Route Jones. From all appearances, it seems the man was parking his car next to the firehouse when it blew up on him. We believe he was part of an RPG team, and that he had an armed RPG round loose in his car when it detonated.

Of all the places in the world to blow up, right next to a firehouse is the way to go. The man was rescued by the firefighters there, who put out the fire in his car and pulled him out alive. We were not summoned to the scene, but we heard the explosion from across town and we responded to investigate. I was shocked that they actually carried water in their tank, and they really did know how to use it.

The bomber was lying on a stretcher, being largely ignored. Unlike in the United States, Iraqi firefighters don't seem to have any medical training. On the other hand, maybe they just figured he was dead. I didn't have anything else to do, so I figured I might as well try to save the guy. I got him intubated and we loaded him into the back seat of the humvee on a litter. As we were transporting him to the FOB, he went into cardiac arrest. Although the docs at C Med did everything they could to save him, even cracked his chest, he was done.

Working on insurgent casualties was not a wasted effort in my book; they were good practice. Our medical rules of engagement were very clear—anyone injured as a result of contact with U.S. forces would be treated. At first, I thought treating people who tried to kill us would waste our resources, but the more I thought about it, the more I realized the good that could come from it. First, for the benefit of our troops, we were not being placed in situations where our guys would be seeing people die and we could do nothing. The very thought of that is dehumanizing and demoralizing. Our troops would also benefit from practicing their medical skills, before they would be needed on our own troops. However, helping the injured in a very public and visible way showed the Iraqis that we are not the barbarians that radical Islam claims we are. Iraqi people would thank me for my efforts afterwards. Even the insurgents have families. It was the family members who were not necessarily insurgents themselves that we hoped to influence. Some of the biggest names in terrorism have been brought to justice by a relative. Kick Momma's door in often enough, and eventually she wants Junior out of the house.

9 Midnight Raid on Al Qaeda

Two days after Christmas was my thirty-eighth birthday. What better way to celebrate than to ride along with SSG Murtha on a raid? We had intelligence reports that the occupants of a particular house were heavily involved in the insurgency. We kicked their door in and caught them completely off guard.

The man in the house published propaganda and handled money for the insurgents. He had detailed notes about terrorist cells and boxes of pamphlets in his house. Evidently he was no stranger to our game of cat and mouse. He and his wife were asleep in the middle of the day. Apparently they moved around in the middle of the night to avoid detection. In the closet near the bed we found two suitcases, packed and ready to go. This couple was prepared to bug out at the first sign of trouble. We were fortunate to catch them asleep. As was my custom, I stood guard over the prisoners while the other guys searched the house. The man mistook my professionalism for a sign of weakness. When we confronted him with the evidence we found, he did not deny being an insurgent. Instead the man became indignant and raised his voice to me, trying to establish his dominance and order us around like children. Having seen the evidence of his involvement with the terrorists who killed so many of my brothers and spread terror among their own countrymen, I was not inclined to take any crap from him.

SSG Murtha started toward him, but I was all over the guy. I spun him around and threw him up against the wall, kicking his feet wide apart to keep him off balance while I commanded him and his wife in Arabic to "shut the fuck up!" I frisked him with one hand and jammed my pistol into the small of his back with the other. He was handcuffed,

This insurgent was found sleeping during a random house search in the middle of the afternoon. He had lots of cash, maps and insurgent propaganda and his and his wife's bags were packed. (Photo by SGT Brandon Allmond)

blindfolded, and cooperative in no time. SSG Murtha just looked at me and smiled, "Well, all right then, Doc!"

Later that night, we conducted a targeted raid on a known IED-making team. The judge that one Irhabee faced that moment needs no jury, offers no appeals, and the jail . . . no parole.

In the middle of the night we slipped silently through the darkened streets of Ramadi toward our objective. The streets were dirt in this neighborhood—an area we seldom drove through, as the enemy buried IEDs everywhere.

Arriving at our first objective, we kicked in the door and rushed into the darkened home yelling commands in Arabic. I found the sleeping teenage triggerman in bed with his younger brothers. He was all of thirteen and already a terrorist. I paused for a moment before I yanked him out of bed . . . thinking how it could very well have been this kid who had killed so many of our men. I did not hold back while I slapped him awake and threw him up against the wall. We knew this kid was the triggerman, but we needed to find the adults he worked with who made the

Night vision view of the area where we raided the
IED making cell. (Photo by SGT Brandon Allmond)

bombs. The boy's uncle was the IED maker and had recruited him to the cause. It sickened me to see our enemy send children forward to do their killing, while they lurked in the safety of shadows—shattering youthful innocence much as their bomb blasts squandered so many lives.

Instantly, the whole area lit up. It was as if every light in the town came on at once. I scanned for targets and found him. Two hundred meters away, standing on a rooftop silhouetted against the moonlit sky was the figure of a man overwatching our position. "Man on a roof, two hundred meters!" I called to our squad leader. "Take him out!" came the terse reply.

It was easy, really. With the monocular night-vision device on my left eye, the red dot scope in my right eye lined up on the target's chest. One round and he was gone.

CRAZY MAN AND THE TANK

Around midnight that adventure-filled night, we were returning to the base when we spotted a man crossing the street behind one of our tanks. He was not armed, but was walking around erratically, and trying to sneak up on our tank. We stopped and SSG Hegg in the lead humvee got out and confronted the guy. With our interpreter yelling Arabic commands, the suspect refused to stop, would not comply, and generally wanted to continue his unarmed pedestrian attack on our tank. In his civilian life, SSgt. Hegg is a correction officer, and in his world, one does not carry a weapon, but instead kicks ass the old-fashioned way.

In a flash, Hegg was on the guy. The suspect was very aggressive, and it took a lot to subdue him. As they fought, Joe Lewis kept our crew inside our vehicle, conducting overwatch for snipers. "You want me to shoot him if I get a clear shot?" Our gunner asked.

"Well, technically he does pose a threat. I mean, if he gets one of Hegg's weapons he could be trouble. Yeah, if he gets away from him, shoot him." Joe then asked me, "What do you think, Doc? Is it the right thing to do?" A fallen-away altar boy, Joe was a Catholic, with the accompanying guilt-riddled conscience.

"I don't think you would be wrong either way. He won't comply with orders to stop attacking the tank, and wrestling with him is too dangerous. Yeah, I guess you could shoot him."

"Yes! Holy man says Kill him!" Joe announced, throwing up his hands to signal a touchdown.

We brought the guy back to the FOB and interrogated him. It turns out he spoke some other language besides Arabic. He did not understand the commands he was given. He was also obviously drugged, and we figured the insurgents sent him out as a test, to see how close they could get to our tanks. In the end, we released him outside our gates with a glow stick tied around his neck. He spent the rest of the night trying to get back into our FOB—driving the Utah Guardsmen there bananas all night long.

The following text is from an e-mail that I sent after the midnight raid to Pat Murphy, a brother firefighter back home.

> January 1, 2006
> Brother Pat—
> I am looking and acting less and less like a medic these days, and more like an infantryman. The other day I had to open fire on a possible VBIED. (vehicle born improvised explosive device). I don't think I killed anyone, but I will never know.

We conducted a raid on a warehouse used by the insurgents. We captured an Al Qaida financier, and confiscated a weapons cache there. My role was to be part of the security cordon outside. A vehicle approached us at a high rate of speed, aimed right at us. In Iraq, that means they want to blow us up, and they must die.

I put a three round burst into the ground in front of the vehicle, and he ignored it. The next three went in the grill, then three in the hood, and finally six through the center of the windshield. The last six finally got his attention, and he turned away. There were two people still sitting upright in the front seat at the time, so hopefully they are OK. Since they turned away, they probably had no explosives, but they may have been probing our defenses. I will never know . . .

. . . Honestly Pat, I used to say I didn't want to kill anyone, but now this is getting personal. I want to kill these despicable cowards. I want to kill a lot of them, in the most violent manner possible. They are constantly trying to kill us, and I am tired of being on the defensive. I want to go to their homes, yank them out of the beds made safe by the ultimate sacrifices of my brothers, drag them out into the cold dark streets by their hair, and end their lives with vengeance and malice. I want to desecrate their bodies in humiliation, and leave them for the dogs.

That's how I feel these days. What am I doing about it? Well, not much. I cannot do these things in good conscience, and honestly, I am really taken aback at the intensity of my own emotions. I am generally not one to lose my composure.

So, remaining within the rules of war, I am more aggressive against targets. They say the best defense is a good offense, and I am very offensive. At the same time, though, I am equally committed to being humane to the innocent populace. I have visited homebound Iraqi civilians and provided home health care, given out soccer balls to the kids, and I always have a bag of candy in my pocket for them. I am just as committed to helping these people, and convincing them to be a participant in the democratic process, rather than a terrorist attacking it. Many of the people here simply want to be left alone. Even among those who hate our presence here, they really want to have a peaceful democratic society someday, and are willing to work towards it.

But, alas, I ramble on. I look forward to working with you again someday.

Tom

NO BETTER FRIEND . . .

I was riding along with Alpha Company's Red Platoon one night in December when they told me they wanted to stop in and visit a relative's house. Earlier on in their deployment, this platoon had engaged a suspected VBIED. Their rounds missed the intended target and struck another vehicle, severely wounding a woman inside. A young newlywed, she was married to an Iraqi policeman stationed near the Syrian border, and as a result of this engagement, she had lost one of her arms and part of her breast. She was staying at the house so that her female relatives could nurse her back to health while her husband was away at work.

The guys felt terrible about what had happened, and they wanted very much to make it right. In bringing me to see her, they sought reassurance that she would pull through. Iraqi health care was not the greatest, and the guys were worried about her.

We inserted into the target house by stopping our vehicles on the next block and conducting house-to-house searches until we reached our objective. In this manner, we hoped to conceal the fact that we were really trying to look in on this woman. We did not want the insurgents to target this woman because of her association with us.

Once we reached the home, the guys introduced me to the family as a "doctor." The Arabic word for doctor sounds a lot like the English version, and this was simple enough. I was amazed by the trust these perfect strangers placed in me. The other women in the family seemed very willing to help me care for her. I examined the patient and found she had several wounds on her chest and abdomen, along with the amputation of her right arm above the elbow. Some of her wounds had some nasty drainage, and she was running a fever. I cleaned her wounds with sterile water and applied fresh bandages. I did not have any antibiotics, though, but I was determined that we would help this poor woman through her recovery.

We explained to the family through our interpreter that she was infected and needed her wounds cultured and the appropriate antibiotics. They promised they would bring her to a civilian doctor in Baghdad. I had our interpreter write a note in Arabic for the doctor, offering our help, and asking if there were any medications or other treatments she might need.

I was not confident in the Iraqi doctors to properly treat this patient, so when we got back to the FOB, I had a talk with Col. McGuinness, our physician. I was only asking for a broad spectrum antibiotic to deliver to the patient, but Col. McGuinness was an old Army Ranger from the Vietnam era. He was not the least bit intimidated by going into Ramadi with us, and asked me to coordinate a house call. In the meantime, he started discussions with the Army about bringing her to the FOB for an evaluation by an orthopedic surgeon.

It required some serious diplomatic efforts from both of us, but in short order, we had arranged for his house call. We could not call ahead because we could not be certain that her family would keep our visit secret. We anticipated that the patient might be in tough shape by the time we arrived. So instead of the doctor riding along unescorted, we brought along a 113 ambulance. We were ready to extract the patient on his say-so alone.

For all our preparations, we still could not know if she would be there when we arrived. Apparently, she and her husband had a house of their own somewhere else, since he was away frequently with his work.

We surprised her relatives that night, but she was not there. They assured us that her Iraqi doctors had made her better, and that she was home with her husband. Their home was not in our area, so we could not visit her there. Perhaps she was placed on a more effective antibiotic; we never learned. Although we would never see her again, from time to time our interpreter would call her on the telephone. She seemed to be OK on the phone, but she never would be connected with our orthopedic surgeons or receive the artificial arm we hoped to arrange for her.

CORPORAL BOSS RIDES ALONG

With so much enemy contact in our sector, the area was known as the worst part of Ramadi, the worst place on earth. I learned later that the Marines in downtown Ramadi considered Tameem to be a lot worse than their battle space. Ironically, we figured the only place worse than Tameem was downtown Ramadi. I guess the bombs are always bigger on the other side of the river.

Our priest's marine bodyguard, Cpl. Zach Boss, was getting restless. It was just after Christmas, and his tour would be ending soon. Although he had traveled far and wide across Iraq, he had never been in combat. Zach told me the only time he ever fired his weapon was when he fired warning shots at an approaching vehicle while he was riding in the back of a Marine seven-ton transport truck.

Father Deusterhause was very understanding of Cpl. Boss's frustration, so when Zach and I asked Father for permission for me to take Zach along on a mission, Father graciously approved. Father had received several soccer balls from parishioners back home, and had not figured out a way to give them to the Iraqi children. This mission would suit both purposes.

After all the enemy contact we had faced in recent weeks, I was confident that we would find some action for Zach. Most of our guys were worn down and in no mood for a goodwill mission, but they respected me and the Marine Corps enough to humor us.

We purposefully avoided Tameem that afternoon, and went through 5K looking for a group of children we always saw playing soccer in a field. We pulled over and Zach and I got out. At first the kids were a little scared—we had never stopped to talk with them before. I approached them with a big smile and greeted the boys with the traditional Arabic greetings. I knelt down and spoke with them, giving them candy from my stash. Zach and I gave them the soccer balls, and the kids' faces lit up. We got some great pictures for Father to send back to his parishioners, and went on our way.

Try as we might, after all that goodwill, we could not buy enemy contact for the rest of the shift. Maybe the bad guys saw us being nice and gave us the night off. Maybe the Good Lord was trying to tell us something. We searched several houses at random, but found only friendly law-abiding families. Our night was a total bust—but most enriching.

. . . NO WORSE ENEMY

The next day after Cpl. Boss rode along we were attacked. One sadsack insurgent actually got his buddy to come along for his suicide ride. His plan was to drop the buddy off on the side of the road to set an IED, then drive himself into one of our vehicles and blow himself up. They chose 1500 hour shift change on Route Jones for their attack. Our tanks on the day shift were in position on both ends of Jones, when a tank and a Bradley from another platoon came out to relieve them.

A Chevy Suburban pulled over to the side of the road as the tank

Making friends with the local kids. (Photo by Corporal Zach Boss)

drove by, and the buddy got out with his IED. As the Bradley passed him, the driver gunned the engine and crashed his vehicle into the back end of the Bradley. The bomb inside failed to detonate, and the impact appeared to knock the driver of the suburban unconscious. The Bradley continued forward, leaving the Suburban sitting in the middle of the road.

The tank on OP Jones had a clear shot, and promptly destroyed the suburban with a main gun round. As for the buddy who had gotten out to set an IED, he was quickly cut to shreds by the coaxial machine guns on the tank. Just another day in Paradise.

SHOPPING

Not all of our interactions with Iraqis involved searches or violence. Every once in a while we would stop into a market just to make small talk with the merchants and make a purchase or two. Iraqis are all interested in commerce, and even merchants who might not like us would not turn away an American dollar. Some of our guys smoked cigarettes, and when they found out they could buy American-made cigarettes in Iraqi markets for as little as two dollars a carton, we became regular custom-

SGT Brandon Almond speaking with local merchants.
(Photo provided by SGT Brandon Allmond)

ers. I was always amused when we would pull into a small store at random, and mingle in with the regular shoppers. Much to the amazement of the Iraqis, we would politely wait our turn in line at the cash register, and pay fair price for the things we bought. Everything in the Middle East is negotiable, and it is customary to haggle over the price of every single purchase. One such transaction really left me laughing.

"How much for the satellite dish?" one of the guys in Joe Lewis's squad asked a merchant, through our interpreter.

"For you? Two hundred dollars, not a penny less," came the reply.

"Two hundred dollars? That's crazy, that thing is worth way more than that!"

A puzzled look came over the interpreter's face. He didn't understand that this haggling was for show, that we were going to give the man a fair price and leave him happy, in spite of our interpreter's efforts to negotiate a lower price. This was no modern "Dish TV" eighteen-inch satellite dish. This thing was huge. It was the old-school, six-foot-wide, humongous dish that had all but disappeared from American homes. It was probably worth two thousand dollars, never mind two hundred.

"No sir, please I must have two hundred dollars for this," the merchant haggled.

A quick huddle with Joe and we figured out a way to transport it in one of the trucks. Each humvee had a huge area for the gunner to stand on between the seats. The CROW truck, however, had its gunner sitting in the back seat, operating the gun by remote control. No one stood in the empty center of the truck.

"Look, I'm giving you three hundred dollars, and that's all there is to it," our guy finally said, handing over three crisp American one hundred dollar bills.

And with that, he became the proud owner of one enormous satellite dish, mounted it on the roof of the barracks, and was suddenly capable of receiving all sorts of television programming. Knowing Joe, I half expected him to have the guy come to the barracks and install it. Somewhere in FOB Ramadi, a soldier or marine is probably still enjoying that dish.

The Glass Factory Disaster

Overlooking our forward operating base was an abandoned glass factory. The place was huge, with smokestacks and tall buildings that loomed over the base like the scepter of death. Our predecessors took sniper fire from the glass factory, and closed it down. It stood, towering over the perimeter of our base, acting as a barrier between us and some of the most violent neighborhoods in Iraq.

It was January 5 and I was in my room on the computer when Lt. Gunn came into the area, yelling for everyone to respond to a mass casualty incident. A bomber wearing a suicide vest had detonated himself near the glass factory in a crowd of people applying for jobs as Iraqi Police. There were hundreds of applicants lined up outside the pedestrian gate to the factory, with the vast majority of our troops inside the perimeter walls.

Chaos broke out as all of us scrambled to get our weapons, body armor and medical gear on. I was the crew chief on one of the first 113s to respond. As we raced toward the gate, we were passed by dozens of vehicles, civilian, Iraqi Police, and U.S. all loaded with casualties and heading in to the hospital. I tried in vain to estimate the number, but it was futile. At least forty or fifty casualties were brought in by these bystanders before our units even arrived on the scene; none of them had any type of bandages applied, and in passing, most looked like critical multisystems trauma patients.

I radioed an alert to C Med (our hospital on the base) and pressed through the rush of incoming vehicles out to the objective. The scene was a sea of mangled bodies, a hundred yards long and thirty yards wide. Life was a suffering madness for the living, and a jumbled bloody mess for the dead. With three 113 ambulances, we had the capacity for twelve litter patients. There were almost a hundred.

I got out and thought calmly through the disaster training I had received from numerous sources both military and civilian throughout my twenty years in the business. I thought about what to do first and remembered that in every disaster chaos reigns. In this instance, there were dozens of responders from several U.S. military branches, a flood of well-meaning Iraqi civilian bystanders, numerous Iraqi Police, a smattering of Iraqi civilian ambulances, and a river of blood.

Under the best of circumstances, with all of the responders having the same training, speaking one language, and using the same radio frequency, a scene like this would be extremely difficult to manage. In this setting we had no portable radios to speak with one another, no visible means of discerning medical personnel from everyone else (no one wore red crosses since snipers would aim for the medics) and with body armor on, we could not even read names or ranks on most of our people. Once dismounted, the only way to communicate with our medics was to find them in the crowd, run over to them, and yell in their ear. There was such a cacophony of noise no one could hear anything.

I quickly surmised that command and control would be impossible, and incoming medical vehicles would have to find their own way through the madness. The best we could hope for was to triage the mass of patients and get to those who needed help the most. In hindsight, the one thing we could have done was establish control of the entry and exit points for evac vehicles, loading each one to the fullest before sending it to the rear.

I jumped in and started triaging patients. I did not stop moving much, just did quick checks of major hemorrhage, airway status, and level of consciousness. The one thing that struck me was that there were no critical patients. Except for one man I considered expectant (mortally wounded and soon to die), all of the people I examined were either not that bad or were already dead. In all I must have triaged over forty casualties, but I lacked any type of tag system to attach to the patients after I examined them. The only thing I hoped to do was to turn around and physically direct medics and litter teams to the critical patients, but when I found none, it was apparent that since almost all of the patients had less critical wounds, it really didn't matter in what order they were evacuated. Apparently the most critical were already en route to C Med via the bystanders or had died.

It was a relief, actually, to realize that the scene was not as bad as it could have been, with more critical patients all vying for the same evacuation and treatment resources. Although it sounds terribly callous, it was also comforting to realize that almost all of the casualties were Iraqis. There were only two U.S. troops killed in action, and four wounded. On a conceptual level, I knew that all human life was sacred. In practice, I worked just as hard to save enemy combatants as I did to save our own guys. On an emotional level, however, the loss of Iraqi life was so commonplace in Ramadi that I was numb to it. When innocent people were hurt or killed I was still saddened, but I was indifferent to the loss of enemy combatants. These people who tried to kill me and my buddies were already dead to me. I looked upon them as a way for us to hone our trauma skills with no emotional involvement. After six months in combat, I looked upon enemy combatants as targets. They were cowardly vermin who would rarely fight us straight on. They would turn on their brother in a heartbeat, and lie, steal, and murder without a second thought. I had no use for the evil they represented or the domination that their brand of radical Islam tried to force on the world.

We loaded up our 113 and headed back to the FOB. There were two medics aboard, and I was not needed inside. As the track commander, I was also the gunner, so I climbed atop the track for the trip inside. We were in bandit country, after all, and our defenses were thin.

We dropped off our casualties and headed back out to the scene of the disaster. We helped load up the remaining casualties onto other Coalition vehicles and assumed a defensive posture along the perimeter. It became clear that the Iraqis would pick up their own dead. We were not needed any longer in a medical role, but there were only a handful of vehicles guarding the scene from the hundreds of onlookers, any one of whom could have been an additional bomber or carried an RPG. I spent the rest of the disaster looking down the barrel of a .50-caliber machine gun at crowds of people. It was here that I thought about how twenty minutes earlier the scene was completely overrun by many of these same civilian bystanders. For better or worse, we had all let our guard down in reaction to the human tragedy before us. Anyone in the crowd who wanted to harm us could have picked up a discarded weapon and opened fire. No one did. I thought perhaps there might be hope for these people after all.

IRHABEE AMBULANCE
Later that same night, SSG Murtha and his gunner, SPC Rittenburg, were manning OP 293 when they spotted a civilian ambulance moving through 5K. It was well past curfew, and civilian vehicles were forbidden

to travel during the night, but our forces were under orders not to inter-fere with Iraqi emergency services, provided their dispatch notified our command center when the ambulances were responding, where they were going, and their destination hospital afterward.

In this case, there was a radio call ahead of time advising of a medical emergency in Tameem. The ambulance made several stops around 5K and Tameem—not going to the house in Tameem and back to the hos-pital as one would expect. SSG Murtha grew suspicious, and he radioed in an inquiry through the TOC. There was no legitimate reason for this ambulance to be traveling through 5K. SSG Murtha radioed the roving patrol to investigate, and they stopped the vehicle on a side street near Route Barry within view of OP 293, on the far side of Route Michigan.

The rovers ordered the crew out of the vehicle and they complied. When the interpreter told them to shut off the engine, the crew jumped back into the ambulance and fled. The rovers fired warning shots at the vehicle, but it did not stop.

At OP 293, SPC Rittenburg saw the rovers firing at the ambulance as it entered his field of fire. He engaged the vehicle, aiming at the engine compartment. The rounds disabled the engine and killed both the driver and the frontseat passenger. Another Iraqi ran for the cover of a nearby house but was engaged with 5.56 mm M-16 rifles while Spec. Rittenburg directed the fire using the CROW's night sight.

The roving patrol discovered three Iraqis in the back of the vehicle; the patient (who had suffered from a heart attack and was already dead), his son, and a third Iraqi who had two gunshot wounds. One was fresh and probably from the dismounted troops from the roving patrol, while the second was to the lower torso and had already received first aid. We later discovered that the third Iraqi was actually an IED triggerman who had been shot by marines while fleeing an ambush north of our area. The triggerman fled into 5K where he received shelter and was able to call for help. The ambulance crew waited for a legitimate emergency so they could use it to enter our area and pick up the insurgent at the cost of an innocent man's life. Our guys felt bad for opening fire on an am-bulance at first—until they learned what really happened.

It was not until further reflection that I came to think of the victims of the glass factory disaster as true victims. These men were trying to become Iraqi Police. Of all the indifference in Ramadi, of all the coward-ice, greed, and betrayal, these men were actually standing up for a cause.

True, many of the Iraqi Police were insurgents, but not all of them. The applicants who stood in those long lines that day had not yet become part of the corrupt police system.

When we were finally relieved that day, I went back to the battalion aid station and found it awash in patients. Over thirty casualties were treated by our BAS, and all survived. In the moments following the disaster, our aid station crew, known as steady-state operations section, mobilized the majority of our emergency vehicles and went to the scene. We were fortunate to have a board-certified emergency room physician working with us. Col. McGuiness and Lt. Gunn reconstituted the aid station crew by calling in every off-duty line medic in the battalion. In most cases, the patients received at the BAS were not critical—those who were went to C Med—but in at least one case, a patient arrived with cardiac tamponade (blood filling the sac around the heart, preventing it from pumping effectively). Our Dr.McGuiness performed a pericardiocentesis (inserted a needle into the sac to drain the blood), while paramedic Sgt. Patrick Padilla performed an endotracheal intubation. But in the process of medicating the patient, Pat also stuck himself with a morphine auto-injector and intubated the patient while under the influence of morphine. The patient was stabilized before he was taken to C Med. Sgt. Padilla was given a narcotic antidote known as Narcan, which reversed the effects of the drug, and he continued to care for patients.

There was still quite a scene when I got back to the BAS. Patients were lined up on the sidewalks in an orderly manner. Each of them had someone attending to them. Generally, at least one nonmedical soldier remained with each patient while the medics circulated as needed. Troops from the Mortar Platoon, Support Platoon, and all over the base came together to act as litter bearers. Before we left Camp Shelby, we had trained almost all of them as combat lifesavers, and it really paid off.

For all of our faults as National Guardsmen—we are old and some of us are out of shape—we bring a lot of strength and maturity to the urban battlefield. The average medic in our task force had several years of clinical experience under his belt. Most of our NCOs in our line units were husbands and fathers. We could all sympathize with the plight of the Iraqi families trying to survive in their war-torn nation.

We later learned that a marine named Sgt. Adam Leigh Cann and his bomb-sniffing dog had detected the bomber's presence just before he detonated himself. If that dog had not sniffed out the bomb and caused him to prematurely detonate himself outside the gates, he might have made it inside where dozens of U.S. and Coalition forces were working to process the Iraqi Police applicants. The marine was killed instantly, but the dog survived.

Months after this disaster I met an Army veterinarian who had known Sgt. Cann and his dog. She told me that at the time of the blast she was at Al-Asad, a remote air base near the Syrian border. Unlike most cases where trauma cases are flown to either Baghdad or Balad for surgery, in this case patients were evacuated to any available U.S. military medical facility that could care for them. She was helping out in the emergency room at Al-Asad when the very dog who saved the day arrived by helicopter, in need of her care. While we were all saddened by the loss of the marine handler, our spirits were buoyed, at least a little bit, at the news that his dog survived.

As the sun set over Ramadi that evening, I headed west on patrol with the guys from Alpha Company's Blue Platoon. We were all treated to the most beautiful blood-red colored sunset. I captured the view on camera. I could not help but think that it was the blood of innocents that stained the skies that night, only to fade quickly into darkness.

Target: Irhabee

There were some areas of Ramadi that we just simply did not go into. The insurgency knew this, and they sought shelter there. One of the most frustrating things about tracking down radical Islam is the Muslim duty to take in strangers and to provide nourishment, shelter, and protection to anyone who seeks it. It is considered a sin not to fulfill this duty.

When the insurgents needed to hide, they could go into an area and ask for protection. The average Iraqi did not necessarily subscribe to the radical ideology that Al Qaeda professed, but he was not terribly fond of the Americans, and he faced the requirement of hospitality. In any case, if he refused, he was killed.

Such was the case with one particularly nasty insurgent cell leader. He had a large extended family, and he would slip through the streets, staying with different relatives, often spending only one night in a given location. The neighborhood he was staying in was one we simply did not patrol. This was the heart of the insurgency, and we did not have the forces needed to control it. The best we could do was to develop intelligence and act on it when we could.

We had been seeking this character for a while now. He was responsible for many attacks on U.S. and Coalition forces. We knew that his extended family occupied most of the neighborhood around the house where he was staying, and that at the sound of an alarm, we could easily be surrounded by hundreds of armed insurgents. Given the remote location—deep in enemy territory, through streets known to be filled with IEDs—our leaders elected to use a small force of dismounted troops. We took only eight men with us, and we left our vehicles behind.

With our night-vision equipment and accurate weapons, we owned the night. We crept silently through darkened streets. It was late—after midnight—but surprisingly, many of the local people were awake. No one was out in the streets, of course, it was far too dangerous for that, but the sound of people talking, laughing, and going about their business could be heard coming through open windows. In all of our other interactions with Iraqi civilians, I don't recall ever hearing the sound of a neighborhood full of ordinary families through their open windows. Except for this night when we operated dismounted, the people were always fully aware of our presence and on their guard. It seemed so normal to hear the sounds of televisions blaring, children playing, and people talking.

We always spread out when we dismounted—so a single attack could not take us all out—and we covered almost an entire city block as we moved, ten-meter intervals between us, sweeping the streets, rooftops, and windows for targets. We hoped we would not find any, because even a single shot out here could give away our presence and spell big trouble. Our advantage was in our concealment. Our backup humvee gun trucks and our tanks could probably get to us and bail us out if we needed them, but our mission would not succeed. We preferred to keep the enemy off balance, and not let them know we were so deep in their backyards.

The target house was in the middle of a block—relatives living in the houses on each side—and across a large open area. We had no other way to get there but through the open. Our plan was to stick to the shadows as much as possible, but we could not remain concealed the entire time. One of our concerns was the proximity of the nearby houses, and the ease with which the enemy could flee from one house to the next. Many of the back doors were only a few feet from the neighbors' back doors, and the rooftops were an easy leap. Once we announced our presence, our prey was likely to vanish. Cutting off his escape was paramount. Doing so without firing a shot was preferable.

We were far enough into enemy territory that we figured it could take quite a while for us to get out of here. The possibility of us having to hole up in a house somewhere and wait for help was strong. For this reason, the squad leader was even more concerned than normal with keeping his doc alive. The guys all knew that if they were ever hurt, I would stop at nothing to save them. The knowledge that if they survived the initial injury they were probably going to survive was comforting for them. They also knew that I had their back. I was twenty years older and fifty pounds heavier than some of them, but I went from medic to soldier in an instant. I never let my guys down, and I fought viciously right beside them.

Some of our soldiers slip silently through the streets in the darkness. (Photo taken through night vision equipment, provided by VTARNG Public Affairs)

As much as I wanted to be in on the initial entry, SSG Murtha would not allow it. We all knew the likelihood that we were going to take or inflict casualties during our initial assault, and he wanted me on the outside looking in. I was assigned to watch the back door for anyone fleeing our assault, and my orders were to kill anyone I saw. People fleeing from our assault were likely to be our targets, and they would sound the alarm and possibly cut off our escape if they got away.

Normally, we engaged the enemy from a distance when we could. Our rifles were effective at very long distances. In this case, however, I did not want to give away my position with gunfire if I didn't have to. I let my rifle fall on its sling, and I held my Marine Corps K-Bar fighting knife in my hand. If anyone came out the back door, they would have to stop and slip around a tight corner in the darkness. I hid in the shadows with my night-vision equipment, poised to strike. I had minimal training in hand-to-hand combat, but I knew enough to know that slicing the neck would stifle a scream. I kept my other hand free, so that as my target slipped through the narrow alleyway around my corner, I could grab them from behind, yank their head to one side, and slash their throat. If the knife didn't do it, my pistol was easy enough to grab in its quick-draw holster.

Our entry team stacked up at the door. At the signal, they kicked it in and ran inside. I could hear muffled sounds, and then it was quiet. It seemed like an eternity while they searched the house. I maintained my post like a coiled spring, ready to pounce if anyone came through that door, but no one did. Finally, the squad leader called me and one of the other guys in to help with the search. We wanted to spend as little time on target as possible, but we had to find our target, and we had to find evidence on him.

Unlike our predecessor unit, we now operated in a new and sovereign Iraq. The elections we oversaw were the beginning of their new democracy, and they now operated under constitutional law. We could no longer take prisoners and send them away indefinitely. We had to collect evidence, witness statements, and photographs. Our prisoners faced trial in an Iraqi court. This was a good idea in theory, but in practice it was unreliable. We could not reveal our methods for gathering intelligence to the Iraqi court system, and frequently the targets we sought would purposefully keep an arms-length distance from any weapons, munitions, or documents that could incriminate them. We relied heavily upon finding evidence with the target when we detained them. If we did not find any, they were often released. A bigger hurdle was the Iraqi court system itself. The judges were reluctant to take the word of an American against an Iraqi. They also considered killing an American to be commendable. The standard penalty for killing one of us was two months in Abu Ghraib Prison. During their two-month stay, the insurgents we captured in Ramadi would network with others from around Iraq, train together, and emerge from prison a whole lot more lethal than when they went in.

Our initial search came up empty. Our target was here, but this house was too clean. We found the requisite single AK-47—and three magazines. They were only allowed one magazine, but having three was not a big enough crime to keep this guy behind bars for very long. We could not reveal the real evidence—information from insurgents—against him in an Iraqi court, for to do so would be signing the death warrant of our informants.

I could feel the tension as I came in. The target was in handcuffs and blindfolded, but sneering and smug. He was defiant toward us and verbally abusive to the family. Our interpreter gave us an idea of what he was saying to them, and it was not nice. They sat stone-faced while we searched. I looked at them and I had the distinct impression they would not miss this jerk when he was gone.

The initial entry team was beginning their second round of searching, more thoroughly this time, desperate to find enough evidence to send this known terrorist away for a long time. He had been responsible a lot of attacks, and we had been seeking him for quite a while. We were not likely to have this opportunity again, but we could not stay here long. The longer we stayed here, the greater the risk of being discovered.

I looked at the room where our target had been sleeping. Clearly it was a guest room, normally used as a sitting room, with a spare mattress on the floor and a few blankets. On one wall was the usual wall cabinet full of drawers with blankets, pillows, and mattresses stacked on top, all the way to the ceiling. There was something about this Iraqi hospitality. Most homes had a supply of spare bedding big enough to house an army—and they sometimes did.

The room had a few drawers open, but most of the furnishings were still intact and undisturbed. Little had been touched on the first sweep, probably because the guys were busy arresting the bad guy. We divided the rooms between us, and worked furiously to search the place. I worked with another soldier in the room where the target was found sleeping. If he had any time at all to hide his weapons, they would be in this room.

I thought back to the fire scenes I had processed back home. We would spend hours digging through the rubble to expose the floor, where we would find the tell-tale burn patterns left by a flammable liquid. We left no stone unturned there, and I was not about to do so here. Every drawer was dumped and pawed through. Every mattress, blanket and pillow was shaken out and thoroughly examined. I was extremely thorough, and as we worked, the young soldier with me began to despair, thinking we would find nothing.

Finally, in the bottom of the lowest drawer, I found something. This particular device looked innocent enough—it was a small black tubular object, only a few inches long and maybe an inch across. It was the sort of thing that anyone might have kicking around in their junk drawer or toolbox—a forgotten gizmo that attaches to a tool we no longer use.

It was a rifle grenade adapter, the same type we found months earlier in the house of the red-headed merchant. I turned with a smile, and held the adapter up. Finally, we had our man. Ironically, he probably did not put that adapter in the drawer. It had probably been there for a long time but it was enough to send him away. AK-47s were allowed for home defense against common criminals, but rifle grenades were clearly an offensive weapon used by the insurgents to kill Americans.

The target seemed incredulous that we found something. He had been so smug, defiantly cursing us and his Iraqi hosts in Arabic while we searched. He refused to obey our commands to be quiet, and was really getting on everyone's nerves. He was calling the men worthless traitors and insinuating that the women were all whores. The more noise he made, the more likely we were to be discovered. Meant to be quick and silent, an ex-fil ("exfiltrate," the opposite of infiltrate) could turn into a real problem if we woke up the neighbors.

We photographed the rifle grenade adapter and the extra magazines. The real evidence on this guy was probably human intelligence gathered by secret means—and it would never see the light of day in an Iraqi court. To reveal it would be to compromise our ability to gather further evidence, endangering many lives. I really did not know or care if the stuff we found belonged to him, we were taking a killer off the streets either way, and this evidence was going to work.

By some Arabic words known only to our interpreter and the prisoner, our interpreter somehow managed to convince him to shut up. I suspect he promised to kill him instantly if he attracted any attention, and that was fine with us. Somehow we made it back out to our trucks without being discovered. The Iraqi family seemed just as happy as we were to have this jerk out of their house, quietly whispering "Shukran" as we slipped out the door—Arabic for "thank you." The unfortunate truth was that their adherence to the tenets of their religion forced them to shelter this infidel in their house while he defiled Islam, insulted their women, and promised brutal and horrible vengeance on the men.

We all slept pretty good the next day, knowing we had done some good that night.

DUNCAN, JAKE, AND THE IED FAMILY

Late one hot afternoon I was on patrol with Blue Platoon and SFC Duncan. We got a radio call that our observation post had observed a man setting an IED up near their position, but he had escaped before they got a clear shot at him. As soon as they swung their weapons toward

The little girl who distracted her parents into talking while my camera recorded every Arabic word. (Photo by author)

him, he had escaped into a nearby house. The guys in the tank made a note of which house he ran into, and we waited for the cover of darkness to pay them a visit. By approaching the home after dark, we hoped to avoid sniper and RPG fire from a nearby apartment complex that we called the "Detroit Apartments." We also figured the bomber was more likely to be home later in the evening.

We found the family home and awake, but no one there matched the description of the bomber we had from the tank crew. One by one, SFC Duncan took the men of the family into another room alone with Jamie, our interpreter. By separating the men for individual questioning, they hoped to discover any inconsistencies in their stories that could help discern who might be lying.

In the meantime, I was assigned to corral the women and children in one room. They all sat quietly while we talked among ourselves. Before long, this little Iraqi girl was giving me what for. She was probably only four years old, and did not grasp that I could not understand her Arabic. She was pointing at my rifle and my muddy boots and going on and on, dressing me down as if I could understand her.

Alpha Company's Blue Platoon guard several prisoners after explosives were found in their vehicle during a routine traffic stop. (Photo by SGT Brandon Allmond)

She was so cute; I thought I would snap a photo. I pulled out my camera and using pantomime, I asked the mother if I could take the little girl's picture. Mom smiled and nodded, and I got the photo. With all of the laughing and joking going on, no one noticed that I switched my digital camera over to video. The adults were talking among themselves in Arabic now, and every word they uttered was being recorded.

Our interpreter listened to the recording later. Turns out, they were laughing at us, remarking to each other that we were idiots, and if we had any real brains we would be going next door to catch Mohammed, as he was the one setting the IEDs.

Mohammed became our guest at Abu Ghraib Prison.

RPGS AT EVERY TURN AND THE DEATH OF SGT. JOHNSON

With our success against IEDs and VBIEDs, the enemy grew increasingly frustrated. We started to see their tactics change during our tour in Ramadi, and saw greater use of RPGs. Toward the end of our year in Ramadi, the use of RPGs was very common. Our vehicles could not stop moving for more than ten or fifteen minutes before there would be an

RPG team firing on them. Fortunately for us, the enemy was not a good shot, and their rockets usually missed.

A friend of mine was not so lucky, however. Sgt. Johnson was killed in Ramadi when a rocket went right through the windshield of his humvee. It was a direct hit and he died later in surgery. He was a great guy, and his loss was felt deeply. Sgt. Johnson was a veteran of the war in Afghanistan and was a squad leader with Alpha Company's White Platoon. I remember him for his quick, constant smile. It seemed like he was always smiling, and he buoyed the spirits of all those around him.

I went home on leave right about the time Johnson was killed, and while I was home I went to his wake.

Shootout in Tameem

"What was that?" I asked our gunner, Spec. Swartz. "Somebody's flipping pigeons on that roof in front of us!" I was sitting in the back seat, and looking forward through the windshield, I saw a flock of birds launch from the roof of an apartment building.

It was a routine patrol in the Tameem section of Ramadi. I was riding in the backseat.

"I didn't see anything behind us," Swartz piped in from above, but he was facing backwards. No one else saw the birds take off, but I knew I had spotted the enemy. Launching pigeons was a means of signaling one another that we were approaching.

"Everyone on your toes!" Joe Lewis said from the front seat. Joe was our vehicle commander. He had fully recovered from his gunshot wound, and he had a sixth sense about him that could sniff out trouble a mile away. Honed when he was on the street as a cop in South Philly, Joe's instincts were usually dead on.

Our two-humvee patrol rounded the corner at the end of the block and started down the next street. All of a sudden, our world lit up with machine-gun fire coming from everywhere. Swartz screamed and slumped low in his seat. I looked up into his turret and saw sparks fly as bullets impacted and ricocheted around the inside. There was blood on his face as he slunk down in his seat.

"Gunner's down!" I yelled. There was blood on his nose, but not much. He was sliding down into the vehicle trying to get below the bullets impacting all around his head. I checked his nose, and there was only a superficial wound.

"Dude, you're fine, it's just a scratch!" I hollered to him.

"Really? Those motherfuckers!" he hollered, as he stood back up in his turret, grabbed his M-60 machine gun and opened fire. From over one hundred meters in a moving vehicle, Swartz shot the first gunman through the eye, killing him instantly. A second gunman was also hit and would later die.

"The roof! Check the roof!" Joe yelled. "I think there's another one on the roof, four o'clock!"

"I got nothing!" Swartz called out.

"Hit 'em with an HE round!" Joe yelled. "I *know* there was somebody up there!"

Swartz loaded his M-203 grenade launcher with a high-explosive round and fired at the roof of the house we had just taken fire from. The first round went right over the top and, we later learned, landed on the mosque on the next block.

"Firing again!" Swartz called out, and this time his aim was true. Everything went flying off the roof when his second round landed right on target—the gunman, the laundry, the pigeon cages, everything went flying.

"Anybody got anything else?" Joe asked, as we all scanned for targets. No one did. "Get us out of here!" He yelled to SPC Forsburg, our driver. We were in an ambush, and needed to get out of the kill zone. "Regroup on the next block!"

We went down the street and around the corner just long enough for SSG Hegg, the squad leader in our other humvee, to call in a radio report and get reinforcements heading our way. With help on the way, we immediately counterattacked. The tanks we had positioned on an observation post nearby roared to life and came storming up the street behind us. As luck would have it, a platoon from the Nebraska National Guard's 1/167th Cavalry was nearby, and responded immediately. They came up the far end of the block, and we started on our end, kicking in every door and chasing down the guys who had just ambushed us. We didn't get far before we found the two guys Swartz had just shot.

The first guy was obviously dead, shot through the eye from 150 meters away. The second guy, though, was quite a sight. Sitting in a pool of blood, he was screaming at us in Arabic, with an arterial bleed from his right arm squirting bright red blood all over the place. His arm was obviously broken, and he was hitting me with it, flailing the broken section wildly.

"The house is clear, Doc, we are going next door! Forsburg, stay with

Doc!" Joe and SSG Hegg called out, and they dashed out to the next house.

I put a tourniquet on the man's arm, and pushed him down onto his back. "Doctor!" I yelled in English. The Arabic word for medic sounds a lot like doctor, and the man seemed to understand. He kept yelling, but he quit fighting me.

Working with my night vision mounted over my left eye, and using the feeble beam of a mini-mag flashlight, I cut away the man's clothes and found an entrance wound on the right upper quadrant of his swelling abdomen. Knowing his liver was in there and he was likely to lose a lot of blood from it, I went to his uninjured side. I pulled out a morphine auto-injector in the darkness and tried to give him something for the pain, and to calm him down.

"Yeeooow!!" I hollered, as the needle launched into my thumb. "I just shot myself with morphine!" I yelled to Forsburg.

"Oh fuck, Doc's down! Doc's down!" Forsburg called to Joe Lewis over the radio.

"I'm fine, I'm fine, Charlie Mike!" I yelled to Joe. He was back in the room in an instant.

"Are you OK, Doc? What's going to happen?" Joe asked, as I continued to work. I used another auto-injector on the patient, and started an IV on him with my now unfeeling hand. I had motor function in my right hand, but could feel nothing from the wrist down.

"I don't know, Joe; it's supposed to go in the muscle. Ten milligrams is a lot to go into a thumb, and I have no idea how fast it will be absorbed. I might pass out, and I might stop breathing, but for now, I am fine. Keep going, and get these bastards!"

"Keep a close eye on Doc, Forsburg, and let me know right away if he goes down," Joe said, and was gone as quickly as he had come.

The patient was unconscious now, and having a lot of trouble breathing. Blood and vomit was filling his throat. I moved to his head and turned him to the side, clearing his airway as best I could. I was beginning to wonder if the patient would survive. I had no suction device, and his airway was full of fluid. I pulled out a laryngoscope (a lighted scope used to see the vocal cords and so to insert an airway) and tried twice to intubate the patient, but could not find his vocal cords in all the blood and vomit.

Gunfire erupted again. I knew I would have to move on soon, and the best I could do for this guy was give him an airway and hope for the best. Others were soon to need me, and even if there were no other casualties, my squad was down to just two people, Lewis and Hegg, while Forsburg and I were tied up with this guy.

I had one more trick up my sleeve before I moved on. Grabbing my scalpel, I made an incision over his trachea. Army medics are trained to do cricothyrotomy, but in all my years in this business, I had never had to do it.

Of course in the textbooks, the patients are all young and healthy. This guy was fat, and all I could see was fat inside the skin of his neck. "What the hell?" I asked out loud.

"What is it, Doc? What's the matter?" Forsburg asked, looking over, "Oh my GOD!! That's so gross . . . what are you doing?" Incredulous, Forsburg had never seen anything like what I was doing to try to save this guy. For that matter, neither had I.

Gunfire erupted outside, punctuating each moment that I struggled to save the life of a man who had tried to kill me. I was losing him.

"He's too fat, I can't see a thing!" I answered, and grabbed my scalpel for another cut. This time I made a much bigger incision and grabbed the wound edges, ripping them apart, then slicing and digging through the fat to find his trachea.

"Doc, forget this guy, we got another one, and she's hurt bad—shot in the face!" Joe Lewis yelled, coming in from the street outside.

"Gimme one more minute, Joe, I am almost there!" Finally, I found the cricoid membrane. Stuffing an endotracheal tube through it, I finally had an airway, and it was time to move on. He would live or he would die, but I could do nothing further for him.

"Doc, I love you man, but you gotta move! This woman is hurt real bad!"

I stuffed my gear into my backpack and snatched up my rifle. Just before we ran out the door, I reached down and checked his pulse. He was gone.

The woman next door was in her first-floor apartment when the ambush started. Her apartment did not connect to the roof, but we did not know that. Joe and SSG Hegg kicked in her door, and she slammed it in their faces, knocking Hegg backwards into the street. Hegg fired half a magazine through the door with his M-4 carbine.

The woman was conscious and making the most God-awful noises through what was left of her face. One eye was all that remained, with an enormous bloody hole in her head where there should have been a mouth and nose. Each time she inhaled, she was sucking in blood, and as she would cry out, blood flew out of her head. She was aspirating huge amounts of blood into her lungs, and bleeding out. Her right hand was blown apart, and her lower right leg was gone.

I took another ET tube, and just aimed it through the bloody mess into the hole in there through which she seemed to be breathing and inflated the cuff. Stuffing the rest of the wound with a roll of kerlix (gauze), I wrapped her head with a field dressing. She began breathing through the tube right away, and the kerlix wrap slowed down her blood loss. I put two tourniquets on and moved to her uninjured arm to start an IV.

Obese middle-aged women have poor veins to begin with, and this woman had lost a lot of blood. I looked everywhere and could not find a vein. I couldn't see anything, but with my left hand, I felt a small vein buried deep inside her elbow, completely hidden in her fat arm. With my unfeeling right hand full of morphine, I tried to line up for the shot. It was tough to tell where to put the needle, and as I looked around, Joe came in to check on our progress.

"Doc, you don't look so good. Are you sure you can do that?" he asked.

The morphine was really starting to kick in now, and I felt like hell. I was kneeling in a pool of blood, dizzy and lightheaded, about to throw up, and I could not feel my hand at all. Joe told me later I was turning blue, and just swaying as I knelt there, staring at her arm.

"You want me to do the IV for you?" he asked. Like all of our troops, Joe was a combat lifesaver, trained to do IVs. I wasn't sure anyone would be able to get this stick, let alone an inexperienced combat lifesaver.

"No, I can do it, Joe . . . at least I think I can get it . . . well, I hope I can do it." And with that, to everyone's surprise, I did.

With the patient effectively stabilized, I tried to get up. We still had a firefight going on in the streets outside, and I wanted to get back to it. Standing was not such a good idea.

"I don't think I can make it, Joe," I said as my knees buckled and waves of nausea swept over me. "You better get on the horn and get yourself another medic before I pass out."

Fortunately, the 167th Cavalry had their own medic with them, and he was brought to my location quickly while a medic track was summoned to the scene. I explained the situation to him. It occurred to me that as long as I was moving and my adrenaline was flowing, I seemed to be able to overcome the morphine. It was only when I stopped moving that I seemed to be in trouble. I started to shadow box while I knelt there, and it seemed to help. I explained to the other medic what I was doing, but apparently, Jamie, our Iraqi interpreter, did not understand. He thought I had completely lost my marbles. After a few minutes of shadow boxing, I was able to get to my feet, where I started running in place, doing jumping jacks . . . everything I could do to keep my heart rate up and stay with it.

After about half an hour the fighting outside calmed down to the point that the medic track was able to make it to the scene. Sgt. Pat Padilla, a Los Angeles Paramedic in his civilian life, was on board. Once we loaded the female patient up, Pat asked me if I would ride in with him.

"NO!" I insisted, "My guys are still in a fight out here, and I am not leaving until they do!" Joe Lewis had briefed him on my condition ahead of time, although I did not know it.

"Just help me get the patient loaded, will you?" Pat asked. I did, and before I knew it, the ramp was closing behind me. I popped out the top, and started yelling at Joe.

"Don't worry about us, Doc, we are all going in. We are your security escort!" He called to me. Reassured now that I would not be leaving my men behind, I relented. Before I knew it, we were headed back to the FOB. I looked backwards at Joe as we were pulling away, and he just waved and smiled.

"You bastards!" I yelled at him. They tricked me into going back to the FOB, but it was for the best. I was in no condition to argue.

A short time later we were in the ER, and my patient was being carried on into the operating room. With the adrenaline subsiding once again, I felt me knees grow weak. I lay down on an empty stretcher, and two of the medics there put me on oxygen and started an IV.

Finally, I could relax. A few minutes later, one of the female medics that I knew through church walked in. She had been unaware of the situation I was in, and was shocked to see me lying there, covered in blood, with an IV and oxygen running.

"Oh, My God! Sgt. Middleton, are you OK?" She asked.

I just smiled up at her, loopy on drugs. "I'm feeling groovy baby, how 'bout you?"

Charlie Company and the Jundii Raid

One of the things that amazed me while serving in Ramadi was our sophisticated radar system that would track incoming mortars and pinpoint their launch sites. Our own mortars and artillery would use the information provided by these radar systems and immediately counterattack. This strategy was effective, and in many cases, the terrorists and their equipment were annihilated. There were some limits to counterfire, however. In some cases, the point of origin would be in a residential area or some other protected site, and we would not direct our indirect fire there. It did not take long for the insurgents to figure this out.

In one such case, the insurgents were consistently firing mortars at our FOB from the courtyard of a private home just a few kilometers from our FOB, north of the Euphrates River. The area was difficult to reach. The only approach was along a narrow, elevated road with muddy fields on both sides, funneling all of our vehicles into a very long choke point where IEDs and other impediments could be very effective.

Charlie Company was the smallest in our battalion. Like our other units that patrolled MSR Mobile, their primary mission was to keep this critical supply route open. They were also tasked with a secondary mission to patrol the villages and farmlands north of the highway. Lacking sufficient troops to control their assigned sector, they focused on their primary mission—to keep the highway open. When it was necessary to mount a patrol off the highway, Charlie Company would usually send a platoon out for an extra mission after their normal shift.

This particular morning raid was just such a mission. The private home used to launch mortars at our FOB was a wealthy home by Iraqi standards, made mostly of reinforced concrete and stone, with marble floors and expensive fixtures.

Nothing says good morning like an armored vehicle crashing through the front
gate into a courtyard used to launch mortars at our FOB. (Photo by author)

We rolled out late that morning, delayed by Iraqi soldiers who were
to accompany us. We would have preferred to conduct operations under the cover of darkness using our night-vision goggles, but the Iraqis
were not equipped with them, so as a compromise we planned to attack
at daybreak. We rolled out with a 113 armored personnel carrier in the
lead. Inside were eight of our guardsmen, who were there to set up a cordon around the target house while the Iraqi troops were to be the entry
team. The lieutenant in charge rode in a humvee directly behind the 113
with a driver, a gunner, me, and a newly arrived female medic named
Sgt. Alaria O'Brien, riding along for her first trip outside the wire.

Although we were running late and the sun had been up for a while,
we still managed to catch the inhabitants in bed. Most Iraquis sleep late.
Nothing says good morning like an armored vehicle crashing through
your front gate and a bunch of infantrymen charging in behind it. We
were right behind them and as the eight guys in the 113 jumped out and
encircled the house, guarding every exit, we took up a position beside
the 113 near the front door.

Our initial assault was perfect; we reached the limits of our advance with speed and violence, just as we planned. The problem was that the Iraqi entry team lacked any sense of urgency with which to capitalize on our surprise. There we stood, poised at the door, with all the escaped routes sealed. Two medics and a lieutenant guarded the front door . . . and we waited.

The five-ton truck the Iraqis were riding in was not designed for rapid egress, but that was not the only issue. The Iraqis were notoriously lazy. They worked only when they felt like it, and at this unreasonably early hour, they were in no hurry to go anywhere. It is also likely that many of them were insurgent infiltrators who knew that if they dragged their feet they might buy enough time for the target to escape or even counterattack.

"Where the hell are they?" The lieutenant asked, incredulously. We turned and heard rather than saw the Iraqi soldiers lollygagging around the target. None of them seemed particularly interested in offending anyone, especially our sleeping target. They were chattering away in Arabic, exchanging pleasantries with one another.

"We should move away from this doorway," I thought to myself, and as if on cue, a military-age male appeared in the shadows inside the large window. I could not see his hands.

"QUIF!!! IRFAA EDAK!" I yelled at him, pointing my rifle at him and ordering him in Arabic to stop and put his hands up. I reached through the open doorway and grabbed the man by the front of his man-dress (our slang for the traditional Arab robes most men wore), yanking him out the door. He was yammering away in Arabic as I hauled him out and around the corner, threw him up against the wall, and frisked him.

The noise of our 113 crashing down his gate was obviously enough to awaken even the sleepiest of Iraqis. Everyone began yelling at once, the lieutenant yelling at the Iraqi soldiers, the prisoner protesting, and just as I looked back at the door, another person appeared from the shadows within.

"QUIF!! IRFAA EDAK!" I commanded, once again, and this time yanked a woman through the door. "Search her!" I yelled at Sgt. O'Brien, and in short order we had both of them in custody.

The Iraqi soldiers finally seemed to understand the situation, and finally they began moving with a purpose, streaming through the door of the house. They found a teenage boy asleep upstairs. There was no one else home.

We searched the home thoroughly, but came up empty. Our radar system gave us enough evidence to take these people to jail, but with mortars being launched from their backyard so frequently, we were certain they must have had information on the insurgents carrying out the attacks, even if they were not doing it themselves.

They all claimed to know nothing of the men who came frequently to their yard to attack our base. The man, woman, and the boy were separated and grilled by teams of U.S. and Iraqi soldiers, along with our interpreters. Sometimes the man would start to talk, but the woman would invariably yell at him from across the courtyard and tell him to shut up. For over half an hour they continued and got nowhere.

Eventually, someone came up with the idea to use the boy to leverage the parents into talking. The plan was to tell the parents that unless they revealed the identity of the mortar teams, their fifteen-year-old boy was going to Abu Ghraib prison.

The job of visibly arresting the boy was given to the Iraqi soldiers. They understood that it was largely for show, and they took on the job in earnest. A particularly handsome young Iraqi soldier went over to the family's garden and picked a red rose. He placed it behind his ear, and held hands with the boy as he led him slowly to a point clearly visible to the parents. He smiled broadly, as he took his time frisking the boy. The boy started to cry and looked imploringly at his parents as the young Iraqi soldier ran his hands over his body.

The parents fell silent as they stared in shock. When he finished frisking the boy, the soldier took the rose from behind his ear, sniffed it, and then slowly ran the rose over the boy's cheeks, caressing his face with his other hand. Finally, he led the boy away, hand in hand, smiling and looking lovingly at his new prize. The boy was taken from the parents' view and the acting stopped. He was simply led around the corner and out of view, where other Iraq soldiers quietly reassured him that he was not going to be anyone's girlfriend.

The hoax worked like a charm. The mother stood frozen while she watched. As the boy was led away, she cracked. She completely spilled her guts, telling us all about the insurgents who came to her yard and threatened to kill her family unless they could use her property for their attacks. The father, too, had a lot to tell us about the insurgents in his village, and even the boy volunteered to go with the Iraq soldiers into Ramadi to point out where the insurgents lived.

In the end, the mission was successful, of course, but it could easily have turned out very badly. If the targets had wanted to fight back, they could easily have seized on our moments of inaction to take us out. The lieutenant, Sgt. O'Brien, and I were in plain sight of the door and could easily have been taken out.

Our crashing in the gate with a 113 certainly revealed our presence to the village. There could have been IEDs or an ambush awaiting us as we left the area on the one road. Thankfully, there were none.

The Iraqi soldiers we worked with lacked discipline and training. With the training they did have, they did not necessarily have the fortitude to stick to it when the going got tough. Many of them came from an impoverished background simply to earn an easy paycheck. The leaders in the Iraqi Army tolerated laziness and disloyalty in their ranks. Some of these same leaders were later found to have been stealing the payroll from their own troops. It was no surprise, then, that many of these troops were unmotivated.

The 5K Mosque Bandits

I spent the latter part of December and most of January working exclusively with the men of Alpha Company's Blue Platoon while their medic was home on leave. It was a fun-filled time of shootouts and explosions, busting bad guys, and narrowly escaping death. I wouldn't have traded it for the world. I was finally getting my crack at the bad guys, and taking the fight to them, rather than waiting for them to come to us. It was dangerous, but very gratifying.

The 5K section of Tameem sat up on a hill overlooking our FOB. It was a slightly less hellish place than the rest of Tameem, with slightly wider streets, a little bit better drainage of the sewage dumped there, and fewer IED strikes. Our suspicion was that a lot of the insurgent hierarchy lived in 5K and did their devil work in other parts of Ramadi. No one makes a mess in their own backyard.

In 5K was an old Iraqi Police (IP) station, a few mosques, and some thriving markets and plazas. Also in 5K was the notorious apartment complex, filled with insurgents, known as the Detroit Apartments. We frequently received small-arms fire from the roofs of the Detroit Apartments, and RPG teams could be seen ducking in there from time to time. A short distance away, the IP station was closed after the majority of the policemen were found to be insurgents. It had recently been taken over by an element of the Iraqi Army called the Public Order Brigade. These troops were responsible for maintaining the peace, but they were clearly not up to the job. Instead, they became the targets of constant attacks with small arms and RPGs. The Iraqis hated them.

At one point, it seems the insurgents had figured out the pattern to our patrols. At one of our observation posts, our four humvees would switch out every two hours. For two hours we would patrol, and for the

The men of Alpha Co, Blue Platoon. (Photo provided by SFC Duncan)

other two we would stay at the OP. We began to get calls for help from the 5K IP station every two hours and always while we were all at the other end of town swapping out.

During one of the earlier attacks, I was riding with SSG Murtha and his squad. We responded into the area between the 5k mosque and the police station. Street by street we combed the neighborhoods, until all of a sudden shots rang out.

"Contact, roof, two o'clock!" our gunner called out. "I had a muzzle flash, now it's gone!"

While we returned fire, the driver headed in the direction the shots came from. There was a house under construction on the end of the block and we thought the insurgents might be on the roof.

"Park down there and we will come in through the back!" SSG Murtha called.

We dropped out of sight of the building on a cross street, and dashed up through an alleyway, invisible from the roof. SSG Hegg had the other crew, and he had a twelve-gauge shotgun along for breaching doors. We got to the back door of the building and surveyed it very quietly through the windows. There was no sign of activity in the construction site, and the back door was locked.

"Take the door!" Murtha commanded, and in a moment, the shotgun blasted the silence. If the insurgents were still in there, they knew we were coming now. The door held, not giving an inch after repeated blasts with the twelve-gauge.

"You guys stay here; Doc, come with me," Murtha called out, and the two of us went around front.

SSG Murtha found another door on the front of the building, exposed to the street. He gave it a mule kick with all he had. The top of the door bounced a little, but the bottom did not budge. Kick after kick yielded the same result. Finally, he gave up. I had watched how the top of the door would go in a foot or more with each blow, and then bounce back, shutting us out.

"Let me have a try at it," I asked, and with that, I backed up, took a running start, and hit the door with all my weight. With all my gear on, I tip the scales at over 350 pounds, and this was the first time the extra pounds were coming in handy.

Murtha covered me through the window while I worked, and I hit the door again and again, finally bending it enough to allow Murtha to slip through it. I took over covering him while he stripped off his body armor and slid sideways through the door. The other guys gave up on the back door, and came around to join us. Inside, Murtha found cinder blocks piled up against the base of the door, creating a blockade that we were not going to get through. From the inside, though, it was a simple matter to lift them out of the way, and in no time, we were in.

Room to room the four of us searched, confident that we had finally found the insurgent stronghold. We split at the top of the stairs and I took point. In the narrow confines, I could not swing my rifle, so I led the way with my pistol. The place was empty but there was evidence we had scared the bad guys away in a hurry. They had left plenty of bottled water and bottled urine behind on their rooftop observation posts.

Eventually we left the area, creeping back to our vehicles in the darkness. We reached the two humvees just as more shots rang out.

"Contact west!" Murtha yelled, and laid down suppressive fire while we clambered into the armored humvees. Our gunners opened up, and we fired for effect, though we had no targets we could find.

We never did find the insurgents who hunted us that night, but we spent the whole night trying. Every two hours we changed shifts, and tried again with the other two rovers. This continued for a week, until our platoon leader, SFC Duncan, came up with an idea.

The IP station was under Iraqi Army control, and the Iraqi Army was supposed to be responsible for this section of town. We would wait until they attacked again, and respond in force. This time, however, instead of driving into their kill zone with only two humvees, we would use our entire platoon to surround the neighborhood, then call out the Iraqi Army from our base. They would conduct a house-to-house search and hopefully find the bad guys.

The first part of the plan worked exactly as planned; the IP station was attacked right on schedule, and we all responded, sealing off the neighborhood. The Iraqi Army, however, took over two hours to arrive on station. When they finally arrived, it was clear what took so long. None of the troops were the least bit motivated to actually do anything. We sat in our armored humvees at the end of the block, and we watched them do absolutely nothing. Fifty men responded, and forty-two of them sat around in the streets doing nothing while eight men politely searched one house at a time. In the course of the next two hours, they searched a whopping four houses. Needless to say, the bad guys got away again. The Iraqi Army, such as it was, was a lazy and undisciplined gang of slugs. Those that weren't actively involved in the insurgency did nothing to stop it, coming as many did from a desperate unemployed population only for a paycheck.

• • •

The following is an excerpt from an e-mail to my Dad.

It gets a little rough over here at times. I patrol one of the worst parts of Ramadi, and there is plenty to do. I don't sweat it though, I am working at the tip of the spear, fighting Al Qaida where it lives and breeds. Our nation has asked a heavy task of its part time warriors, thrusting us into the most dangerous area with less combat power than we need to do our jobs. With the level of risk our troops face here, I am right where they need me, and there is nowhere else I would rather be. I did not have to be here. I volunteered for this assignment, because I believe in our guys and the mission we are here to accomplish. Politically, they are trying to stand up the Iraqi Army and Police, and move us to a backup role. They have moved a little too quickly in pinning their hopes on a force I do not feel is up to the job yet. It is good to turn the fight over to them, but we need a larger force to hold this ground in the mean time.

There is a benefit in having National Guardsmen do this job. We tend to be more mature, make better decisions, identify and sympathize more with the innocent families trying to go about their day here. On the other hand, all of us leave our own children fatherless while we are here.

Tactically, it is good to see the Iraqi Army out there, and in time, they will get better. It was their first time in a quick reaction force role, and they did not grasp the sense of urgency required to catch the shooters before they melted away. Next time our commanders will fix that. I am not into taking needless chances, but I do take calculated risks. I try to stay one step ahead of the bad guys. I also stay in touch with God, and ask that he look after my family if something does happen to me. I'm in good hands.

ALPHA COMPANY AND THE MARINES

Jade Phillips and I were talking about his prospects for promotion. One of the things holding him back was his lack of a current weapons qualification for record. Soldiers must qualify periodically, but we had not had the opportunity lately, and our last scores were too old to use for this round of promotions.

I looked into the requirements for an official qualification for record, and got approval to take him out to the range set up just inside our perimeter, within range of 5K. We borrowed a humvee, scrounged lots of ammunition, and headed out. We both had a great time out there, dealing with stress, escaping the war for a day, and having fun.

We had been out there for a couple of hours when we heard a huge explosion in Ramadi. We figured something big must have happened, but didn't know what. From a distance we heard traffic on the vehicle's radio, but didn't catch the details.

We had completed Jade's qualification for record earlier, and at this point, we were skipping bottle caps across the desert, shooting them with a 5.56 mm gun pushing the tiny targets further away, making them more challenging each time we hit them. We had burned through all the extra ammo we brought with us, and we were down to our combat loads. It was time to head back to the base—and to find out what blew up. I was assigned to Voodoo QRF, and I might be needed. I had someone covering for me so we could go to the range, but it was my duty, and I should be there.

As we drove back, we learned more from the radio traffic on the command net. The U.S. Marine forces in downtown Ramadi were attacked by a large band of insurgents. The marines counterattacked, and pushed the insurgents back across the bridge into Tameem—straight at the other marines located at a checkpoint on our side of the bridge, right behind the glass factory, and just outside our FOB.

Alpha Company's White Platoon was in sector, and they responded to back up the marines. It was a target rich environment. White Platoon lit up the insurgents, fighting side by side with their marine counterparts, but there were too many of them. Many of the insurgents fell, but a substantial number of them fought their way across the bridge and made it into a couple of buildings near the water's edge. From their elevated vantage points in the buildings, they pinned the dismounted marines down in an alcove. The marines were taking blistering fire, barely able to get off a shot before the enemy bullets drove them back. It became a standoff, and it was not going well for our guys.

Other insurgents circled around the next block and attacked Ogden Gate, cutting off our guys, pinning them down between two bases of fire from ample cover in the concrete buildings. Units responding out Ogden Gate came under immediate enemy fire, slowing down their efforts to assist White Platoon and the marines.

As all hell broke loose at Ogden Gate, Jade and I pulled up to the intersection right behind the guard shack. It would be so easy to just take a right and jump into the fight. We talked about it as we sat there, humvees and tanks racing past us. Did the reinforcements have a medic with them? We had no way of knowing. Were there casualties out there? Probably. We had my one aid bag, and we both had our combat loads of ammunition.

Jade was my best friend, and the warrior spirit ran strong in him; a soldier's soldier, he would have backed me up assaulting the very gates of hell if I told him to. Deferring to my rank, he checked his weapons and got his game face on. It was up to me.

Meanwhile, riding in his new position as a tank gunner was Joe Lewis. He and his crew, along with SSG Murtha and the rest of his squad, raced out the gate, through the heavy enemy fire, and took up exposed positions from which they had a clear field of fire at the enemy's far superior positions in one of the concrete buildings across the road. Joe and his tank crew ignored the small-arms fire, protected as they were in seventy tons of armor. They pulled out into Route Michigan and saw the marines pinned down there. The superior optics on the tank helped Joe identify the enemy positions quickly. They were arrayed in the third-floor windows of a building with a commanding view. The marines could not hit them, but the insurgents were able to place accurate fire right on top of our marines, effectively taking them out of the fight. One of the marines struggled to line up for a shot with an AT-4 anti-tank rocket. It was the squad's only shot. Their rifles were not effective, and they carried only one rocket.

Finally the traffic cleared enough for us to get across. Decision time. We had no communications with the elements out there in the fight. The Voodoo QRF might be rolling out any minute. I should get back. Mad as hell, fuming like a caged beast, I gunned the engine and headed back to the BAS. I had a job to do.

Back in the open field outside Ogden Gate, SSG Murtha and his crew heard the enemy bullets impacting their vehicles. They searched for targets and laid down sporadic suppressive fire, unable to locate all of the insurgent positions. In the backseat, SPC Rittenburg sat before a video screen, protected from IEDs and small arms fire, operating a joy stick. Atop the humvee was a high-tech weapon system called the CROW, a remote control .50-caliber machine gun with a ten-power day/night/ thermal optical system. Linked together, the incredible range and firepower of the .50 and the advanced targeting system could drive tacks from a mile away.

Rittenburg had a problem—the gun was not working. There was no human gunner on top of the CROW truck, so there was no armored turret protecting the weapon. As he struggled to fix it, Murtha and the driver, Spec. Sharkey, got out and engaged the enemy with their rifles. There was very little cover.

"Get that fucking gun up and running, Rittenburg!" Murtha yelled, blasting away.

Nothing was working. They needed that .50-cal in the fight in the worst way. There was another way, Rittenburg thought, looking up. He jumped out of his seat and threw open the roof hatch. Standing up chest high in the unprotected hatch, he took the big gun in his hands, targeting down the barrel the old-fashioned way.

Murtha heard the big gun come back into the fight, and saw the enemy fall. The tide was finally turning in their favor, and he was thankful to have Rittenburg in the back seat, operating the CROW system with incredible accuracy. He stole a look up at the million-dollar weapon on the roof, and was shocked to see Rittenburg standing up behind it, completely exposed to enemy fire, firing manually.

"Are you out of your mind? Get your ass down in the truck you idiot!" Murtha screamed at Rittenburg.

Meanwhile, as Joe's tank approached, the marine squad leader waved the tank off in typical marine fashion. He had this under control and did not need the Army to bail him out. It was insane, and naturally Joe and his tank crew ignored him. Joe picked out the enemy location, and fired the main gun. Nothing says hello like a 120 mm high-explosive round flying in your living room window.

In quick order, Joe and his tank crew annihilated the insurgents. White Platoon and the marines advanced on the building cautiously, expecting booby-trapped bodies and IEDs everywhere. There might have been hidden explosives, but there was no one left alive to detonate them. Joe's tank crew made all the difference, and all of the bad guys in the building were dead.

The soldiers guarding the gate, though, were still taking fire. There could be casualties anywhere. But Rittenburg's bold move worked to turn the tide of battle back in Alpha Company's favor. The insurgents fell back, some of them slipping out of the other buildings, escaping, while the others covered their retreat. Alpha Company pressed the counterattack, running and gunning through the streets of Tameem, in a battle that raged on for several hours.

Eventually, they pushed back what was left of the insurgents all the way down to the river, and soon the enemy was no more. The insurgents' last stand lasted a long time before their last guns fell silent. There was plenty of time for them to set traps before they died. Low on ammo, Alpha Company set up a cordon around the other building and waited. There was no sense rushing in when time was now in their favor.

When our guys finally entered the building, there was no one left. Using the river under the cover of darkness, someone had removed the bodies. Blood was everywhere, but haji took care of his fallen. We never learned how many insurgents died that day, but there was a palpable void in hostile action from that day forward. Intel later reported that all of them were wiped out. Somehow they found out that every single one of the insurgents involved in that battle was dead.

There was no worse feeling than knowing that my Alpha Company brothers were pinned down and I could not help them. I was a soldier first, armed well, with a fine soldier next to me. But I was also a doc, and assigned to QRF duty. I prayed they had enough firepower, knowing that without a crew-served weapon on the roof, we could only do just so much. If things went really bad, I'd be dispatched to go out there, and I could certainly make a difference as a doc.

It was incredibly emasculating not to take that right-hand turn and rush into the fight. I talked about it later with SSG Murtha. He said he would have been really glad to see me that day. They were in a tough spot. Thankfully, there was no need for Voodoo QRF to roll. We took no casualties that day, and our guys annihilated the enemy.

 **The Battle of OP 2**

In February 2006, the 2nd Marine Division finished its tour and was replaced by the 1st Marine Division, which established its headquarters in Fallujah rather than at Camp Blue Diamond, outside Ramadi.

COBRA TO BLUE DIAMOND

The men of Bravo Company, 109th Infantry, did a great job of clearing their sector and killed, captured, or chased away almost all of the insurgents. It was a long hard fight, and they paid a price for their victory. The men had accomplished much, and they had earned a break. The 109th was pulled out of FOB Ramadi. They moved to Camp Blue Diamond, and were given a new battle space. The Danger Element of the Kentucky National Guard's D/149th infantry took over where the Cobra Element left off. Every man in D/149 Had volunteered for this deployment, and they had spent the first part of the deployment at Al-Asad, where enemy contact was comparatively light. They were fresh and ready to fight.

Camp Blue Diamond had once been a palace occupied by Saddam Hussein's sons, Uday and Qusay. It was considered too much of a prize to leave abandoned. With the Marines' division headquarters pulling out, the 109th Infantry became the de facto landlords of the entire camp.

With this movement to Blue Diamond, everyone needed to figure out how to provide services at both bases. Our own medical platoon detached a small squad to go over and work in a battalion aid station, and Chaplain Lawson, a truly pious man and an excellent preacher, began, providing services on both sides of the ancient biblical river.

My old friend Lt. Gunn needed a ride to Blue Diamond and so did the brigade chaplain. I put the two together and gave up my day off—New Years Day—to ferry them both over there so they could set things up. I commandeered our LMTV—the brand new two-and-a-half-ton cargo truck that we outfitted as a mass casualty ambulance—and the three of us headed out. What a strange crew we were: a medical officer driving, a chaplain riding shotgun, and me—a combat medic—as a roof gunner. Fortunately it was only a five-minute trip across the bridge.

We did not anticipate just how long everyone wanted to spend at Blue Diamond. It was well past darkness by the time we were ready to leave. What we had not realized was that this brand-new truck had not yet been equipped with black-out lights. All of our military vehicles had factory-standard black-out drive lights, but they were tiny, invented before the advent of night-vision equipment and only designed for a few feet of visibility at extremely low speeds. In Ramadi, we modified all of our vehicles with special infrared headlights, powerful high beams comparable to normal headlights, but visible only through night-vision equipment. Unfortunately, we overlooked retrofitting this truck with the special lights, and we were blind for the ride back. With practically no visibility, we were also traveling over a road known for IEDs and small-arms attacks. Speed was of the essence in order to avoid falling victim.

Unlike the weapons carried by the rear-echelon troops, my rifle was outfitted with a PEC 2 infrared laser sight, capable of shining an invisible floodlight beam comparable to a large mag (flash)light. The lieutenant and I wore night-vision goggles, but the chaplain did not. I climbed up into the gunner's hatch and shined my invisible light at the road in front of us. The lieutenant gunned the engine, and drove like a bat out of hell.

The experience was rather unsettling for the good chaplain, riding blind through the night at forty miles per hour over pothole-strewn roads. Although he couldn't see it, the lieutenant had a pretty good beam of light to see with.

"L . . . L . . . L . . . Lieutenant, don't you think you should slow down a little?" I heard him stutter imploringly in the darkness. "O Ye of little faith," I thought to myself, smiling.

With B 109th moving, and additional Iraqi forces coming online in our area, our battalion was tasked with sending medics both to Blue Diamond and out to work with the Iraqi Army. I went on leave in February while all these changes were under way. When I got back, much of our medical platoon was shuffled around. I found a new assignment waiting for me with B Troop, 104th Cavalry. I would not be a floating medic any longer, but would be assigned to 3rd Platoon on a full-time basis. I arrived there in late February, at about the same time as the new platoon leader, Lt. Harry Golden.

B Troop's 3rd Platoon was a mixture of troops detailed to B Troop from HHC, 1/172nd. Included in this platoon were volunteers from the New Hampshire Army National Guard, a handful of guys detailed over from the Philadelphia-based B Troop, and a collection of guys from HHC. Most of the men in this platoon were not infantry. There were cooks, mechanics, artillerymen, tankers, and military police. There was a lot of variance in the combat skills of these men, and with that came differences in their levels of motivation.

This platoon had lost a lot of guys to injuries and death. They suffered one of the highest attrition rates in the battalion. March 1, 2006, would be one of the hardest days of my life and it would be my defining moment.

The early morning hours of March 1 began very peacefully. I had just started my new assignment as the medic for 3rd Platoon. We had our morning briefing in the darkness before dawn, and SSG Pratt, the platoon sergeant, explained that he would be riding with the new platoon leader, Lt. Golden, and introducing the lieutenant to our area. We would try to locate some schoolchildren today. A small group of boys had been spotted a couple of days before, playing in an abandoned building close to our OP 2. We stopped and talked with them, and they promised to keep an eye on our position in return for some school supplies. We gave them all the candy we carried, and I even gave them each a toothbrush, courtesy of my own dentist back in Vermont.

Like me, Lt. Golden joined the platoon just a few days before this mission. He had been deployed to Saudi Arabia with D Company, 1/172nd Armor out of Lyndonville, Vermont, where he patrolled the desert and saw little action. Lt. Golden had been a Navy man in a past life, and this was now his fourth trip to the Middle East. When D Company returned from their deployment, he volunteered to join Task Force Saber in Ramadi, knowing full well that this mission was extremely dangerous. There was a war on, and the lieutenant wanted to do his part. A highly intelligent man, Lt. Golden had a quick smile and a complex sense of humor. He immediately grasped the importance of being on the offensive against this insurgency, steadfast in his view that the Iraqis had been oppressed for so long that they only respected the powerful.

Our first stop that morning was OP 1, where we swapped stories with the previous shift, played with our dog, Booger, and took in the glorious red sunrise. The outline of the glass factory was just visible on the horizon as the fiery desert sun burned through the morning haze—splashing its bloody red hue into the stillness of our morning.

The previous platoon commander had been a solid and charismatic leader who tried hard to befriend the locals. He loved to get out and kick a soccer ball with the kids, and everyone liked him. If he had a weakness, it was reluctance to fire. To me, it seemed as if he would rather he be killed than to lose another one of his men or to be wrong in taking the life of another.

SSG Pratt had worked many jobs in his lifetime, from drill sergeant to bouncer to handyman, and he had an easygoing manner that belied the inner conflict brewing beneath his thick skin. An older man, not unlike me, he felt an obligation to bring his boys home in one piece. His platoon had taken many casualties early in this deployment, and in his view he had failed the men he lost. He had little use for the war he found himself in, and I suspect he would have preferred to spend his last few months in Iraq just focusing on his primary mission: keeping the main supply route open. He felt there were too few of us to really make a difference, and the apathy that the Iraqis displayed toward their own fate made men like SSG Pratt want to pull the plug on our entire operation and just go home.

I listened patiently and smiled while getting to know the platoon. In the past, I had occasionally filled in as a relief medic with these guys, but not often. I was content as a relief medic, but I worked out a deal with our medical platoon leader where SPC Lancette and I basically traded places. I was now assigned as the platoon medic, and Lancette went to work with the Iraqi Army.

With a different platoon of infantry to work with every day, I had become very close with my friends in the chapel. I did not want to leave our parish at FOB Ramadi or the music ministry that I shared with our troops there. Jade Phillips, Glen Woods and I leaned on one another for strength, prayed together for guidance through this mess, and found an escape in our ministry each week. For a few hours each week, we got to sing the Lord's praises, follow in His footsteps, and forget about the war. With each other, we insisted on using our first names. We shared our musical decisions together, supporting each other in harmony and rhythm. The last thing I wanted to do was move to another FOB and lose the only close friends I had in this forsaken wasteland.

The captain wanted me to move to Camp Blue Diamond and be assigned to a MITT team—training the Iraqi Army. Instead, I moved over to B Troop, 3rd Platoon, and Lancette went to Blue Diamond to work with the Iraqi Army.

My travels through the streets of Tameem with Alpha Company taught me to embody the warrior ethos. There was no better friend, and no worse enemy than me. I did not hesitate to jump into the fight and tear up the insurgents. The men of Alpha Company had taught me the importance of dominating the battlefield. The enemy won't fire at you when he is cowering in fear. Putting on a bold face was crucial; suppressive fire took the concept to another level. I had developed a keen sense of when danger lurked. Guys like Joe Lewis and SFC Duncan showed me what to look for and taught me to recognize the actions the enemy took to engage us. By recognizing the hostile intent early, we were able to engage and destroy him before he could execute his attacks on us. I was a quick study in the ways of war—and a good shot with my rifle.

With Booger skittering about playfully and the guys all laughing and stretching the morning kinks out of their armor, I thought about the differences in our approaches to battle. The glass factory in the distance loomed over Tameem like the specter of death, the bloody horrors in its shadows merely an intangible tale of carnage to the men who were not there—while the blood of innocents still stained my own well-traveled boots. (I refer here to an actual pair of boots that I wore through most of my tour. They were literally stained with lots of human blood—that of insurgents, innocent bystanders, and U.S. soldiers. That one pair of boots was irreplaceable since they were my only pair that fit properly. I still have the boots, but I have cleaned them up.)

Lt. Golden joined me on the quiet edge of our position, staring thoughtfully into the sunrise and wondering what the day would bring. He had heard I traveled far through these war-torn sands, and he wanted to hear about my war. I shared with him a tale or two, telling more with my eyes than my words.

As the desert sun broke free of its bloody reverie we mounted our humvees and headed out . . . west at first, though only for a while.

Sunrise over FOB Ramadi on the morning of March 1,
just before the battle of OP2. (Photo by author)

In the hummer behind us, PFC Snodgrass was riding high in his own private world—that in which the gunners gun. Boldly he stood, exposed from the waist up, riding high as always, to better see the threats he faced.

Our own gunner, Brevet, hummed happily to himself, enjoying the cool of the morning air for now. Brevet often seemed unfazed to the casual observer, his deliberate disconnect from reality a mystery to the uninitiated. Nothing bothered Brevet in his world, because nothing bad ever happened there . . . nothing.

"KABOOM!!" From behind us the explosion came, shattering our morning reprieve and throwing us headlong into the day. "Contact, IED, six o'clock," I said, unthinking, to the lieutenant, forgetting for the moment that our other hummer was at our six. Roadside bombs were nothing new to me, but they were less common out here on the highway.

"Gunner's down!" came the radio call, and instantly I shifted into gear. We cleared out of the blast area a few hundred meters and pulled over. The trucks hadn't stopped rolling yet before I was out the door. My butt pack aid bag strapped to my side, I dashed toward our wingman's truck. Snoddy rocked back in his seat, reeling. Tears ran down his cheeks from his clenched eyes as his mouth tried to form words that he couldn't hear.

At a full sprint, I planted one foot on the bumper and was on the gunner's turret in a flash. Snoddy and his TC were banged up, but weren't bleeding. Snoddy was making a lot of noise, but not a lot of sense. Clearly the blast wave had scrambled him up. Keenly aware of the exposed desert around us, we got him down into the truck as quickly as we could. There was little to do for a closed head injury out here, and no way to quickly immobilize his cervical spine. Every second we stayed in this ambush made us more of a target.

The complex attack was becoming the norm in Ramadi—IED blasts to stop us, then secondary attacks with small arms and rockets to finish off our survivors. We had to be alert now—with a huge explosion to announce us and lots of sand dunes nearby to hide behind—and we were a long way from our FOB.

We were lucky: a dirt shower and a concussion were the only injuries, and the vehicle was not disabled. We raced back to the FOB and dropped them off at the hospital. A quick CT scan at Balad and a few days off were all that were needed.

We got a couple of guys out of bed and went back out there. This time we were lucky. The triggerman was nowhere in sight, if there was one. This was just an IED. No one took advantage of our moment of weakness as we recovered and evacuated our casualties.

We headed back out into sector and made our usual stops at our OPs, checking on the guys, looking out for trouble, checking the hot spots. Nothing unusual going on today, so by midmorning we headed into the village near OP 2 to try and track down the boys we met yesterday. The village was a flurry of activity, with families going about their business, herds of goats grazing in the dirt, women cooking in the concrete houses. We showed the pictures of the boys to a few people and they pointed out their house. Mom and big sister showed us where their school was, and we dropped in on them.

The boys we sought had played hooky that day, their teachers said, but we dropped off a few boxes of school supplies anyway, and tried to be as friendly as we could. An air of tension was palpable in the school—our presence upsetting the daily routine. I could not help but draw comparisons between this impoverished Iraqi school and our own elementary schools back home, where I often taught fire safety.

We gave up and headed back out toward the highway. On a whim we stopped at the ice cream store across the street from the local sheik's house. One of the boys was there, visiting with his uncle and at least half a dozen adult men. We spread out, initially, and gave every appearance that we just stopped by to shop. Some of the guys bought sodas, and LT even picked up a pair of sandals. We distracted the men with our shopping and our casual conversations with them—albeit in a combination of broken Arabic, limited English, and a lot of pantomime. None of them noticed our interpreter speaking fluently and quietly with the boy.

I struck up a conversation with the cashier. A portly man about my age, he wore a windbreaker in spite of the heat. He seemed very interested in the weapons I carried, and pointed at my pistol and K-Bar fighting knife. I bought a few things from him, and then I pulled out my knife and handed it to him, handle first.

This show of trust with a perfect stranger was extraordinary in its own right, and the men in the store were all impressed, but the lieutenant sitting down on the floor, taking his boots off and trying on shoes, was even more of a spectacle. These men just couldn't believe we were so naïve as to go shopping in the middle of their war zone.

The cashier felt the razor-sharp edge of my blade, and a quizzical look came over his face. He asked me why I carried such a knife. The smile left my face. Then, as I accepted the knife back, I drew it across my own neck. "It's for Irhabee," I said. The color drained out of the man's face as I uttered the filthiest slander I could call someone—a Godless terrorist. To the Muslims, Ali Baba was an honorable thief, and Mujehadeen was a holy warrior, but Irhabee was in it only for himself—a low-life despicable creature.

"No Irhabee, Mister," he replied, quietly. "IP," he added, almost under his breath. The cashier pulled back his windbreaker and showed me a Glock pistol, secured in a shoulder holster. He discreetly showed me his Iraqi Police ID card, held low behind the counter so that only I could see it.

After making our rounds again, we stopped in at the gate to our FOB, where we had a late lunch and took a break In the entrance's protected area, sheltered from enemy snipers and in view of the gate guards, but still able to respond in our sector.

From the entrance to our FOB, a massive explosion rocked the afternoon. A column of smoke was visible as we scrambled into our humvees and raced out toward the source of the blast. The crew of the medic track and 88 ran to their tracks, firing up the engines as SSG Jose Pequeno came on the radio, reporting that the Iraqi Police station near OP 2 had just been hit. He was describing the scene when his radio stopped transmitting. We were only two minutes away, and Voodoo Mobile and Mobile Wrench were right behind us.

While we raced to their aid, SPC Ghent was in the gunner's hatch of SSG Pequeno's humvee on the bridge at OP 2 when the VBIED hit the IP station. (The account here of Kent's actions during that fight is re-created from what he and Frank Sorrento told me up on the bridge during the fight while I dressed Ghent's wounds.) A few minutes later, a grenade hit him in the chest and fell into the humvee. He yelled "GRENADE!!" and sprang upwards out of the gunner's hatch. The explosion threw him clear of the truck, and he found himself on the ground facing a three-man rifle and RPG team armed only with his 9 mm pistol.

AK-47 fire lit up his world as SPC Ghent got to his feet. In an instant his pistol was in his hand and he charged right at them. The RPG fired, but did not explode. Ghent ran straight at them, firing round after round from his pistol.

Caught totally by surprise, Irhabee did not expect to be facing an American soldier charging at them, firing furiously. Ghent hit at least one of them, and possibly two.

Reaching the guardrail, Ghent raised his pistol and aimed carefully. Irhabee was much further away now, having fallen down a forty-foot embankment and landing near a car parked below. As Ghent's last round left his pistol and his action locked it to the rear, Irhabee turned and fired a burst at him. Burning hot pain shot through his left side and across his back as the bullet spun him around and threw him to the ground. Dozens more rounds tore through the guardrail inches above him and whistled by him.

As quickly as it began, the gunfire stopped. Tires screeched as Irhabee took off. Kent got to his feet and looked around. Blood ran down his back, and his legs were burning, but he could move. He ran to the humvee and stopped. There was his friend Chris Merchant, not moving. He was gone.

Running around the other side of the truck, Ghent found SSG Pequeno lying on his back in a pool of blood, his feet still in the humvee, his arms stretched out, deformed and broken. "Oh my God! They're dead!" he screamed. "They're all dead!"

"Ghent!" someone hollered from behind him. As he whirled around, bewildered, pistol in hand, there was Frank Sorrento and the crew from OP 1. "Get in!" Sorrento commanded.

Sounds began to reach his ears again, and Ghent realized he was taking more fire. "Get in the truck!" Sorrento yelled. "They're dead, Sergeant, they're all dead!" was all he could say as Frank grabbed him and threw him into the backseat.

"Go around to the north; get me up on that bridge!" LT commanded. SSG Pratt skidded the humvee off the highway onto the access road at full speed.

"Blackjack 31, this is 34, I've got two KIA on the ground and one casualty on board with me," Sorrento called over the radio. "I'm taking him to C Med, he's hurt bad!"

We rounded the corner at the base of the bridge and raced right at 34 in a bizarre game of chicken. "Hold up, I've got Doc with me, hold up!" the lieutenant commanded. We pulled up alongside Sorrento's humvee and I flew out of the back seat. Ghent opened the rear door of the other vehicle. The sound of gunfire was everywhere, and I could hear bullets impacting all around, bouncing off the vehicles, punching through the guardrails, and ricocheting off the pavement as they whistled by us.

"They're dead, Doc, they're all dead!" was all Ghent could say. I refused to believe it until I saw it for myself. His words were having a chilling impact on the other men, and I knew I had to snap him out of it. I grabbed him by both shoulders and bored into him with my eyes. "They're not dead until I say they're dead!" I commanded, as if death itself would obey me. Turning to the lieutenant, I said, "We've got to get up on that bridge, sir; we've got wounded men up there!"

LT and SSG Pratt let this sink in for a second while I turned back to Ghent. "Strip!" I commanded him. "What?!?" he replied. "I said strip! You're hit!" I yelled at Ghent. His pants were soaked in thick dark blood, and he was looking pale.

"But Doc, I'm not wearing any underwear!" the bashful soldier resisted.

"I don't give a fuck! Strip—now!" and with that, I started tearing his clothes off. The two humvees provided us cover, and I had two more casualties to attend to. This was no time for modesty.

Incredibly, Ghent's wounds were not life-threatening. A rifle bullet had hit him in the side of his rib cage below his armpit. The bullet struck just in front of his rear SAPI (armored plate of his body armor) plate, and tracked a route around the inside of the body armor, digging a three-inch trench through the soft tissue, just below the shoulder blades. There was a lot of bleeding, but the lungs were intact. I threw an Israeli bandage around him and tightened it as much as I could. There were only minor shrapnel wounds in his legs, with minimal bleeding. While I dressed his gunshot wound, Ghent told me what happened.

I threw him into the backseat of our hummer, and turned to see Lt. Golden running up the bridge toward our wounded soldiers. We were taking fire from three directions, and LT had just left the only cover we had. Sparks flew up off the pavement near his feet as he ran. "Get in and drive, Doc!" SSG Pratt yelled at me, and he began to run after the lieutenant.

I drove the humvee up the bridge and tried to shield SSG Pratt as best I could, but fire was coming in from everywhere. Ahead of us I spotted SSG Pequeno lying on the ground in a pool of blood, motionless. I assumed for the moment that Ghent was right. I stopped our humvee right next to Pequeno's vehicle, blocking the incoming fire from our east, with his truck covering our west. I grabbed my rifle and threw my door open. "Ping Ping Ping, Pop Pop Ping!" bullets impacted all around me. I slammed the door and took my weapon off safe. I threw the door open again, and laid down suppressive fire. I got out and moved to the rear corner of my truck. More rounds impacted, and my gunner began to open up with his .50. I looked to my northeast at the IP station, and it was in ruins. There were no people visible in the wreckage, and no muzzle flashes. I looked to the northwest at Sheik Achmed Abood's compound, and I could see muzzle flashes all along his roofline. I lined up my rifle and squeezed off several carefully aimed shots.

Every one of my magazines was loaded with a tracer every third round. I could see from my tracers that my rounds were going low. I switched to three-round burst and again lined up carefully aimed shots. As I walked my rounds onto target, with the barrel resting on the back of the humvee, some of the enemy positions stopped firing. I worked from right to left across the roofline, as the lieutenant was firing from the other end of Pequeno's vehicle. I stole a quick glance back at SSG Pequeno lying there and thought I saw him move a little. SSG Pratt was inside the disabled hummer, and called out that Merchant was dead. I wasn't so sure about Pequeno. I continued to pick away at the sheik's men. For the life of me, I could not imagine why they were shooting at us. I remembered someone telling us that Sheik Abood did not like Americans, but this was crazy!

Lt. Golden just kept blazing away. His rifle had been modified to fire on full automatic, and he was putting out a lot of lead. SSG Pratt climbed up through the gunner's hatch of Pequeno's truck and began working on the .50-caliber machine gun still mounted up there. I just kept firing three-round bursts at the roofline, eight hundred meters away. My CCO scope was useless at this range, but the tracers were just what old Doc ordered.

To the south, I spotted some IP vehicles rounding the corner of the sheik's compound. Each of them had a crew-served weapon in the back of it, and they were firing at us!

Incredulous, I adjusted fire. These targets were not as protected as the men hiding behind the parapet walls on the sheik's roof. Many of the IP officers fell as we lit them up. All of a sudden, SSG Pratt's .50 came to life. I paused for a minute and looked back at SSG Pequeno. Clearly he was still breathing, and we now had a lot more firepower on line with that .50 up and running. To our north, Sorrento's .50 was blazing away from the bottom of the bridge. One of the IP trucks burst into flames and exploded. I broke contact and spun around toward Pequeno.

He was slumped on the ground with his feet still in the vehicle. I dragged him out, opened his airway, removed his IBA, and opened his shirt to assess his wounds. I could see that his left arm was bloody, and he had a nasty head wound. My friend was breathing spontaneously, at a rate of approximately fourteen times per minute. He was unable to maintain his airway in the open position, and there was bloody fluid present in his throat. When I released the head-tilt chin-lift maneuver, he had snoring respirations, with difficulty breathing. I did a quick sweep for other injuries, determined that the bleeding from his left arm was not immediately life threatening, and began preparing for an endotracheal intubation.

The rovers from Charlie Company arrived next, and they dropped their medic off at the north end of the bridge before taking up positions along the road to our north and turning to engage targets. Dismounted, Sgt. James Morrisette, ran through a hail of enemy fire coming in from three directions to get to our positions. He appeared out of nowhere in the middle of hell. Moments later I heard the unmistakable roaring of the 88 recovery vehicle as it rounded the corner and charged up the bridge, .50-cal blazing away. Voodoo Mobile was right behind them. As we were working on SSG Pequeno, Lt. Golden ran over and told us he was out of ammo. I pulled all of SSG Pequeno's magazines out and handed them to the lieutenant.

Morrisette cut away the patient's clothing, and controlled the bleeding in his left arm. As I was attempting to intubate the patient, SGT Cole and SPC Hardy arrived with Voodoo Mobile. SPC Urban did a flat spin, placing the rear gate of the 113 near us. Little did they know that there was an unexploded RPG round lying on the ground, not three feet from their track. The 113 was under fire, and our forces were firing continuously with suppressive fire and engaging the enemy elements on the ground.

Like SGT Morrisette, SGT Cole and SPC Hardy proceeded through the enemy fire, dismounted, at great personal risk, to arrive at SSG Pequeno's side. Their courageous actions under fire are in keeping with the highest traditions of the U.S. Army, and reflect great credit upon themselves, their units, and the Vermont Army National Guard.

With Sgt. Cole pushing down on SSG Pequeno's neck, providing cricoid (pushing down on his adam's apple) pressure, I was able to intubate him on my second attempt. We confirmed tube placement by observing equal bilateral chest rise and tube condensation. SGT Cole reported feeling the tactile sensation of the tube passing beneath his fingers. Because of the noise of the two .50-caliber machine guns firing on both sides of me, I was unable to auscultate lung sounds. We loaded SSG Pequeno onto a folding litter and I called for suppressive fire. The guns began firing, and we carried him through an open area, while receiving enemy fire, to the rear gate of the 113, and loaded him in.

After Voodoo Mobile and Mobile Wrench left, we found ourselves alone on the bridge. I picked up my rifle and got back in the fight. Running low on ammunition, we continued to engage targets. SSG Pratt called out that there was UXO (unexploded ordinance) on the ground right next to his vehicle. He told me and Morrisette to pull Merchant's body out from the driver's seat and try to move the vehicle. SGT Morrisette provided suppressive fire and covered me while I moved Merchant out onto the ground. He was a large man, and it was all I could do to move him. Incredibly, the humvees started. I backed the hummer down the hill away from the UXO. Continuing to fire, SSG Pratt and Lt. Golden discussed abandoning the bridge.

I could not fathom the thought of SPC Merchant's body falling into the enemy's hands. I pictured the CNN images of the American contractors' bodies being hung from bridges in Fallujah and our dead helicopter pilots being dragged through the streets of Mogadishu. I considered the effect on the war effort and the effect on Merchant's family if such a fate were to befall him. I could not let it happen. I knew Pratt would not go along with it, so I didn't ask him. I grabbed Morrisette, hollered at Pratt and Golden for suppressive fire, and we took off running through the field of fire before they could object. Sgt. Morrisette laid down his own suppressive fire, and we ran about fifty to one hundred meters to Merchant's body. I grabbed him and dragged him backwards away from the UXO toward our vehicles.

Miraculously, we were not hit. Morrisette and I took Merchant's ammo and divided it between us, then got back in the fight. Almost out of ammo, and outnumbered ten to one, SSG Pratt was ready to break contact. When reinforcements arrived, he and SGT Morrisette took the disabled humvees and Merchant's body back to the FOB. The rovers from the Utah Army National Guard's 222nd Field Artillery arrived on the bridge, and brought us more ammo and water.

Lt. Golden proceeded to organize the responding elements into a co-ordinated attack on the sheik's compound, where the enemy fire was still coming from, and I remained with him, as his driver.

I grabbed some water and ammo from the 222nd, and lined up again on our enemies. Lieutenant grabbed my arm at that point. "It's OK, Doc, we're surrounded by friendlies." I looked down below our position and realized we had four American tanks online between us and the bad guys. Lieutenant gave the order over the radio that when the tanks saw muzzle flash, they were to answer with main gun rounds. The tanks lit up the sheik's compound with everything they had. The sheik's men were no longer a threat.

We heard a radio call from an unknown element at the IP station, reporting four routine casualties. Lt. Golden was too busy with coordinating the battle to respond, so I asked the 222nd lieutenant to use his radio to make contact with the unknown U.S. forces at the IP station, ascertain whether they had a medic, and see if they needed our assistance. I also asked the lieutenant from the 222nd to confirm that a medical evacuation unit was en route to the IP station, and I informed Lt. Golden.

When the reply came back that the casualties at the IP station had no medic attending to them and that they asked for our help, Lt. Golden had me trade places with the 222nd dismounted soldier, and the 222nd took me to the casualties. I assessed them and found no life-threatening injuries, and a competent combat lifesaver (CLS) providing care. The CLS had triaged the casualties appropriately, and identified the worst of them. Shortly afterwards, another medic track arrived, and I transferred care of these patients to them. I rejoined Lt. Golden as the attack on the sheik's house began.

We proceeded to the area near the ice cream stand, just north of the sheik's house, where a rally point was established, a perimeter was set up, and several detainees were being held. Lt. Golden dismounted and coordinated the battle, while I noted that some of the detainees were wounded, and attended to them.

One detainee, identified to me as an IP, had non-life-threatening wounds to his buttocks and upper thighs, and was complaining of a great deal of pain. These appeared to be shrapnel wounds, and I noted there was a burning IP pickup truck present at the scene. I directed the care administered to this man by a U.S. soldier, and administered 10 mg morphine, via auto-injector, into the man's upper left buttock.

I proceeded to another casualty, wearing partially melted nylon pants, with mostly second and very small third-degree burns to his legs. I had left my only pair of scissors with the combat lifesaver, and when I got to this patient I recognized him as the cashier in the IP station that I had met earlier. Without a thought I whipped out my K-Bar knife and began to cut away his pants.

"NO MISTER!!! NO IRHABEE NO IRHABEE!!!" He screamed. Suddenly it dawned on me that this traitorous Iraqi Police officer must have thought I was about to castrate him. I cut away the man's clothing, determined the wounds were not life threatening, limited to only 18 percent or less of his body surface. I administered 10 mg of morphine to this patient in the upper outer aspect of his right thigh, and left him in the care of the soldiers assigned to guard him, while I rejoined the lieutenant and we advanced into the compound of the sheik's house to coordinate the assault and search of the area.

After we stormed the sheik's compound, we found over thirty-five

The author and a soldier from Charlie Company treat wounded enemy prisoners of war following the battle of OP2. Photo by SPC Luis Beveraggi)

fighting positions with thousands of rounds of spent brass strewn everywhere. We had been outnumbered ten to one, and still prevailed. It was a miracle that we survived.

Lt. Harry Golden deserves the highest accolades, first for leading an advance through enemy fire ahead of the cover provided by the humvee I was driving to reach our wounded soldiers. He and SSG Todd Pratt engaged and presumably destroyed the enemy who were firing on our position. After our casualties were evacuated, Lt. Golden did a phenomenal job of managing numerous elements from multiple units, who arrived to support us. He coordinated an assault on the sheik's compound, from where we were continuously receiving hostile fire, and showed remarkable composure.

SSG Pratt and PFC Brevet were exposed to hostile fire from the waist up. With countless rounds impacting all around us, they remained at their gunner's posts, actively engaging and destroying the enemy. Lt. Golden, Sgt. Morrisette, and I also engaged the enemy with our rifles.

The entire crew of the Voodoo Mobile element proceeded into the middle of a firefight, directly into the enemy fire, to come to our aid, and evacuate casualties. SGT Frank Sorrento and his crew from OP 1, who evacuated Ghent off the bridge should be commended for their actions, proceeding alone into the fight, and directly into the enemy fire, to retrieve the wounded.

SPC Christopher Scott Merchant was killed in this engagement. SSG Jose Pequeno sustained severe permanent brain damage. He remained hospitalized for over three years.

Seven enemies were killed in the engagement, eight were wounded, and twenty-eight were captured. From the captured enemy prisoners, we learned that over 2,250 rounds were fired at us. The engagement lasted over forty minutes, but after the initial ambush, no additional U.S. soldiers were wounded or killed.

For our actions in combat during the battle of OP 2, SPC Ghent received the Silver Star; Lt. Golden, SSgt. Pratt, and I received the Bronze Star for Valor; Sgt. Morrisette, Sgt. Cole, and SPC Hardy all received the Army Commendation Medal for Valor.

BETRAYAL

Of all the bad things I had to face while in Ramadi, betrayal was the hardest. I could stomach being blown up and shot at, but when people we trusted betrayed us, that was the worst. In the case of the battle of OP 2, we didn't know who betrayed us, but it was clear to us that the Iraqi Highway Patrol knew this attack was coming. There was no other explanation for the absence of their vehicles, all three of their machine guns, and so many of their people when the VBIEDs struck.

As a matter of necessity, our leadership had to work with the local sheiks. In practice, they were the local law. The newly formed Iraqi government in Baghdad had little control over Ramadi, but everyone belonged to a tribe. Governments come and go, but family stays forever. When it came to getting stuff done, the local sheiks were the power brokers.

It was Sheik Abood's people who joined in the attack on OP 2, and whose compound we stormed in return. His people worked at the local Iraqi Highway Patrol station that was attacked with the truck bomb.

It was the Sheik's people who fired on us as we advanced up the bridge at OP 2 to get to our wounded. It was the Sheik's people in the IHP station who dismounted all three of their heavy machine guns prior to the attack, and just "happened" to be in the village when their station was attacked. These same IHP officers, who almost never ventured outside their station compound, always notified us and coordinated their patrols with our command. For them to be out in the village with no prior notice, armed with all three of their heavy machine guns mounted in trucks, was too much of a coincidence for me.

We tried to foster good relations with the Iraqi Police as much as we could. We knew the country would eventually have to be turned over to them, and we had to build them up before we could withdraw U.S. forces. When we saw them advancing on our positions, guns a-blazing, we were outraged. We all knew that some of the Iraqi Highway Patrol were insurgents. We did not suspect, however, that they were infiltrated to such an extent that they would use marked police vehicles to attack our position in broad daylight.

The thing that upset us the most was how quickly the sheik and his people were released following this attack. After the fighting was over, our platoon was relieved at about 1700 hours. We returned to the FOB with clear orders to get cleaned up and immediately write out the details of the encounter in a statement. We did so, and after chow we went to meet the helicopter that would pick up SPC Merchant's body—the angel flight. Lt. Golden and I were returning from the angel flight and had not turned in our statements yet when we learned the sheik and his people were to be released.

Furious, we went to the building where the prisoners were being held. In all, twenty-eight men were captured unharmed. Most of them were sitting outside handcuffed and blindfolded in the dark. Sheik Abu and his key people, however, were sitting in our dayroom, on our couches, watching our television, eating our food, and generally having a great time. They were not even finished being interrogated yet, and no one had even read the statements we wrote, when the brigade commander came in and ordered that they be released.

Lt. Golden managed to at least convince the powers-that-be to hold these men until our statements were read. The end result was the same, however—our leadership needed this sheik and his people to work with us, not against us. Our brigade and battalion commanders had a global view of this battle space that we could not see at the time. They knew that Sheik Bezia and his cousin Sheik Abood were key to gaining the upper hand over the insurgency in Iraq. The only publicly palatable explanation for what had just occurred was that Al Qaeda attacked the IHP station with a VBIED and simultaneously attacked our crew at OP 2. There was no explanation given for the IHP trucks attacking us, except that perhaps they might have been aiming at targets that we did not see. The subsequent investigation of this incident could not rule out a friendly fire incident between us, the sheik's people, and the IHP.

No explanation was offered at the time for why the crew-served machine guns were all removed from the IHP station prior to the attack. In retrospect, the IHP people who knew this attack was coming probably would have been killed if they tried to prevent it. Instead, they pulled most of their assets and most of their people out. The few who remained were in the back of the building, far from the blast. I believe the Sheik also knew of the attack and it was probably he who warned the IHP—after all, many of them were his relatives. It is very likely that his family was threatened and he was told to look away. He may not have orchestrated the attack, but he did not warn us.

Our platoon returned to our sector twenty-four hours later full of rage, hatred, and bloodlust. I wish I could say I was above these base feelings, but I was not. I was angry with the insurgents and more than anything, I wanted to hunt them down and kill them. I was dumbfounded at the actions of our commanders.

My demeanor changed after March 1. I had been attacked before, but never outnumbered ten to one and almost overrun. I had never been betrayed like this. I could not do anything about our chain of command, but I could certainly take out my frustrations on the insurgents we encountered. Before this incident, I would generally try to treat all civilians with courtesy and respect. No more. Being almost overtaken made me hard, being betrayed made me furious.

MORTARED BY THE SHEIK'S MEN

Shortly after the attack on OP 2, Lt. Golden and I were in the front seat of our humvee with Peshi on the gun. We were all fuming over the way our command had betrayed us when there was a huge explosion just off our right front fender. We took a dirt shower, but our vehicle was not damaged. I slammed on the brakes and just as I did, a second explosion occurred just to my left. We were getting mortared, and they were dialing in on our moving vehicle. The third shot was not likely to miss.

I gunned the engine and we scanned for targets. A third mortar landed just behind us as we raced ahead, out of the kill zone. There, in a field three hundred meters away, was a man throwing something small and tubular into the back of a bongo truck. "Contact! Nine o'clock!"

I whipped the humvee around, and our gunner tried to line up a shot. The Iraqi Highway Patrol station was in his line of fire. We could not fire without hitting them. The bongo truck raced behind the IP station and straight toward Sheik Abood's compound.

We had the advantage of paved roads, and moved quickly to intercept the bongo truck on the road between the sheik's compound and the IP station. The fields had narrow unpaved canal roads in poor condition, and the bongo truck could not move very fast.

We pulled around behind the IP station in time to see the truck turn and run the other way. Still we had no clear shot without hitting houses and businesses, so back out onto the highway we raced, passing the bongo truck just as it neared Sheik Bezia's compound. We stopped on the edge of the highway and watched as the man who had just mortared us got out, spoke quickly with Bezia's guards, and was allowed into the compound.

We had strict orders not to enter the sheik's compound, so we snapped a cordon in place around it, and called for permission to enter from higher headquarters. With three ways out and only two humvees to cover them, it was not perfect security. Within a few minutes, the gates on the far side of the compound opened and three separate vehicles left, headed in three separate directions. It was obvious the mortar man was in one of them, but we could not chase them all. On the orders of the battalion commander, we broke contact. He probably had frank words with Sheik Bezia in private about these attacks, but we were not privy to them. Bezia's guards followed the Iraqi custom of taking in a stranger in need. His guards did not have time to weigh the totality of the situation, and probably did not know that this guy had just fired mortars at us. He asked for shelter, and they let him in.

• • •

. . . Not long after the battle of OP 2, Lt. Golden and I were on patrol when we received a radio call from the battalion TOC. The TOC advised us that the Marines were releasing two hundred prisoners from Abu Ghraib Prison at the Iraqi Police station near OP 2.

Every once in a while we heard about a prisoner release in our sector. It never made sense—risking our lives day in and day out, gathering evidence on hard-core insurgents, exercising incredible restraint, not killing the enemy when we had the opportunity . . . and the Iraqi Court System sentenced them to only two months in prison.

Some of the members of B Troop, 3rd Platoon at Trooper Gate. (Photo by author)

Sometimes the prisoners were released not because their time was served but because there was some unknown political purpose to further by the gesture. To a fighting soldier, such logic was unfathomable. It seemed as if someone above us in the chain of command was a disgusting traitor, betraying us at every turn. The same spit-and-polish son of a bitch probably carried around a chest full of garrison ribbons and looked down his nose at the real warriors who dragged our dead assess into the chow hall at the end of a hard day at war, reeking of sweat in our blood-soaked boots. At least one thing was clear in this case: three of the prisoners were insurgents who should not have been released, and our battalion commander learned of the mistake and ordered their recapture. Whoever made this mistake, it was not one of our people.

How in the hell three very-high-value targets managed to mingle in with the others was beyond us. The name of every single prisoner released was sent ahead to our headquarters. It was our people in Ramadi who received the list and realized what was about to happen. Whichever authority approved the release either did not have any clue about the American lives sacrificed to capture these prisoners, or they just didn't give a damn.

Lt. Golden and I already felt betrayed after the Battle of OP 2. When they mortared our patrol and we had to break off pursuit, our wounds deepened. With this prisoner release, we were positively incredulous, and began to wonder if we were alone in our struggle to defeat the insurgents. It would be years before I could put aside my own anger and consider that our chain of command must have made their decisions in good faith, based on information and perspective that we did not have. I hope that they are someday able to fully appreciate the foot soldier's point of view.

We were ordered to intercept the Marine convoy at the release point, pick out the three men who should not have been released, and take them back into custody. I gunned the engine and we raced to OP 2, the very scene of the horrific battle only days before in which we had lost SPC Merchant and SSG Pequeno.

Our notification came late in the process. The military higher-ups purposefully waited until the last moment to announce prisoner releases. It made sense not to give the enemy time to set up an ambush. We knew the release was coming, but did not know who they were releasing until it was about to happen. After all, the prisoners' families were probably insurgents themselves—they just hadn't been caught or they were honored graduates of the insurgent catch-and-release program that some of us called the terrorist academy. Trouble could break out at any minute, and with hundreds of potential enemy combatants, it could get ugly fast.

I whipped into the Iraqi Highway Patrol station, and the lieutenant was out of the truck before it stopped moving. He grabbed the first marine he found and demanded to speak with their leader. It did not take long to find him. The marines did not know we were coming, and they were shocked. Their orders were to release the prisoners. Our orders were to recapture three of them.

The rest of us fanned out on the perimeter around the prisoners. With the lieutenant busy talking with the head marine, there were only three of us standing dismounted, shoulder to shoulder with the marines, our two gun trucks taking up positions in their perimeter.

The marine acted as if we were insane, to stand there with two hundred insurgents and their families in an open field. He would not allow his men to stay there any longer than it took to get the prisoners off the buses, and for him to get the hell out of there. (Hadn't we heard about the horrific battle on this very spot only days before?) He had no idea that we were the very men who stood our ground atop the bridge that day, outnumbered ten to one and almost out of ammo.

I was close enough to the lieutenant and the head marine to overhear much of their conversation. The two of them were yelling at each other at the top of their lungs now. Our lieutenant insisted that the marines stand their ground and help separate the three high-value targets out of the crowd. The marine basically told our lieutenant to go to hell.

At that, the lieutenant exploded. The prisoners were all off the buses by this point, and they squatted in the field, hands over their heads, waiting for whatever was about to happen next.

I stood at their front, facing two hundred insurgents, every one of whom was caught fair and square, every one of whom stood trial in an Iraqi court, was convicted by his own countrymen . . . and was about to taste freedoms to which he was not entitled.

The marines had their orders. They had no choice. They shouldered their rifles and walked slowly back to their trucks. From my perspective, I seemed alone in my willingness to kill every single one of them single-handedly. Mentally, I took stock of my weapons and calculated the number I could likely kill before they overtook me with their sheer numbers.

No longer satisfied with the basic combat load of 210 rounds, I carried at least a dozen 30-round rifle magazines, five 15-round pistol magazines, a couple of grenades, and my Marine Corps K-Bar fighting knife. I doubted I would live long enough to use the knife. Damn shame, too, for it was a fine blade, and deserving of enemy blood.

From the moment of my first contact with the enemy in southern Iraq almost a year earlier, I had struggled to get my hands on these filthy bastards, and to wrap my hands around the throats of every one of them. If it wasn't these men who took out 343 of my brother firefighters at the World Trade Center on September 11, it was their brethren. I knew full well that Al Qaeda was everywhere in Al Anbar Province, their treacherous tentacles reaching into every corner of this impoverished, chaotic mess. My only regret was that the traitorous bastards who ordered this scum released would not die with them on this day.

By the time the last marine drove out of sight, I was ready to explode . . . weapons ready . . . safety off . . . finger tight around the trigger . . .

I glared at them—some of these men probably killed American soldiers and marines. These beasts would suck the life out of their own children.

I held all of them in a cold, deadly stare. One by one I stared them down, making all of them squirm and wonder if they had been brought out here only to be executed.

One by one they faded. Not one of them had the courage even to meet my gaze.

AFTERMATH

For six weeks following the battle of OP 2 on March 1, I remained with the men of 3rd Platoon, B Troop. The group dynamic changed dramatically following that battle. There was a palpable split between those who wanted to pursue the enemy and those who did not. Both positions were understandable, but we were at war and we had a job to do. Lt. Golden, Peschi, I, and a few of the other guys were pushing the envelope and taking the fight to the enemy, but we met a lot of resistance from some of the platoon who wanted to put out the minimum effort possible. The result was a lot of tension, which permeated our days like a malignant cyst, only to come to a head six weeks later at the Battle of Low Water Bridge.

Real Stories from the Highway Patrol

Not everything that happened in Ramadi was bad. Some of it was downright funny. In the days and weeks following the Battle of OP 2, we were aggressive in our dealings with the local population. Our minds were made up: we would stop *every* car we suspected of carrying insurgents and try to gather evidence of their activities. In addition, *every* traffic stop we did became a felony stop: weapons aimed, thorough searches, and so on.

On one such traffic stop, we thought we had the mother load. A carload of wealthy-looking men drove by us. We pulled them over, as they fit the description of a known bolo (be on the lookout) vehicle. Lt. Golden and I advanced on the vehicle and commanded the driver to get his hands up and get out of the car.

The man was clearly flustered. He would take his hands off the wheel and the car would roll forward. LT yelled at him to stop and he would stop and put his hands back on the wheel. LT commanded him to get out and he just sat there looking dumb. In frustration, the lieutenant advanced on the car screaming at the driver to get out, and the driver got more scared and nervous with each passing second. Finally, LT reached through the window and yanked the driver out through it. As the startled driver was pulled out the window, his leg fell off and bounced down the road. There he stood, terrified, keeping his hands up and bouncing around on his one leg, with four of us all training our weapons on him.

Although we tried to remain serious, we couldn't contain ourselves. Howls of laughter erupted from our guys. We had not laughed in days, and we needed it. The poor man just stood there, dumfounded, wondering what we thought was so funny.

I gave up trying to keep up the tough exterior act. I picked up his leg and handed it to him. "Put your leg back on, and keep your hands up!"

He tried hard to do both, but watching him bounce around like a one-legged Tigger was too much to take. I broke down laughing, too. Turns out the men were not connected to anyone in our area. They were wealthy businessmen traveling through the area, and the one-legged bandit was their mentally challenged driver. Being pulled over at gunpoint was too much for him. Losing his fake leg in the process was more than he could take.

BOOGER AND THE BAD GUYS

After the Battle of OP 2, being mortared below OP 2 shortly afterward, and all the rest of the excitement we had, when our platoon rotated to the night shift it was a welcome relief. The nights on the highway were long, cold, and boring . . . just the ticket for a platoon worn thin by intense combat.

It was on one such night that Lt. Golden and I found ourselves out behind OP 1, taking a break. We had the radio on and the doors open, and both of us were a little sleepy. Somewhere in the darkness was our dog, Booger, probably asleep under a humvee.

The radio crackled to life, telling us that two Iraqis were just leaving our base and giving us a description of their vehicle. They were working for us, and we were to let them go by if we saw them. We didn't pay much attention, and got back to our conversation.

About fifteen minutes later, we heard Booger jump up and start barking wildly. She ran up over the berm and down toward the highway. The gunner on OP 1 called the lieutenant, to report that two unknown humvees had pulled over a vehicle down in front of their position, and had two Iraqi men jacked up. LT and I looked at each other and wondered if perchance these men were the same ones who just left the FOB. He confirmed the description of the vehicle, and we headed out to see what we could do.

There in the darkness were two marine humvees. We came around the end of our dirt berm in complete darkness. We all wore night-vision equipment, but we could see that the marines did not. They could not see us coming at all, but they could clearly hear us. Their gunner peered over the top of his .50 cal at us, turning his head this way and that like a curious puppy. When we got closer he started waving for us to stop, but we just ignored him and drove right past him and up to the two marines who had the Iraqis all jacked up.

There before us was the funniest thing I ever saw. These two marines were all serious and focused on the bad guys. They were itching to arrest them or shoot them, and were clearly proud of themselves for having caught them. They yelled commands at the men in English, while all around them Booger barked excitedly. She skittered in and around the marines' legs, while they tried to shoo her away and snarl at the "bad guys."

Booger hated the Iraqis. They smelled very different, and she knew they didn't like dogs. In their culture, dogs are dirty and mistreated. Booger was Iraqi, but had been raised by us to be one of us. She would protect all of our guys from the nasty-smelling Iraqis, and her definition of us included these ignorant marines. They dressed like us and drove humvees. That was good enough for Booger, and she instantly adopted them—even though they didn't know it.

Lt. Golden walked up next to the senior marine. "You're going to have to let these guys go; they work for us," he said quietly.

"I am not letting anybody go; these guys have AK-47s and they are out past curfew!" came the rapid-fire reply. "And who the hell are you, anyway?"

LT didn't bother to answer the marine; he just walked past him, and right up to the two Iraqis. He spoke briefly with them in Arabic, just long enough to confirm that they were working for us. They knew the right names of our key people.

LT told the men to put their arms down, handed them back their AKs, and sent them away. He turned to face the marines. They were furious, and protested loudly.

"Who the hell do you think you are? I need your name mister!!" the senior marine demanded.

"Look, who I am is not important. Those guys work for us."

"You? Who the hell are you?"

"That's on a need-to-know basis. We have a base a few miles from here."

The lieutenant just turned and walked away. I could not resist having a little fun with them.

"By the way, guys . . . we were never here."

I let that sink in for a second, then I called Booger over.

". . . and that's *our* dog."

With that, I scooped Booger up, put her in the humvee with us, and we drove off smiling into the darkness.

THE 20K BRIDGE LOVERS

At the far western end of our patrol area was a bridge that we seldom visited. It was about twenty kilometers from our FOB. On the far side of the bridge was another unit's sector, and they had to drive through our area to get there, so we didn't get out there much.

One afternoon we got a radio call that there had been an IED detonated near the 20K Bridge. There were no U.S. or Coalition forces injured in the attack, but the other unit (222nd Field Artillery, Utah Army National Guard) was requesting our help in setting up a cordon. We responded to their call cautiously, scanning the roadsides and passing vehicles for possible triggermen. As we got closer to the scene of the explosion, all of a sudden two men jumped up from the desert, got into their car, and raced off, heading south across the desert toward a parallel road a few miles away. We whipped our humvees over, off the side of the road, and gave chase. The little Kia could not move over the desert well, and we quickly overtook them. We had one vehicle to their right and one to their left. We had the advantage off road, but if they got to the paved road before we did, they might get away from us. We reached the other road just ahead of the suspect, and they turned toward us. I jumped the humvee up over the edge of the road and onto the pavement. We jumped out, screaming at the suspects and throwing them around. We were sure we had found the triggermen, and we were not letting them go. We had no interpreter with us, so the interrogation would have to wait until we got back to the base.

It took a lot of effort, but eventually their story came out. The two men were cousins and they were in love. They had gone out into the middle of the desert to an abandoned house for a romantic interlude. While they were at it, an enormous explosion rocked their world. They ran out and saw our humvees racing at them. They did not know there was an IED nearby, but thought we had attacked them. These two guys were not terrorists, but they were willing to risk death in order to avoid discovery. The younger of them was only fifteen years old, and they could not bear the shame of discovery in front of their family and village. We let them go.

B Troop on Patrol

One of the most frustrating things for a soldier to do is to sit on the sidelines while others fight. This was the case with the company commander, who had not been out in the fighting much since arriving in Iraq. He was a man of ambition, whose National Guard career meant a great deal to him. Very young at twenty-six, he looked fourteen. The tough inner-city troops from Philadelphia that he commanded found him annoying. They viewed him as a spoiled little rich kid from the suburbs—an only child with limited social skills who was desperate to prove himself. Most of the guys were OK with going into combat, but they were frustrated that the commanding officer (CO) did not listen to their advice well. They were concerned that he would get them killed through his mistakes.

We would listen to the CO sign on to the radio, using all the strict, by-the-book procedures that we had long since stopped using. We would wonder about the wisdom that the CO seemed to lack—he would scrape together extra patrols out of whatever troops he could find. It was not uncommon for him to roll out into sector with a couple of radio operators from the headquarters element, some civil affairs people, and a few psychological warfare (psy-ops) guys. With his ragtag band of misfits, the CO roamed the area looking for trouble. The guys he took with him were not accustomed to the area, and so they were at higher risk than those of us who were more familiar with the enemy threats we faced every day.

As much as the guys liked to laugh at the boss behind his back, I had to hand it to him: at least he had the balls to get out there and try to do some good. It was on one of these special patrols that the CO and his boys found their prey.

Lt. Golden and I were out on patrol near OP 1 when we heard the CO begin his radio ritual and debarked on his mission. We all joked about him and his hunt for irhabee. We had no idea where he was headed today, and did not really care.

"Blackjack X-ray, this is Blackjack 6, we are approximately ten kilometers north of OP 2 on Route Miserable, and we have found a military-aged male making a VBIED. We have detained him, and our interpreter is questioning him.

"What the hell is he doing way the hell up there?" Lt. Golden asked, rhetorically. It was bad enough that the CO was out by himself with only minimal firepower, but for him to venture so far from our area without backup was even more of a concern.

"Blackjack X-Ray, this is Blackjack 6, send the rovers up here to assist us."

"You've got to be kidding!" The lieutenant exclaimed, as I whipped the humvee around and headed their way.

We raced across the desert, taking a short cut that would save us time. It was a rough route, and our vehicles banged around, dust blowing everywhere. After almost fifteen minutes, we found the CO's patrol. He had three humvees, including a psy-ops team, a civil affairs team, and his own vehicle. There beside the road was an old car up on blocks, with all the glass gone out of it, the doors and trunk wide open. A young male, perhaps sixteen years old, was handcuffed.

The CO's patrol had found this young man working with cutting torches, taking everything out of the car except the driver's seat. This was a VBIED in the making, and the CO caught him red-handed.

The kid was scared. This area did not see many American patrols. Like many Iraqis who had never met us, he thought we were going to torture and kill him. He was so desperate to save himself that he rolled over on his entire village. He told us that there was a junkyard about ten miles north of our position where VBIEDs were made. He said the sheik in the young man's village hated Americans and that he organized all of the men there to work in his junkyard, making car bombs.

We had only seen a handful of VBIEDs in this area, but Baghdad was getting hit with them all the time. We bundled the kid into our humvee and took off. The CO got together with the lieutenant and they formed a quick plan. We would sweep into the village at high speed, spread our five gun trucks out to form a perimeter, and storm the compound with our limited manpower. What we lacked in manpower we hoped to make up for with speed and the element of surprise. None of us had a good feeling about this, since we were so far from the FOB now, in unfamiliar territory. It would take almost an hour for reinforcements to reach us, if they could even find us up here.

This was exactly what we needed to do in order to defeat this insurgency. In spite of the inherent risks, we were out there working the territory, developing our own actionable intelligence, and then leaping into bold action before the enemy could react to us.

We roared into the isolated village, and there to our right were the concrete walls the boy described. We pulled up at the main entrance, right in the middle of the village. Our vehicles spread out, snapping a cordon around this target-rich environment. Iraqi men were everywhere. They stood, frozen, mouths agape and tools hanging limp at their sides, while our guys swarmed out of the vehicles, yelling commands in Arabic.

Our gunner, Peschi, trained his gun inward, covering our guys and turning his back on the village. Told to stay with the vehicle, I got out of the driver's seat and did a quick visual sweep of our surroundings.

"QUIF! IRFAA EDAK!!" I yelled as I spotted at least twenty men on a rooftop directly across the street from the junkyard. The men all dropped their masonry tools and put their hands up. I covered them from my driver's door. There we stood while I tried to figure out what I would do with these prisoners.

"It's OK; you can put your hands down!" I heard someone call out in English. Incredulous, I turned and saw two marines walking up the road, weapons slung at their sides.

Suddenly, one of the men dropped down into the house, and people scurried everywhere in the shadows within. I saw an AK-47 dash across the doorway. "QUIF! IRFAA EDAK!!" I yelled at them.

"One of them inside has an AK!" I yelled to the two marines. They sprang into action, racing up the last of the hill toward me, just as a military-aged male sprinted out the back door.

"Get him!" I yelled, and the marines complied. The three of us ran after the man. He was young and in good shape. He ran like I've never seen anyone run before. We were weighted down with almost one hundred pounds of gear, and we were losing him.

He took a left and ran down a side street; children came out of no-where and joined in, running with him, making a clear shot impossible. The houses were very small, and an alley ran behind them. "Take the street, I've got the alley!" I yelled at the marines.

They followed the sprinter down the street and I dashed into the alley, hoping to cut him off. Shots rang out. From a gap between the houses, the young man emerged, still sprinting. I raised my rifle and aimed at his back. It was an easy shot—less than thirty yards . . .

". . . this is it," I thought to myself, "Do I take him out?" There was no one else there in that alley. No squad leader, no infantry, just me and the bad guy.

He really didn't do anything, I considered, he just ran away from us when I ordered him to stop. The AK flashing across the doorway was all I had on him, and it wasn't much—every house in Iraq had an AK. As far as I knew he was just a scared kid who panicked.

I lowered my rifle and kept after him. We got to the end of the block and there was a wide-open area. He dashed across it and ran toward a house on the other side. The two marines emerged from the end of the street.

"There he goes!" I yelled to them. The suspect led us through narrow yards, leapt over ditches, and finally disappeared into a house.

Chests heaving from the effort, sweat pouring off us in the desert heat, I linked up with the marines. We stopped for a minute to plan our next move.

"What do you want to do?" they asked me.

"We can keep an eye on this house and get some more guys here to take it down. Either of you guys got a radio?"

"No, do you?" The older marine asked me.

None of us wore our rank or name tapes. We didn't want to let the en-emy know who our leaders were.

"No. By the way, who are you guys?" I didn't remember there being marines on this mission, and it occurred to me we had not been properly introduced.

"I am Major Smith, with Civil Affairs; this is Sgt. Ricker. Who are you?"

"Civil Affairs?" I replied, shaking my head in disbelief. "Holy shit." Then I added, "Pleased to meet you, sir," smiling and extending my hand. "I am Doc Middleton—and I'm the medic."

CRAZY ABDUL AND THE CAMPER ROBBERS

I was driving for Frank Sorrento one sleepy afternoon when we took a break out behind OP 1, an isolated position high on a hill overlooking a remote section of highway, where we would often take breaks in relative safety. It was a long way across open desert from anywhere, and we all felt secure, knowing that no one could sneak up on us out there. We noticed a parachute flare go up from way out across the desert. It was not that unusual to see flares fired off now and then. We used them to warn traffic to stay away, and we used them to signal each other occasionally. It meant nothing to us, so we ignored it. About twenty minutes later, we saw another one and ignored it too.

Frank and I had the doors propped open and were half asleep when I heard him say something like "holy shit," and he got out of the truck. I half woke up and looked over in his direction to see him running with his pistol out. Twenty meters in front of him was an Iraqi with an AK-47.

"QUIF! IRFAA EDAK!!" Frank yelled at him.

The Iraqi was talking a mile a minute, and waving his hands wildly. He was not pointing his weapon at us, but was trying as hard as he could to tell us something. Unfortunately for him, our interpreter had the day off. With what little Arabic we understood, it was clear to us that something bad had happened. He kept pointing out into the desert, and talking excitedly. We were really frustrated that we could not understand anything he said.

We left Abdullah with the guys at OP 1, went back to the FOB, and picked up an interpreter. Forty minutes after he first showed up at our position we finally heard his story.

Abdullah was well known to Lt. Abe Begins and his platoon of B Troopers, but not to our platoon. They knew him to be a little crazy, but for reasons unbeknownst to Begins, Abdullah hated the insurgents and provided him information about insurgent activity in Tameem. Abdullah's information proved accurate, and it was very useful. He went out into the desert and found mortar launch sites for Begins. He even brought them an entire mortar tube with ammunition that he found. In return for his information, Begins's platoon protected Abdullah, and set him up in an old camper they found in the desert.

On the day that we met him, two men had shown up at his new home and demanded that he give them the camper. Abdullah shot them.

He claimed they threatened him, and he opened fire on them with his AK-47. He fired the flares given to him by our other platoon in an effort to summon our help, but we did not know he was trying to signal us. We ignored the flares, assuming that Alpha Company fired them at a vehicle.

When we finally heard the story, we were dumbstruck. We headed out across the desert to his house, not knowing what we might find when we got there, and we expected the worst. A platoon of tanks was at the firing range nearby, and we requested they come along for added security. There were two men lying there. One of them was already dead, but the second still had a pulse and some respirations. We radioed for an ambulance and I started to work on him. As we looked around, we began to take stock of our situation. We were alone out in the desert, a long way from our positions or reinforcements. We had one dead Iraqi and another one dying in front of us. These guys must have family, and they were all known insurgents. We expected a counterattack at any minute.

I worked hard to save the second man. He had been shot up pretty badly and lost a lot of blood. It was not long before he died. Our ambulance was still at least ten minutes away when he lost his pulse. I knew there was no saving him, so I cancelled the ambulance and said a simple prayer for him. It was not unusual for me to say a brief prayer for the dying, but our Iraqi interpreter was very impressed. He thought it was especially generous for a Christian to pray for a Muslim, and later told me how much it meant to him that we would work so hard to save this man who might be an insurgent, and that we would even pray for him when he died.

The family did show up looking for these two men, but they did not want to fight. Lieutenant Golden and our interpreter explained what had happened, and they accepted his word. They were assured that we had done everything possible to save the men, and even prayed for them when they died. I watched from a respectful distance as they offered up Muslim prayers for their cousins, then picked up their bodies and took them away. Afterwards, we all thought Abdullah was a dead man. He actually lived for quite a while before they came for him, but in the end he was executed. Another unit found his body dumped along a road in the desert. The men who killed him left a death note, stating that Abdullah died for helping the infidels and being unfaithful to Allah.

Crazy Abdul and the mortar tube he brought Lt Begins. (Photo by 1Lt Abraham Begins)

SATAN'S VILLAGE

The medical platoon received a lot of requests for forward support for larger missions. Often these involved deploying a forward aid station and an evac ambulance to support a company-sized operation. Typically the medics assigned to these tasks were not participants in the mission, and they usually stayed buttoned up inside their armored vehicles.

My role, and that of the other line medics with the infantry, could not have been more different. Our nighttime raid on one Irhabi village was one such event.

Military intelligence is not only an odd oxymoron but it is also a quirky, secretive business. Most of us out there actually fighting the war felt that intel normally only flowed in one direction—up. It was not really that the intel folks refused to share information with us, it was just that it had to be solid, confirmed data before they would put it out there for us to act on. Often the subtle hints and innuendos that went without corroboration were ignored.

This particular raid was quite different. We received a comprehensive intel brief on this village. There were numerous targets there, including an Iraqi policeman whom we knew to be a spy, a number of insurgents conducting operations against Coalition forces on a regular basis, and a sizable weapons cache. The surprising part for me was not that these elements existed, but that they thrived for as long as they did while we continued to gather more intel on them.

Finally, the time came for action against this insurgent cell. We assembled a company-sized force, augmented with a forward aid station and numerous trucks to haul away prisoners and confiscated weapons. The operation would be at night, and would involve members of several platoons. Our mission was to storm a house on the south side of the village where the known Iraqi Police spy lived, and to take him into custody—alive if possible—so that our intel folks could try to get more information from him.

I often worked with troops much younger than me. Sometimes, when they did not know me very well, they would size me up—twenty years older than them and fifty pounds heavier—and shake their heads in disbelief. It was especially entertaining when the young bucks were so full of themselves. This was one of those nights.

The kids were debating who would carry the battering ram when we assaulted the house. This particular platoon had not been with me in Tameem, conducting raids on targets like this with only half a dozen men. To these guys who patrolled the highway for a living, this was a very different and exciting adventure. None of these guys wanted me in any danger at all, and they had not quite come to grips with the doc being very much an active participant in the combat. The guy with the battering ram was expected to break the door open and then step aside while the other guys stormed into the house. None of these young fire-pissers wanted to be passed by while everyone else got in on the action.

I took one look at the bucks struggling for position, and figured out a way to get in on the action. I took the battering ram. It was heavy, and often required two men to handle it. I took it alone, and used all of my weight to slam it through the door. I just didn't bother to step aside, and I allowed my momentum to carry me through the door and into the lion's den.

We stormed through the place with maximum speed and shock effect. We had considered entering with high-explosive hand grenades first, but decided against it due to the presence of women and children. The men in the house were Iraqi Police, and were all issued body armor in addition to their Glock pistols and AK-47 rifles. If they wanted to fight, they were well equipped for it.

None of the targets ever expected to be taken down in the middle of the night in their isolated village. They did not have anyone on watch in this remote village, and none of them put up a fight. They assumed that once they identified themselves as Iraqi Police, we would consider them friends. They had no idea that we already knew they were spies.

We dashed through the house, grabbing one man after another and tossing them up against the wall in the front hall. There were only supposed to be one or two men here, but we found six of them staying there. Such arrangements were not uncommon in Iraq, with large extended families all living together in one house with frequent guests.

We corralled the women and children into one room on the first floor, and then turned our attention to a thorough search of the place. One of the Iraqi women just kept screaming that her child was still asleep upstairs. With my limited Arabic, I understood her. I went upstairs with our guys, and found a young boy, perhaps four years old, sound asleep in one of the bedrooms. I scooped him up in his blankets gently, and carried him downstairs to his mother. The kid awoke in my arms, took one look at me in my helmet and night-vision goggles, and started screaming "Ali Baba! Ali Baba!"

In this part of the world, Ali Baba was a term for an honorable thief. Thievery was generally tolerated, and there was honor in stealing from the rich to give to the poor. In common use, however, Ali Baba just meant thief or criminal.

"No irhabee," I told him softly. "Jundii American." Surprisingly, the boy calmed down. I delivered him safely into his grateful mother's arms. They seemed to know that we were not about to harm women or children.

Pile after pile of weapons, body armor, ammunition, and grenades were discovered in this house. These Iraqi Police had enough stuff in this house to take down an entire platoon. I worked with one of our guys searching, handcuffing, and guarding the prisoners. It was good to make a difference for a change. These terrorists took the cloak of righteousness and perverted it. I had nothing but respect for the police officers I knew back home, but these men had nothing in common with their American counterparts. They brutalized innocent people, and used their police powers to hide their terrorist activities.

We quickly finished our search and moved on to our next target. The house next door belonged to a man we suspected was the major arms supplier for the insurgents in this area. We knew for a fact that he was a major player, and hoped to catch him. Again we broke in the door with the battering ram, avoiding the high-explosive grenades that would have ensured our safety by killing everyone inside—too many women and children present.

The house was right next door to the mosque. We did a hard entry, and quickly gained control of the objective. The man was surprisingly cooperative. He sat down calmly while we overturned his house looking for weapons and explosives. There were none to be found, and he seemed overly confident. He must have heard us in the house next door and known we were coming. Somehow he managed to get rid of his weapons and explosives.

"Wheen rushasha?" Our lieutenant demanded, asking him in Arabic where the weapons were. He calmly pointed next door at the mosque.

Our rules of engagement forbade us from entering a mosque without permission from very high up the chain of command. A request was quickly transmitted.

The lieutenant and I stood in a room with the man of the house while our squad searched the rest of the place. Finding nothing, they turned to the room where the women were held. The women were brought out of the room and into the room where the lieutenant and I guarded them.

There were three generations of Iraqi women here, a grandmother, a mother, and her teenage daughter. The young woman was probably about sixteen or seventeen and she held a blanket in her arms like a baby. The blanket just didn't look right to us.

"GUN!!" the lieutenant yelled, ripping the blanket from her arms. I was on her in an instant. "Doc, search the women!"

I had already grabbed the first one and thrown her up against the wall. In a matter of seconds I threw the other two up against the wall as well. I was none too gentle with any of them, and quickly frisked them.

There was only the one gun. It was a World War II–era British Sten gun in immaculate condition. One of the early machine guns, it was effective and deadly.

We probably could have killed the woman who tried to sneak the weapon past us, but we didn't. In Iraq, a man would pay for the crimes of the family, and it was taboo to take a woman into custody. We detained him, but let the women go free.

We marched the prisoners from both houses to our detainee collection point—a large house on the other side of the village. Inside this large house was a motley crew of interrogators. There were Iraqi soldiers, civilian interpreters, and a few Arabic-speaking Americans.

We told them about the Sten gun and the large supply of weapons, and they took it from there. Our guys filtered out to the assembly area outside as they finished turning over their prisoners.

I was the last to leave, and I walked out alone. As I walked past one of our humvee gun trucks pulling security in the yard, the gunner on top was calling for the company commander on the radio with no luck. It struck me as very odd that a gunner would be calling the boss directly like this, so I stopped in the darkness and asked him what was up.

"I've got a man on a rooftop, observing our position. It looks like he is talking into a cell phone."

"So shoot him!" I urged.

The gunner hesitated. "But how do I know who he is?"

"Doesn't matter. He is observing and reporting our activities. That's an enemy tactic, now shoot him!" Still he would not fire. I clambered up the humvee to see what he was looking at, ready to take the shot myself, but could see nothing. The man had gone back inside.

I thought about that engagement later. What a contrast from the streets of Tameem, where there would be no hesitation. Even if the man was innocent, we could not allow the enemy to conduct tactical observation and report on our movements. He could be a dead enemy combatant or he could be an unfortunate bystander, but either way he would pose no more threat. When you are outnumbered fifty thousand to one, you can't take chances.

We maintained our cordon around the mosque, waiting for permission from higher headquarters to enter and search it. Eventually our request was denied. We packed up our prisoners and left. The insurgents lost the use of about thirty men for a few months, but in the end, they kept their weapons and the men were all released. Is it any wonder the fight continued for as long as it did?

It was not only the lush vegetation and knee-deep waters here that made Vietnam spring to mind, it was the utter mismanagement, the taking and retaking of the same ground, and the waste of young lives that left so many of our troops bitter and disillusioned.

SOLDIERS OF CONSCIENCE

As time passed, the Iraqi Security Forces (ISF) established more of a presence in our battle space. New Iraqi soldiers were recruited and trained by U.S. soldiers and marines embedded into their units. To our east, SPC Androsov and SFC Esposito's platoon of Rhode Island National Guardsmen often worked with the ISF, conducting joint patrols in the orchards and palm groves near Route Duster and the Euphrates River. On April 3, 2006, they were working together on a dismounted patrol mission to confront enemy insurgent activity approximately six kilometers northeast of Ramadi.

During their patrol, the platoon detected and engaged a small group of enemy combatants, south of their patrol in thick vegetation. A company of ISF gave chase to the insurgents, and they were drawn into an exposed area where an ambush awaited them. The insurgents sprang their trap, opening fire on the dismounted ISF elements using concealed and fortified machine-gun positions. While the ISF returned fire, they sustained a casualty, at which time they sent one of their soldiers back to SFC Esposito's 113 to get help.

Two of the four M-113s maneuvered across a canal to retrieve the casualty and provide security for SPC Androsov. The 113s drew immediate enemy machine-gun fire while SPC Androsov and SFC Esposito jumped out to stabilize and evacuate the casualty.

While Sgt. Borden's 113 engaged with .50-cal, Cpl. Moore attempted to fire his M-19 automatic grenade launcher. The M-19 jammed, and Cpl. Moore was unable to get it working again. He braved a heavy rain of enemy fire and climbed out the top hatch of his 113 to get the broken M-19 out of the way. He picked it up and tossed it into the track, replaced it with a 240B machine gun, and got back in the fight.

The casualty was shot in the arm and the leg, and Androsov could not see the wounds through all the blood and contamination. He had to improvise, and flushed the wounds with Gatorade before applying dressings to control the blood loss. Esposito ran back to the 113 to get a make-shift litter, leaving Androsov in an irrigation ditch with only a handful of ISF soldiers providing security. Esposito treated and stabilized another wounded ISF soldier that he found down near the casevac track, and then he ran back to Androsov's position with the litter. While he worked, the exchange of gunfire between the enemy and Coalition forces raged on. Two additional ISF soldiers were wounded during the exchange. One of them sustained a gunshot wound to the head and fell right on top of Androsov while he worked furiously to stop the bleeding on the first casualty. Suddenly, Androsov realized that the enemy was in the same irrigation ditch, only five meters away. He drew his 9 mm pistol and returned fire, eliminating the threat. He then stabilized the other two ISF casualties, and working with Esposito and Sgt. Chambers, dragged the casualties back to the 113.

SPC Aleksey Androsov's actions are a classic example of the incredible selfless bravery Army medics often display while under fire. For his actions that day, he was awarded the Army Commendation Medal for Valor.

Working with an entire platoon of dismounted soldiers, Aleksey remained truer to his role as a medic than I did. While initially I, too, had reservations about going on the offensive, I worked past them out of necessity, and became much more a soldier than a medic. Since I usually worked in the much smaller groups of mounted infantry, I might be one of only four soldiers to get out of the humvees and make entry into a building. There was no room for a noncombatant on such a small team, and I was dedicated to providing the absolute best medical care possible to my men at the point of injury. I was a firefighter first, after all, and firefighters always watch each other's backs.

In coming to terms with my decision to engage, I researched the restrictions on the role of the Army medic, as embodied in the Geneva Convention. I found that the limitations on offensive action applied primarily to medical officers, chaplains, and other noncombatants who wore distinctive insignia (such as the Red Cross) and did not engage the enemy offensively. The medical officers were permitted to defend themselves or their patients, but were not permitted to carry or employ offensive weapons.

I questioned my chain of command about the applicability of these limits on the enlisted medic who does not wear medical insignia or claim any special protection as a noncombatant. I learned that engaging in offensive action would only be considered unethical if I were to wear such insignia. I also learned that the lessons learned on the battlefield far outweigh Army doctrine.

In my year in Iraq, I learned that the insurgents would specifically target the medics, females, or officers if they could figure out who we were. We tried to blend in and look exactly like infantrymen, carrying the same weapons and fighting just as fiercely.

It is important to distinguish, however, that I fought out of necessity, given the small size of our mounted patrols. In Tameem I dismounted with three other soldiers, compared to seventeen in the palm groves. Had I worked primarily with platoon-sized elements in an environment such as Aleksey did, my conscience might have led me in a different direction.

My Last Battle

"Blackjack 31, this is Blackjack X-ray," came the radio call late in the evening. "Danger X-ray is reporting their rovers passing through the area found an IED on South Street, just outside the FOB. They request you take over the security cordon for EOD so that they may continue into their sector."

It was April 2006 and I was on patrol with a man I had come to respect and admire, Lt. Harry Golden. The strain of this combat tour was causing cracks in our resilience. We were worn down, the newfound aches and pains in our middle-aged bodies reminding us constantly that we could not go on like this for long. Some of the guys had figured out exactly how many more days we would spend in Iraq. Lt. Golden and I preferred to think about the impact we could have on Al Qaeda before we left.

We met the rovers from the Danger element (D Company, 149th Infantry) at the IED site. They were good guys, all of them— a unit of the Kentucky National Guard comprising entirely men who volunteered to deploy into combat, they had been relegated to a sideline role at Al Asad Air Force Base for most of the war. Only recently had they been redeployed to Ramadi to bolster our forces here. They took over some of Blog's space and a lightly patrolled area where the insurgency survived while C company stretched itself to the limit trying to chase them around in it.

There was a pressure switch stretched across the road in a shallow trench. The explosives were a shaped charge placed in the shadows of a high wall in front of a house. We set up our cordon and the Danger rovers moved on to their sector. While we waited for the EOD team to arrive, we talked about what to do with the insurgents if we could find them.

"There is no way those bastards set up that IED without being seen. I bet the guys in that house are in on it," I said to the lieutenant.

In the six weeks we had worked together, Lieutenant had listened well to my suggestions. We both took the fight to the enemy at every opportunity—and here was the perfect opportunity.

"You're right, Doc. After EOD clears the IED, we're going in."

EOD came out with the QRF. These QRF guys had a crap job. They were on duty all the time, and rolled out into sectors they were not necessarily familiar with only to stand around in the sun being bullet magnets while the EOD guys disarmed bombs. Always a target, and seldom a shooter, these guys never got the chance to go out after target packages, kick in doors, and bust heads like the rest of us. Tonight we hoped to change that for them.

EOD disabled the IED and we formed up in a stack on the door. This would be a hard entry—the not-so-nice technique we used when we strongly suspected the enemy awaited us inside. Just as we were about to kick the door in, we got an urgent radio call.

"Blackjack 31, this is OP Thumper, we have a boat in the water, approaching our position!" We were only a stone's throw away from OP Thumper, positioned under the MSR bridge on the banks of the Euphrates River. There had been several boats spotted drifting in the water lately. All of them had been empty so far, and we suspected that the insurgency was sending empty boats down the river near our positions to see how we would react.

"This is OP Thumper, we think the boat has three men in it. It is too close to our shore for us to see it or get a shot at it. Blackjack 31, can you intercept the boat on the other side of Low Water Bridge?"

"On the way!" Lieutenant replied, and with that, we were off like a shot. Gunning the humvee into action, we rounded the corner into view of the river in no time.

"I've got a boat in the water, just coming out from under the bridge!" Peschi called down from the gunner's turret.

"Doc, line us up for the shot!" Lieutenant called to me as I brought the humvee on line.

"Engage! Engage! Engage!" Peschi's .50-cal barraged the boat with a torrent of large-caliber lead. I jumped out the driver's door and observed the boat with my night-vision goggles as Peschi's bullets tore into it.

"You're a little high, aim lower!" I called up to him as I brought my rifle up. The stream of tracer fire lowered onto the boat and instantly the side of the boat blew apart. Dark shadowy cargo spilled into the water as the boat broke in half and began to sink. I could not tell what was in the boat, but whatever it was, it was destroyed.

"Blackjack 31, this is Saber X-ray, Blue Diamond Gate is reporting taking incoming small-arms fire!"

The last of Peschi's rounds were still impacting the boat when the first radio call came in. At first we thought they were complaining about our firing. With Peschi's gun quiet now, we realized we were not the only ones out here firing tonight.

"Blackjack 31, Blue Diamond Gate reports three heat signatures, and they are taking fire from small arms and RPGs. "

The front gate to Camp Blue Diamond was only about eight hundred meters away on the opposite bank of the Euphrates. Thick undergrowth lined the steep river bank, and tightly packed houses—filled with insurgents— filled the area in front of the base gates.

"We need to line up for a shot at them!" The lieutenant exclaimed. "Where the hell are they?"

"Let's get out onto the bridge for a better shot! Maybe we can draw their fire!" I yelled back at the lieutenant. I jumped back into the driver's seat, and drove the hummer out onto the lower bridge, stopping right in the middle of the Euphrates River—fully exposed to the enemy fire.

We had no cover on this bridge, but we also had the best vantage point from which to locate the enemy. All three of us got out and scanned for targets. We could hear the enemy AK fire in the distance, and Camp Blue Diamond was on the radio calling for help, but still no enemy revealed themselves.

High above our heads, our guys on the upper bridge used their thermal scopes to search for targets. One of them found the insurgents' heat signatures and lit them up with a laser designator. They called down to us that they had located the bad guys, but we strained to see their laser beam—visible only through a night-vision device. Finally, we spotted it. Peschi and I started squeezing off rounds at the enemy—over eight hundred meters away.

"Where are they, Doc? I don't see them!" The lieutenant called to me. I leaned across the hood of my humvee, the only cover we had, and lined up my red dot scope on the target laser beam with my night vision. "Just follow my tracers, sir!" I said to him.

With those words I unleashed the fiery rounds from hell . . . tracer every third round . . . a torrent of blazing rage streaming across the night sky, ripping apart the enemy flesh as the burning phosphorous left a trail of unquenchable flame in its bloody, shredded wake.

Long I had waited for this moment—month after month of being a target while the unseen enemy maneuvered to ambush us at every turn . . . taking life after life like an insidious plague . . . our medicinal weapons unable to locate the source of this infectious cyst. Finally, the enemy that so cleverly avoided us was in our sights—and I relished every burst as our weapons destroyed him.

The LT came alongside me and joined with my tracer fire. His rifle joined mine in a harmony of vengeance—raining down a furious scourge—and laying waste to the enemy beyond.

Both sides of this river of Babylon were lined with our machine guns, large caliber crew-served weapons guarding the walls of our two bases—Saddam's former palace to the east, his former Iranian death camp to the west. For an eternity it seemed these guns remained silent . . . the men behind them constrained to sit out most of the war on guard duty while we patrolled. An eternity's measure of frustration poured from the west with sudden clarity. At long last these well-oiled sentries unleashed their pent-up fury upon the forces of evil.

My own tracer fire guided these weapons to their targets. What enemy escaped my bullets they shredded with theirs.

High above us on the bridge, the artilleryman turned infantry brought his remarkable skills to bear. Like so many other New Hampshire National Guardsmen, PFC Jonathan Snodgrass volunteered for this deployment. He was assigned as a gunner on a humvee, manning a .50-caliber machine gun. But Snoddy had other tricks up his artilleryman's sleeves. Beneath his M-16 hung an M-203 grenade launcher—the closest thing to artillery that he could carry. Every chance he got, Snoddy practiced with his 203—launching countless rounds into the desert, hitting targets with incredible accuracy.

Finally, the moment of truth came for this New Hampshire Guardsman, and he launched round after round at the enemy. Flares lit up the sky first—the flares we all carried as warning devices against suspected VBIEDS, now being used for their intended purpose— turning the night sky into day above this bloody river battle.

The enemy lit up now, their shadows racing across the darkness as the flares flew overhead, a dozen gunners became more accurate. Methodically, we reconned by fire. Nothing was left alive in the killing field before us.

"I've still got the heat signatures but they're not moving!" came the radio call. Machine-gun fire rained down from all around. Within moments, round after round from Snoddy's 203 landed dead center in the enemy's midst—the high-explosive rounds blowing the enemy dead into the Euphrates River.

"Doc, check it out!" Peschi called down from his turret. I looked up to see so much gun smoke hanging in the night above him that he looked like a demon floating in the darkness. Below us the air was clear. "There! In the water!" He pointed.

In my year of war here, I had seen many men die. The lucky few among them did not die right away, but had time to reconcile with their maker as the life drained out of them. More than once, I had found enemy dead lying prostrate, in the Muslim prayer position, bowed down with their arms outstretched toward their sacred Mecca. Not in this case.

I looked down into the river of Babylon beneath us, and there in the icy water lay the symbol of Christianity—three men splayed out, face down, arms outstretched at their sides, looking like Christ on the cross. Aiming at them, I almost shot them up just for spite, but no, they were already dead—floating face down in the water, they could not breathe— and I smiled at their symbolism: of good triumphing over evil, of evil men crucified for their treachery, splayed out in the image of Christ. Better not to disturb them.

Back on target, my weapon spoke, belching out flame and lead as we raked the target—making sure nothing could survive there. Magazine after magazine I fired at them . . . treasuring every delicious recoil as my vengeance flowed. Hot brass rained down from the LT's rifle, searing my skin as the vengeance spilled from me, scorching my soul even as my spirits soared with treacherous release. Standing there in the middle of the Euphrates River, hot brass searing my neck, the blood of our enemy flowing in the biblical waters beneath us—in that moment, I was a warrior. Six empty magazines skittered across the bridge at my feet, at least five men were dead, and we had not lost any of our own. Our only wounds were the searing burns on my neck—and in our souls.

Many of our fellow soldiers thought we had carelessly opened fire on our own positions, that there never were any enemies out there that night. Our chain of command eventually concluded that our actions were justified, that we had foiled a complex attack on our bases, using land and water-based elements using IEDs, RPGs, IEDs, and other explosives washed away by the Euphrates River.

It took a long time before I was able to distance myself from my actions that night and during my year of combat in Iraq, and to reflect on them from an abstract, detached perspective.

LIVING DEATH

Most of the troops who served primarily on the FOB were somewhat insulated from the full effects of war. They too suffered in isolation from their families, and from the physical discomforts of serving in the desert, but they did not face the trauma of having to take the life of another. While they were exposed to indirect fire and the deaths of others, they did not face enemy bullets on a daily basis. The distinction between the troops who fought the fight and those who did not was almost palpable at times. The term "fobbit" was coined. It referred to those who lived lives of relative safety within the confines of the FOB, not unlike the hobbits in the Shire of Tolkein's Middle Earth, safe from the dangers of Mordor beyond their walls.

In most cases, I tried not to judge others. We all relied on one another to get this job done, and working hard in a rear-area job was honorable. I certainly had my own weaknesses and temptations. The people I lost all respect for were those who cowered in our shadows and refused to support the front line when we needed them. I remembered an old Shakespearean quote that my grandfather, a Canadian Army Reservist, passed on to my mother: "A coward dies a thousand deaths, the valiant never taste of death but once" (from *Julius Caesar*).

When we arrived in Ramadi, our task force was organized mainly as armor. In the armor, casualties are less common than in the infantry, and there is only one medic per company. In the infantry, immediate evacuation from the battlefield is not always available. The infantry generally has one medic per platoon, and sometimes one per squad.

Since we mobilized and deployed as an armor battalion, we only had the one medic per company, and minimal staffing in our treatment and evac squads. When we reached Ramadi and our brigade finally organized our forces the way we would fight, we found ourselves in a newly minted organization, the brigade combat team, with its mix of two parts infantry to one part armor. Suddenly our medical platoon found itself stretched to the limit as we had to find a way to provide one medic per platoon. We needed fifty-four medics, but we only had twenty-eight when we arrived.

Another quirk of this battle space was the use of organic transportation, whatever vehicle we had, for most casualty evacuations. There was little use of dedicated evacuation vehicles, and so our own evac section was reduced in size and merged with the treatment section to become the steady-state operations section. Like me, others of our medics originally assigned to evac were suddenly thrust into ill-fitting roles as dismounted infantry medics. The fact that they were twenty years older and fifty pounds heavier did not matter—we were all medics and the troops needed us.

With our own medical assets tapped out—pulling double duty in many cases, going on back-to-back missions at times—we turned to the brigade field hospital for help. They were fully staffed in their evac section, and did not really have a lot to do since the majority of the casualties were brought in by each unit's own transportation vehicles.

The commander of this hospital unit was not a Vermonter. He was from Pennsylvania, and he could not fathom sending his own troops out into the line of fire. He refused to send us any help, and many of our infantry platoons rolled out with no medics, or with medics who had to work day and night in order to fulfill our mission requirements. Our medics harbored a lot of resentment for the protected medics assigned to the hospital.

In reality, most of their medics wanted to help, but were rarely allowed to do so. Their officers would not cooperate. I wrote off their decision as wrong, but accepted it as something I could not change, and did not lose a lot of sleep over it. It was not until the end of our deployment that I was reminded of the trauma that these hospital medics, nurses, physicians, and staff had to endure day after day. Rear-area troops who worked in offices or other areas did not have blood on their boots, but these people did.

During one of my last few days in Ramadi, a mortar attack struck our base and mortally wounded two Regular Army engineers. From our vantage point standing outside our aid station, we thought the attack had struck the hospital. We ran over to see if we could help, fearing the worst. The casualties were already being carried into the hospital when we arrived. From my many trips into the ER from the field, I knew most of the hospital staff—at least casually.

I was dressed in my PT uniform (shorts and T shirt) and armed only with my pistol in a shoulder holster. I was quickly put to work trying in vain to resuscitate a young man who had taken his last breath. While we worked feverishly to save him, his buddy looked over from the next bed. Fully alert, and with seemingly less life-threatening injuries, the second soldier spoke with us and inquired about his friend, encouraging us to do everything we could for him. We promised we would, but we couldn't do enough, and before long the first soldier was pronounced dead.

Our surgeon was a regular parishioner at our weekly Mass. He was a high-ranking Navy officer of some sort, but I did not know his true rank and I remember him only as Joe. I just remember that he was a friendly and outgoing middle-aged man, a devout Catholic who genuinely cared for his patients, a real doctor in this age of uncaring. Ironically, he was a surgeon, known as the least personable of all physicians.

My friend Joe, the surgeon, had received many of the critical patients I brought in from the battlefield. He knew that I was a part-time ER and ICU nurse back home, and noticed how I was dressed. As we worked to save these men, he asked me if I had to get back to my unit. No, I replied, our tour was over. We were only waiting around for a flight home in the next couple of days, and I had nothing else to do but help him out. Joe invited me into the operating room, and I went in, assisting the anesthesiologist running the blood infusion pumps.

Joe had his hands full. The second patient had two collapsed lungs, various shrapnel wounds all over his body, and a nasty neck wound that would ultimately claim his life. The surgeon had help from another surgeon and a PA. All of them worked feverishly for hours on end in the operating room, inserting chest tubes, reinflating collapsed lungs, setting fractures, and suturing wounds. The patient seemed hemo-dynamically stable, and the atmosphere in the operating room was relaxed and casual. The medical officers were all on a first name basis, and my surgeon friend introduced me only as "Tom," an RN. They did not know I was an enlisted combat medic fresh from the streets. We got to know each other over the course of the next four hours. The patient's wounds were complex, and this was a battle we were clearly winning.

Finally, all of his other wounds were addressed, and it was time to repair his tightly bandaged neck wound. When the bandage was released, the patient began to bleed uncontrollably from his badly damaged jugular vein. We began pumping fresh blood into the patient. It flowed out as fast as we pumped it in. The surgical team worked feverishly to stop the blood loss. We infused the blood as fast as we could, and still the patient slowly deteriorated. We ran low on blood supplies, and the call went out across the FOB for blood donors. Troops lined up by the dozens, all giving their life's blood freely to save the life of this soldier.

More than four hours after he was wounded, having spent most of that time in surgery, this soldier succumbed to his injuries. The formerly casual, optimistic mood in the OR became very somber. None of us saw this death coming, and the surgeons, officers, medics, and blood donors who tried so hard to save this perfect stranger were as profoundly affected as if they had just lost their own child.

I always had my prayer book with me. As I had done so many times in battle, I prayed the Catholic rites of Viaticum for this soldier. The surgical team joined me in prayer. We had no priest on the FOB to administer last rights or to provide support to those left behind, so I did what I could for them. I did not know what else to do, but I offered to go to our tabernacle and bring the staff Holy Communion after we all had a chance to clean up. I showered, changed, and headed for the chapel. As I walked by the morgue, I found a soldier standing nearby, alone. He was a senior NCO, and just stared at the morgue building.

I stopped and stood there with him, silently. He hardly seemed to notice my presence. Eventually I put my hand on his shoulder and shared with him that we did everything we could to save them, and that we prayed for the soldiers before they died. He nodded his thanks, and we prayed together for his men.

"I raised him like my own son," he said. "He came into my platoon right out of AIT, and I raised him like my own. We survived all kinds of stuff out there, only to die on the FOB, doing construction of all things."

As he spoke, an ambulance slowly approached the morgue. "Where are they taking him?" he asked.

"They are bringing them to the morgue for now. They will be cared for, and tonight they will fly out together on an angel flight," I replied.

"Them . . .?!? Oh, God NO! Not both of them!! Dear God, not both my boys, Sweet Jesus, why?" The platoon sergeant knew that two of his men were hurt, and that one had died, but did not know the other man had later succumbed to his injuries. He collapsed on the ground, crying.

We remained together for quite a while there near the morgue, joined by the brigade command sergeant major, who always came to help when men where badly hurt. Finally, after what seemed an eternity, there was just silence. We said one more prayer together, and I left. The sergeant major stayed with him, helping him to regain his strength before he had to go back and break the news to his platoon.

I brought the Holy Eucharist to the surgical team. They received it with the most devout reverence, praying together for the repose of the souls we had just seen leave this world.

While we prayed together for the soldiers we just lost, privately I added my own prayers for healing the wounds that these medics were suffering. For the combat soldier, death was an expected part of the mission. We inflicted it, and sometimes we suffered it, but we usually prepared for it as part of a larger mission, and when the mission was over we returned to safety, able to let down our guard. For the support troops working around the FOB, losing a soldier to indirect fire was a totally random intrusion into their daily routine. They were not ramped up to expect it; they were working in their normal day jobs when suddenly their buddy died. For the hospital-based medics, doctors, and nurses, however, the deaths of others were a constant companion. While they did not kill others or face their own deaths the way we did, their pain and scars were more than most combat troops realize.

At least the U.S. Army did one thing right: they sent a lot more troops to replace us. During our time in Ramadi and the surrounding Al Anbar Province, we stretched our manpower to the breaking point, beating the enemy at every turn, only to lack the strength to hold the ground. When we pulled out at the end of our year there, we were replaced by a unit three times our size. Of course, the Army in its infinite wisdom would not send all of them at once, so there was much confusion as we turned over the entire area to two brigades to replace our one. The first two brigades were augmented by yet another brigade once we left. The incoming units abandoned even more of our hard-won territory as they limited themselves in many cases to only patrolling the territory that they would ultimately control and left their third brigade's future turf for them to win back when they arrived. As the new units took over the battle space, our FOB began receiving mortar fire once again from some of the very same ground that we had once owned.

The two regular army combat engineers died when the newly constructed wooden barracks they built was struck by mortar fire. These buildings were placed precisely where the enemy used to hit us with mortars most frequently, before our troops seized their territory and took away their launching area. The deaths of these two men never should have happened. The buildings should never have been there in the first place. The buildings should not have been hastily constructed out of wood, and the enemy should not have possessed the launch site they used that day—an area we once controlled.

Going Home

Our last few days in Ramadi felt hollow. We had spent the previous year fighting this war with every ounce of strength we could muster. Now we milled about, waiting our turn to leave. We had learned a lot about our battle space, yet many of the Regular Army soldiers who replaced us seemed disinterested in our information and experience as we tried to prepare them for their year of hell that lay ahead. We were National Guardsmen, after all, and they were Regular Army. The First Armored Division launched a major offensive against the insurgency after we left. They did some good, but they lost so many troops that they were rendered combat-ineffective and had to be relieved by the Third Infantry Division.

Our ride home started via helicopter. Routine flights took place only at night, and we waited in the wings in the late afternoon, wondering if the helicopters would actually take us out of there that night. With so much enemy contact, our aircraft were often diverted to higher priority missions. Even when the enemy didn't disrupt their flight plans, dust storms and other environmental factors would often prevent our helicopters from reaching us. We learned not to rely on others to deliver us from evil.

Our success was defined not by others, but by our own actions. Many of us would rather have fought our way out of Ramadi, using our hard-learned knowledge of this battle space and our own firepower.

Instead, we slowly stood down from our battle posture, packed our worn equipment and boarded transport aircraft as passengers for the ride home, leaving green young soldiers to die preventable deaths under the command of arrogant officers.

It was early evening as we sat together at the dusty helicopter pad, gathered en masse in full view of any snipers who cared to climb atop the Detroit Apartments. We still had our rifles, stripped now of the high-tech aiming systems that we carried in combat, and each of us carried one last magazine.

Many of the troops around me patrolled other areas during their year in Ramadi. Most of them had never been near the Michigan Apartments that overlooked our exposed position, kicking in doors and racing up darkened stairs chasing insurgents who fired at our base. Only a few of the relieved soldiers on the helipad that night scanned the rooftops as I did . . . yearning for one last target to appear before we left this urban battleground forever.

Reluctantly, I boarded the old Chinook, dragging my feet up the under-sized ramp left to us by men who drove tiny jeeps in yesterday's wars. I purposefully took the last seat, aiming the iron sights of my trusted rifle out the back door as we lifted off, leaving behind this horrible place that had claimed so many lives.

I continued to scan for targets as the dust clouds around us gave way to crisp open air, the windows faded into buildings, and Ramadi became a beautiful carpet of distant lights. I stared in wonder at the fading tar-gets below, wondering how many insurgents lived through our time in Iraq to end future lives.

Chill winds tore at my soul in the prop-washed darkness. My lungs breathed deep the cold embrace like a long-forgotten friend . . . harken-ing back to so many wintry nights at deer camp in the Adirondack Mountains.

I would have quit this watch an hour ago, I thought to myself, had I been still hunting deer in the remote mountains of home. Not tonight. Not tonight. I stared back at Ramadi as it slowly receded into the distance.

We landed half an hour later at Al Taqadum Air Force Base (TQ), a short trip but far from the violence in the remote desert sands. At TQ, we picked up our old familiar routines of transients, living out of a single duffle bag while we waited for our turn on the plane to Kuwait.

Our flight from to Kuwait could not have been more different. We boarded a cavernous C-1 17 Starlifter, and marveled at the world of our Air Force. The plane was pressurized and air conditioned, with bright lights, semicomfortable seats, real in-flight latrines, and a galley—much like a civilian airliner. It was a very flexible platform, able to convert quickly from troop carrying to cargo handling to mass medical evacuation platform and sky-mobile intensive care unit. The only thing missing was a cute flight attendant with snacks and in-flight movies.

The highlight of my last stay in Kuwait was Mass. I went in search of Glenn Woods, Jade Phillips, and Courtney Allen. Lacking the guitars they had shipped home separately, we got together for one last service in that huge air-conditioned chapel. By this time, I had learned to play much of their guitar music on the piano.

It was a different sound that we sang that day—beautiful yet mournful—with just my piano to accompany our four war-weary voices. Each of us knew this was likely to be the last time the four of us would make music together. In a mixture of sadness and joy, we thanked the Good Lord for being with us through this war together, for bringing us together as friends. We would each return to our homes and families soon, but would carry with us the lamp we lit together in his remote chapel . . . this beautiful oasis of air-conditioned comfort, surrounded by the savage sands.

We settled into our comfortable seats on the chartered jet for the ride back to the United States, half a world away. This was a real civilian airliner, complete with those cute flight attendants, in-flight movies, and snacks. A flight attendant stood at the front of the cabin giving us the brief presentation on how to fasten our seatbelts, don flotation devices and evacuate the plane in case of emergency. We all laughed when she made sure to ask us to please place our rifles on the floor, with the muzzles pointed away from the aisle. There was a round of applause as we lifted off, bound at long last for home. Flying home from war on a civilian airliner reminded me of how this war started in the skies above New York and Pennsylvania. I quickly lost interest in the in-flight movie and pondered our response to the attacks on the World Trade Center, the Pentagon, and Flight 93, and my small role in the larger War on Terror.

To a point, we can defend our shores, cities, and airports, but we must not be lulled into a false sense of security by negotiating with people who are bent on our destruction. We are facing an enemy which measures time in terms of centuries, not days. In the eyes of the radical Islamist, there is no dishonor in a negotiated peace if it allows him time to prepare for his next attack. He is not necessarily committed to peace, but may simply be looking for time and space to regroup. We must not be deceived into a false sense of security based on appeasement. The only way to be truly safe is to be strong.

There comes a point when diplomacy and deterrent measures alone reach their limits, and we must fight. In the face of an enemy such as Al Qaeda, there is no choice. Their most ardent members will not be persuaded to give up. They believe that all must convert to Islam or die. They will try to destroy us to their last dying breath. We are under no obligation to assist them in our own destruction. We had to learn to distrust people, to search out those who murdered and terrorized others, to accept the hard reality that we—that I—must kill such men in order to stop them. I also learned, however, that there are many variants of Islam, with different interpretations of the Koran. Only a small minority are extremists.

During my year in Iraq, I actually found much to admire about Islam. The religious fervor that I witnessed was impressive indeed. References to Allah permeated every sentence, and five different prayer sessions at all times of the day and night required an intense level of dedication. To me, as a western Christian, such devotion was truly remarkable. For so many people to become willing martyrs, their faith must have been very powerful. Still, I could not help but suspect that many of the Muslims who practiced their faith so visibly might be hypocrites—going through the visible motions of their faith, but not really believing in Allah. Some of the more violent Muslims reminded me of the biblical moneychangers that Jesus threw out of the temple.

I recall one brother firefighter asking me before I left for war if I was looking forward to killing. I was slow to answer, and another firefighter chastised him for even asking such a thing. I remember my answer, though

"No," I said to him, "I am not looking forward to killing. I have spent my whole adult life fighting death at every turn. I will kill if I have to, in defense of myself or my patients, but I do not relish the thought, and I refuse to take pleasure in it."

There had been a gradual de-evolution in me, from compassionate healer to dispassionate killer. As a soldier, I grew from an even-tempered and cautious medic to a willing stalker of evil. Perhaps paradoxically to some, my development into a warrior deepened my faith in God. The contrast was stark. Someone said it better than I, "No better friend, no worse enemy." Truly, this exemplifies the combat medic. On the surface it would seem to the uninitiated that these two beings, healer and killer, cannot inhabit the same soul, that the healer would commit the gravest sin by becoming the killer. Consider, however, that we killed others only out of necessity, and that when they were no longer a threat, we recognized the sanctity of human life, and provided medical care to the men who attacked us.

There was a stripping away of the superfluous when we entered the field of battle. The sanctity of life, spirituality, honor, loyalty—all these mattered. Petty thoughts fell aside, and we focused on our mission with an intensity unlike anything we had ever experienced.

In my retrospection, I concluded that indeed, the killing we engaged in was necessary and justified. There was simply no other way to stop those who attacked us and inflicted terror on the civilian populace. There is, however, one burning question that remains for history to answer. Did our use of arms produce chaos and disorder greater than the evil that had to be eliminated?

This question has yet to be answered. Certainly, we eliminated Saddam Hussein and the evils he committed. Unleashed from decades of repression, the Shiite and Kurdish minorities have engaged in retribution. In the ensuing chaos, radical Islam and Al Qaeda furthered their goals—at least for a time.

In my mind, there was justification in ridding the middle east of Saddam Hussein and freeing the Iraqi people from his tyranny. The effort was moral. There were mistakes made in the strategies employed, but no one, including our president, is perfect. From my perspective, we lacked adequate troops to secure the weapons caches located during the initial invasion, and we lacked both the troops and the presence of mind to secure the country after we conquered it. The resulting combination of a disgruntled population, insufficient security, and plentiful weapons gave rise to a well-equipped insurgency. Whether we agree or disagree with this war, each of us had a part in selecting our nation's leaders through a free and democratic election. Our nation's elected leadership—president and Congress, Republican and Democrat—all agreed to undertake this operation. Collectively, therefore, we have a moral obligation to see this through—to restore law and order to a chaotic land.

Were we sinful? No. We endeavored to defend a civilian populace from insurgents and terrorists concealed within it. This endeavor was complex, and the enemy was often difficult to discern.

Being a target for enemy snipers and bombers every day made us frustrated and callous. When the enemy finally showed his face to me and we had the opportunity to shoot back it was a welcome relief. Later, scarred by the loss of my brothers, betrayed by the same sheiks that our leadership befriended—ambushed, pinned down with our dead and almost overrun—I began looking for payback. This is where the thin line blurred between the justified killing of another in the defense of self or others and indulgence in immoral vengeance.

The enemy needed to know we were not to be trifled with. It was necessary to communicate our strength and our resolve. In the dark days following the battle of OP 2 and the Battle of Low Water Bridge, I came to learn just how creative Satan is. Never in my life did I imagine being tempted to commit murder. In the end, I firmly believe that I only killed those who deserved it, but I still recoil at the temptations I felt. I never mistreated anyone, and I honestly fought to improve the lives that I encountered over there.

I believe that one day each of us will stand before God and answer for our sins. I pray for all of our troops—that our moral compass leads us into his kingdom.

HOMECOMING

We flew through the night and approached Gulfport, Mississippi, almost twenty-four hours after we left Kuwait. We still had sand embedded in our uniforms and rifles. As we began our final approach, the lights came on in the cabin, and we raised the window shades.

Everything I could see from the airplane was so green . . . the Mississippi pine belt below was such a contrast from the desert . . . it was a shock to my eyes.

Our troops cheered as our wheels touched down on American soil. We walked out of the aircraft in single file and were met by a delegation of Vermonters who had come to greet us. Major General Dubie, the adjutant general of the Vermont National Guard, personally greeted every one of us as we stepped off the plane. He was followed by Vermont's governor, Jim Douglass, and a host of high-ranking officers and dignitaries too numerous to count.

Being back in America was such a shock. Not wanting to show any emotion, I donned my dark sunglasses and hardly spoke to anyone. I didn't really know any of these dignitaries very well and I didn't feel like engaging in conversation. Still, it was great that they made such an effort to welcome us home.

I had a few minor problems out-processing, and had to stay behind in Mississippi to take care of them while the rest of the unit flew home to Vermont. When I told Lisa I would be delayed, she couldn't stand it any longer. She boarded a plane immediately and flew to Mississippi to be with me. She landed in New Orleans and rented a car so we could get off base. We had a terrific weekend together in Jackson while the Army slowly worked on clearing me to go home. When the pieces all fell into place and they finally allowed me to leave, we went to the military travel office to get a plane ticket, only to discover that all the flights out of Gulfport and Jackson were booked. They could not get me a government plane ticket anytime soon, and told me to return to the barracks and check back with them each day to see if they could find me a flight.

Lisa and I were astounded. I had made it all the way from Kuwait in under twenty-four hours, but it might be days before I could go home to my children. We just stood there in shock for a moment . . . then slowly, I looked down at my discharge paperwork. Yes, the paperwork was in order. I was officially released from active duty and free to go; they just couldn't find me a flight home.

I thanked the travel office for their time, and we left. A quick phone call to Jet Blue and I had my own ticket home on a flight out of New Orleans, with my wife at my side. We landed in Burlington, Vermont, and got off the airplane without any of the embarrassing fanfare. I was still in uniform, but I'd had about enough of being a soldier for a while. We walked through the quiet suburban airport in the late afternoon, and were met by only one man. A Burlington police officer I knew was stationed there, and he alone welcomed me back from the war. With my wife at my side, and my own truck waiting for me in the parking garage, it was the perfect homecoming. I drove the truck home myself, and the rest of our family was waiting at the house. The kids were ecstatic, and did cartwheels in the yard when I pulled in the driveway.

Lisa had another surprise waiting for me too. While I was still in Iraq, we had talked about the camper we always wanted to buy, and how we wanted to travel the country. It was waiting for me in the driveway. A few days later, I bought a new truck to pull the camper with, and our family embarked on a month-long cross-country camping trip down the East Coast . . . together at last.

Our travels took us through western New York and down through Pennsylvania. I stopped in at Walter Reed Army Medical Center in Washington, D.C., and visited SSgt. Pequeno. I met his family—his wonderful mom and sister had remained at his side around the clock since he arrived, and they thanked me profusely for saving him.

We continued on down to the Carolinas, and worked our way back up the coast. We visited Cape Hatteras and camped at a military campground at Fort Story—where we swam with wild dolphins in the waters off Virginia Beach. We toured Washington, D.C., and visited Cape Cod before returning home. We stopped in southern Vermont and visited with Glenn Woods and his family before we finally returned home.

I took three months off from my job with the Fire Department and picked up a few shifts as an ER nurse at Central Vermont Hospital. I worked the midnight shift, where I had plenty of time to write this book in the quiet hours before dawn.

A dad showed up at the triage station one morning, and I was lucky enough to be free and at the nurses' station when he came in.

"Can I help you?" I asked.

"My wife is having a baby, and she needs some help," he said calmly.

"Right now?" I asked.

"She thinks so," was the reply.

We grabbed a wheelchair and went out to the parking lot. There was Mom, standing next to the car, legs apart, calling out to us. Her water had broken and her contractions were nonstop.

"OOOOOhhhhh!!!! I feel the baby's head in my bottom!"

I knew that she meant it, and wasted no time. She had a wet spot on her pants from the water breaking, and when I had her sit in the wheelchair she got right back up again.

Our charge nurse, Ted, was right behind me, and we each took an arm and started walking her into the code room. As we approached the door, she said she didn't think she could make it.

We got her undressed and onto the stretcher. Although the head was not yet visible, it would not be long. Dr. Wilson came in and checked her.

"Well, you are fully effaced and dilated. That's the head!" he informed us with a smile.

I looked over her knee, and I could see the baby's hair. There was no taking her upstairs; this baby was coming out very soon.

As Dr. Wilson slipped a gown on, Mom told us she had the urge to push.

"You go right ahead," I told her, as Dr. Wilson came around and got ready.

With just a little pushing, John Ramon Fernandez came into the world. He was doing great, with a healthy cry, and all his pieces and parts in order.

It was such a happy scene in the ER on that morning. We saw so much pain and misery there, so many people leave this world there, that when we bring someone new into the world, it is just incredible.

It was so calm. The crew we had on were all guys, but we were all experienced dads. Dr. Wilson has delivered over 140 babies. Ted has two children and Tom has a few. Lisa and I have three, and I delivered two in EMS before I was a nurse. Everyone just swung into it calmly.

I was actually sitting at the nurses' station writing this book about the war in Iraq when Mr. Fernandez walked in. Such a contrast, writing about memories of war when the arrival of a new life interrupted my sad retrospection with such joy!

I wheeled Mom and the baby up to labor and delivery with one of the L&D nurses. They were so happy, and thanked us all again and again. What a great feeling! John Ramon Fernandez came into the world in our emergency room at 5:20 in the morning. Mommy, Daddy, and Baby were just fine, and rested safely upstairs in the protective enclave of the labor and delivery ward.

I stopped in our chapel on the way back downstairs, and said a quick prayer for little John, asking God to bless him and his family, and thanking him for bringing life to us this morning.

In this surprise arrival of new life, I finally returned from the war— no longer a killer but a healer once again. For me and my fellow healers, people who tread through suffering and death every day in a never-ending struggle to ease human suffering, saving a life is surpassed only by the rare privilege of delivering new life into a loving family.

THE ANBAR AWAKENING

In the months after the Battle of OP 2, Sheik Abu Sittar and the other leaders in Al Anbar Province came to realize that Al Qaeda was perverting Islam for its own benefit, that it sought only to perpetuate violence, and that there would be no peace with Al Qaeda. Under Sheik Abu Sittar's leadership, the sheiks of Al Anbar Province began a movement they called "The Anbar Awakening." They turned their backs on Al Qaeda and began to work with the Coalition forces and the new Iraqi government. Violence in Al Anbar Province decreased dramatically. After a difficult campaign to eradicate Al Qaeda, the province is now reported to be fairly peaceful.

Sheik Abu Sittar was later killed by a VBIED right outside the gates to his compound—the very same compound into which the sheik's mortar launcher had fled. After his death, the Anbar Awakening did not fold, as Al Qaeda hoped, but it became stronger—more determined than ever to defeat the foreign-born terrorists who plagued their homes with their perverted brand of violent Islam. Sheik Sittar's younger brother, Sheik Achmed Albu Risha, took over as the leader of the Al Anbar Awakening.

In the fall of 2007, Sheik Achmed Bezia Albu Risha traveled to the United States with the key leadership of the Al Anbar Awakening. While they were here, they met with President Bush and Secretary of State Condoleeza Rice. To everyone's surprise, these sheiks insisted on traveling to Vermont to meet with and to thank the men of Task Force Saber for our efforts to bring about peace in Iraq.

Although I did not realize it at the time, our battalion played an instrumental role in bringing peace to Ramadi. While our leadership reached out to the Iraqi sheiks and government officials, we wielded a Saber of righteousness against those who would harm the innocent. It was both our strength and our even-handed sense of justice that Iraqis came to respect, and which brought them hope. Had our battalion and brigade commanders handled the sheiks the way we would have preferred after the Battle of OP 2, it is quite possible that the Al Anbar Awakening might never have occurred. By the same token, had we not responded with force to the attack, it is equally possible that they might have cast their lots with Al Qaeda. With the sheik's visit, I came to appreciate just how much Task Force Saber prepared the way for the Al Anbar Awakening. While Al Qaeda's indiscriminate violence alienated the average Iraqi, the contrast presented by the combat strength and measured diplomacy of our National Guardsmen set the stage for peace. When followed up with the additional combat power brought to bear by a surge of thirty thousand troops, our total force of soldiers, sailors, airmen, marines,

Peace in our time. A dove (the Christian symbol for the Holy Spirit) rests on one of our armored vehicles. "May the peace of God be with us all." (Photo by author)

and Iraqi troops brought a measure of peace to Al Anbar Province. The Al Anbar Awakening is now spreading to the rest of Iraq.

On November 8, 2007, I met Sheik Achmed Bezia Albu Risha at Norwich University. Reflecting on the healing power of forgiveness, I shook his hand.

"Salam Alekum," I said to him.

. . . May the peace of God be with us all.

GLOSSARY

5K—A section of Tameem that bordered the southeast border of our FOB, it was a hotbed of insurgent activity.

88—See M-88.

113—See M-113.

Abu Ghraib Prison—A former Iraqi prison used by U.S. forces to imprison Iraqis, it was the scene of now-famous cases of torture and sexual abuse of prisoners by U.S. Army Reservists.

Agaf—Arabic word meaning "stop."

AIT—An acronym for advanced individual training, the advanced skills training that each soldier attends after graduating from basic training.

AK-47—A 7.62 mm automatic assault rifle that began as a Soviet design, mass produced in many of the countries of the Soviet Bloc, and was adopted by the Iraqi Army. The AK-47 was issued to Iraqi civilians as well, and is extremely common in Iraq. Virtually every family has one. They are limited to one AK and one magazine per household.

Al Anbar Awakening—The name of the movement started by Sheik Abu Sittar Abu Risha a few months after the Battle of OP 2. It refers to the sheiks and their followers who realized that Al Qaeda in Iraq was perverting Islam for its own puposes and bringing nothing but violence and death. They led their people to stop supporting Al Qaeda and to work toward building a peaceful Iraq.

Al Qaeda—Arabic for "the base." The Islamic terrorist group that attacked the United States on September 11, 2001. Al Qaeda has small cells spread throughout the world, including a group known as "Al Qaeda in Iraq."

Allah—The name of God in Islam

Assalamu Alaikum—Arabic phrase meaning "may the peace of Allah be with you." Sometimes shortened to "Salam," it is accompanied by the placing of the right hand over the heart and a slight bowing of the head. The standard response is "Alaikum Am S'Allah," meaning "and also with you."

Auscultate—A verb, meaning to listen to and assess the sound of.

Babylon—An ancient city, dating back to the Old Testament, approximately fifty miles south of modern-day Baghdad.

BAS—Acronym for battalion aid station, the first echelon of medical care after the front line medic. In a traditional battlefield, the BAS would be located one to two kilometers or one major terrain feature from the forward edge of the battle. The BAS is staffed with a physician and a physician's assistant, and six to eight enlisted medics.

Battalion—A large group of soldiers. In the infantry it usually consists of four to five companies, including the headquarters element. The battalion is led by a lieutenant colonel, with a major as second in command, and a sergeant major as the senior noncommissioned officer. In addition, several staff officers, each with a respective function and a small staff of enlisted soldiers, are assigned to the battalion commander. There are sections for operations, intelligence, administration, logistics, air liaison, and communications.

Battle Captain—The officer in command at the tactical operations center.

Battle of OP 2—A pivotal battle that occurred on March 1, 2006, in the vicinity of Sheik Abu Rissa Sittar's compound, an Iraqi Highway Patrol Station, and a U.S. Army observation post manned by soldiers from my unit. The battle began with simultaneous attacks on our observation post and two truck bombs at the Iraqi Highway Patrol station. Our OP was on a highway overpass above Highway 10, which we referred to as Route Mobile. The overpass was the first one west of the Euphrates River on Route Mobile.

Battle space—An area of operations assigned to a given unit.

Blackjack—The radio call sign for Bravo Troop, First Battalion, 104th Cavalry, 28th Infantry Division, Pennsylvania Army National Guard.

Bradley—Short for Bradley Fighting Vehicle, it is the modern replacement for the M-113 armored personnel carrier. Improvements over the 113 include high-powered modern optical targeting systems on par with our best tanks, a 70 mm cannon, thicker armor, and faster speed.

Brigade—A group of soldiers, typically three to four thousand strong, it is led by a colonel. The brigade staff functions include operations, intelligence, administration, logistics, air liaison, and communications. During the Iraq War the brigade has become less singular in focus, and now comprises special groups of different types of units, designed to function as a single combat team. It is now commonly called the brigade combat team, or BCT.

C-4—A putty-like explosive charge commonly used by U.S. combat engineers, it is fairly stable, requires a blasting cap to cause detonation, and can be used like putty to form large or small explosions and to shape the explosive force.

C-117—A modern U.S. Air Force aircraft. It is a versatile and powerful workhorse, capable of multiple configurations, including as cargo carrier, ambulance, troop carrier, and combinations of the three. It is pressurized and air conditioned, and includes latrines and mess facilities (military jargon for bathrooms and kitchens, respectively).

C-130—An older cargo aircraft used by the U.S. Air Force, it can be configured for cargo or personnel, and features a drop-down ramp on the rear of the aircraft, through which vehicles and cargo may be loaded.

Camp Blue Diamond—One of Saddam Hussein's many former palaces, Camp Blue Diamond was used primarily by Saddam's two sons, Uday and Qusay, as a hedonistic pleasure palace. It was the scene of horrific torture, murder, and deviant sexual behaviors. Under U.S. command, Camp Blue Diamond was the location for the 2nd Marine Division headquarters.

Camp Buerhing, Kuwait—A U.S. Military base isolated in the Kuwaiti desert. It is used mainly as a staging point for U.S. forces traveling on into Iraq. It is desolate, barren, isolated, and extremely boring. The best thing about Camp Buerhing is that it actually makes U.S. troops look forward to going to war in Iraq.

Camp Cedar—A U.S. base in Iraq at which we stopped briefly.

Camp Navistar—The last U.S. base on the Kuwaiti side of the Kuwait/Iraq border. It is used as a final jumping-off point for troops traveling on to other destination in Iraq, and as a patrol base for U.S. forces patrolling the border areas of Kuwait and Iraq.

Camp Shelby—A Mississippi Army National Guard Base that serves as a mobilization center and training site (MCTS)station for units called to active duty.

Casevac—Short for casualty evacuation, it refers to vehicles that transport casualties, but offer no medical care while en route.

CAT scan—A high resolution x-ray capable of viewing soft tissue, it is the definitive test used to diagnose internal bleeding and other medical problems. The only CAT scanners in Iraq were in Baghdad or Balad, at one of two Army combat support hospitals.

Cavalry—A term originally adopted by the horse-mounted soldiers of yesteryear, it is a term rich in history, and is now used by modern mounted troops, some of whom ride in tanks, others in helicopters, and still others in up-armored humvees. The cavalry soldier is referred to as a "trooper" and the company is a "troop," while the cavalry battalion is known as a "squadron."

CLS—Acronym for combat lifesaver.

C Med—Short for Company C (Medical) Forward Support Battalion, 28th Infantry Division, Pennsylvania National Guard. C Med was a one-hundred-bed field hospital, complete with laboratory and x-ray facilities. It was augmented by a U.S. Navy field surgical team (FST).

Cobra—The radio call sign for Bravo Company, 109th Infantry, 28th Infantry

Division, attached to the First Battalion, 172nd Armor (Task Force Saber), during the deployment to Ramadi.

Combat lifesaver—A soldier trained as a medical first responder, he or she functions as a fighting member of the squad, performing their secondary medical mission only when the tactical situation permits.

Company—A group of three to four platoons, an infantry company is usually comprised of 80–160 troops, and led by a captain, with a first lieutenant second in command. The senior noncommissioned officer in the company is called the first sergeant.

Counter battery fire—mortar or artillery fire targeting enemy mortars or artillery.

Cricothyrotomy—An emergency surgical airway which involves cutting a hole in the neck through which the patient will breathe. It is used to relieve an obstructed airway.

DFAC—Acronym for dining facility, it is typically operated by civilian contractors on forward operating bases. It is similar to a "mess hall" which is typically operated by military cooks.

Dismounts—Infantry soldiers on foot, out of their vehicles.

Division—A large military force of approximately ten thousand troops, the division is led by a general, and includes all of the staff functions of a brigade, plus other specialized elements, such as artillery, which report to the division commander.

ECP—an acronym for entry control point. This typically refers to a semipermanent position, it can also describe a hastily constructed portable checkpoint often known as a "snap ECP." A variation is a vehicle control point, or VCP.

Eid—The Muslim festival at the end of Ramadan.

Endotracheal intubation—A medical procedure in which a cuffed tube is passed through the mouth past the vocal cords and into the trachea. The cuff is inflated via a very small air tube connected to a syringe. This technique is considered the "gold standard" of airway control, offering 100 percent control of the patient's airway, preventing aspiration and facilitating excellent ventilations.

EOD—Acronym for emergency ordinance disposal, it describes a military bomb-disposal team or technician.

Extraordinary Minister of the Eucharist—Also known as a eucharistic minister, this is a lay minister in the Catholic Church who is specially commissioned to administer the Holy Eucharist to the congregation, either to assist the priest with a very large congregation, or to bring the Eucharist to the people when the priest cannot be there. Catholics believe that the bread and wine at communion are transformed into the body and blood of Christ at Consecration during the Mass. Only a priest may consecrate the Eucharist, though it may be administered by the extraordinary minister.

Euphrates River—One of two main rivers through modern day Iraq, the other being the Tigris, which runs through Baghdad. The area between them is known as the cradle of civilization. It was in these verdant lands that the biblical Garden of Eden was said to be located.

Evac—Short for evacuation, it refers to removing casualties from battle and transporting them to a higher echelon of medical care. See also Medevac and Casevac.

Field-expedient—The military commonly uses this term to mean an acceptable improvisation to meet an immediate need.

Five-ton truck—A workhorse dating back to the 1980s, when it largely replaced the older two-and-a-half ton truck known as a Deuce and a half. The modern five-ton features automatic transmission, air conditioning, and a central tire inflation system, and it can be up-armored for the modern battlefield. It is not as maneuverable as the new two-and-a-half-ton LMTV.

FOB—Acronym for forward operating base, it is a temporary military outpost from which combat operations are conducted. The FOB typically has such amenities as hot water, hot prepared food and showers. Most FOBS in Iraq have heated and air-conditioned facilities, and may use existing hardened buildings, but do not normally include the construction of permanent buildings.

FOB Ramadi—The FOB where I was assigned. It is located on the northwest corner of the city of Ramadi, in the Al Anbar Province of Iraq. The FOB abuts the western shore of the Euphrates River, just downstream from the Route Mobile (Highway 10) Bridge over the Euphrates that we referred to as High Water Bridge.

Fobbit—A derogatory term used to describe soldiers who never left the FOB, it is a take-off on the little people known as "hobbits" in J.R.R. Tolkein's books. The hobbits lived in a peaceful and idyllic world of comfort known as the "Shire" oblivious to the evil that grew far to their south in a land called "Mordor."

Forsaken Stronghold—A remote outpost along Route Duster, it was constructed out of a house we took over and fortified with Hesco barriers and sandbags. It became a base of operations for an Iraqi Army unit augmented with U.S. advisors.

Glass factory—A huge factory complex with enormous twin smokestacks extending over one hundred feet into the desert sky, the factory and its twin stacks were located on the edge of FOB Ramadi, between the FOB and

Tameem. They offered an excellent vantage point from which snipers had a clear shot at our base. Our predecessor unit took enough sniper fire from the factory that it closed the place down, putting hundreds of angry people out of work—stopping the snipers but fueling the insurgency.

Haji—Arabic title used to address a man who has completed a pilgrimage to Mecca, it is used by the U.S. forces incorrectly as a slang term for any Muslim man,which often offends Iraqis.

Hesco barrier—Named after the company which manufactures them, Hesco barriers consist of huge cardboard boxes, reinforced with heavy wire mesh, and filled with dirt. The Hesco barrier is typically eight to ten feet high and about three feet thick; it offers excellent protection against small arms and shrapnel, but does not provide overhead cover from artillery or mortar fire. The advantage to the Hesco barrier is the ease of transport which the disassembled frame offers, and the speed with which it can be set up (of course filling it with dirt goes much faster with earth-moving equipment than with a shovel).

HHC—Headquarters and Headquarters Company.

High Water Bridge—Bridge that carries the four-lane divided highway known as Route Mobile (or Highway 10) across the Euphrates River on the northern edge of the city of Ramadi, in the Al Anbar Province of Iraq.

Humvee—The workhorse vehicle of the U.S. armed forces, it is a four-wheel drive all-terrain small truck, roughly the size of a pickup truck. It is commonly configured with four seats and a crew-served weapon mounted in a turret on the roof. Earlier versions lacked any armored protection, while later varieties included armor—often improvised in the field.

IBA—Acronym for Individual Body Armor, it was issued to every U.S. serviceman or woman. Equipped with armor plates known as SAPI plates, it was capable of stopping a 7.62 mm bullet.

IED—Acronym for Improvised Explosive Device, a field expedient weapon that can be fashioned out of a variety of munitions, it is the most lethal weapon used by insurgents in Iraq.

Ifah—Arabic for "open."

IHP—Acronym for Iraqi Highway Patrol.

Infantry—Soldiers who specialize in ground combat using rifles, machine guns, or hand-to-hand combat. Every soldier and marine is trained as infantry in basic training. For those who specialize in infantry, it is their primary focus, while support troops go on to specialized training in their respective fields.

Intraosseous infusion (IO)— A method of administering fluid to a patient via a needle inserted into the bone marrow. In adults this is done through the top of the sternum or breast bone, while in young children it is done through a lower leg bone, just below the knee.

Intravenous infusion (IV)—A method of administering fluid to a patient via a needle and catheter inserted into a vein.

IP—Acronym for Iraqi Police.

Irfaa-edak—Arabic for "hands up."

Irhabee—Arabic word for "terrorist."

ISF—Acronym for Iraqi Security Forces

Jundii—The Arabic word for soldier. Iraqi soldiers were referred to as "Jundiis" or "ISF," the acronym for Iraqi Security Forces.

Just War Doctrine—The criteria by which the Catholic Church defines when it is appropriate to conduct a war.

K-Bar—A type of fighting knife used by the U.S. Marine Corps, it is a strong blade, about eight inches long, and is carried in a leather sheath.

Kuwait City—The capital of Kuwait, occupied and ravaged by Saddam Hussein's Iraqi Army during the first Gulf War, it was liberated by U.S. forces. The U.S. forces traveling to Iraq and Afghanistan first arrive in Kuwait City and are taken by bus from there to U.S. bases in the desert. Flights travel from the continental U.S. to Kuwait City and back every day.

Litter—A device used to carry casualties, otherwise known as a stretcher.

LMTV—Light mobile tactical vehicle, a newer two-and-a-half-ton truck used by the U.S. military, it is much lighter and more maneuverable than the five-ton. The latest version features an angled cab that will deflect the blast from an IED, and will detach from the frame intact and carry the occupants away from the chassis if an explosion is big enough.

Low Water Bridge—A one-and-a-half lane secondary bridge across the Euphrates River, it is located adjacent to and beneath the High Water Bridge across the Euphrates. Low Water Bridge is only about ten feet above the water line, and its clearance above the water is so low that occupants of small boats have to duck to get under it. A U.S. observation post known as OP Thumper is located on the western shore of the Euphrates, beneath the High Water Bridge and alongside the Low Water Bridge.

M-1—The main battle tank used by the U.S. military.

M-4—The short barreled carbine version of the M-16A4, it is capable of firing either single shot or three-round burst. It is effective to five hundred meters.

M-9—The standard U.S. military sidearm, it is made in Italy by Berretta, and fires a 9 mm bullet. It is accurate up to fifty meters.

M-16—The 5.56 mm assault rifle used by U.S. forces. The early versions (M-16A1) used in the Vietnam War were fully automatic. Later versions (the M-16A2, M-16A4, and the short-barreled carbine known as the M-4) fired either single shot or three-round burst. The full-length versions are accurate up to eight hundred meters.

M-19—A crew-served fully automatic grenade launcher.

M-60—An older 7.62 mm machine gun in service with U.S. forces since the Vietnam War, it is crew served and belt-fed, accurate to a thousand meters, and capable of firing eight hundred rounds per minute.

M-88—A huge armored vehicle, it is the tow truck for tanks. The 88 has been in service since the Vietnam War, and features a turret mount for a crew-served weapon similar to the one atop the 113. It also features a small crane and an anchor mechanism, often used as a plow.

M-113—An older armored personnel carrier used by U.S. forces since the Vietnam War, we used them as ambulances, and in some cases, to carry infantry. The 113 has a turret mount for a crew-served weapon that can be configured for a .50-caliber machine gun, an SAW, a 240B, an M60, or an M19 grenade launcher.

M-203—A breech-loading single shot grenade launcher mounted below the rifle barrel of an M-16.

M-240B—A modern replacement for the M-60, it is a 7.62 mm machine gun, belt fed. It is faster and more accurate than its predecessor.

Magazine—The part of a firearm that holds extra ammunition. In most military weapons, the soldier carries several rapidly interchangeable magazines, and each holds a large amount of ammunition—typically fifteen to thirty rounds.

Main gun—The 120 mm gun mounted in the turret of the M-1 tank.

Marhaba—Arabic phrase meaning "welcome," it is secular, and appropriate for use by anyone, without invoking Allah. It is a regional term, used in Al Anbar, but not a part of classic Arabic.

Medevac—Short for medical evacuation, it usually refers to helicopters that offer medical care during transport.

Medic—A general term used to describe the Army's front-line enlisted medical specialist. The medic is trained to operate alone or in concert with a higher level of medical professional in a treatment facility. The medic can be an armed member of the fighting force, or an unarmed noncombatant. The medic is trained in a sixteen-week course delivered by the army. The training includes the same training delivered to civilian emergency medical technicians, but includes advanced trauma care and basic nursing skills.

MITT team—A small team of U.S. soldiers or marines assigned as military training teams for Iraqi Forces, to train and supervise them during combat operations.

Mobile—Route name for MSR Mobile.

Mobile Wrench—The M-88 day shift crew assigned to Trooper Gate, Mobile Wrench was the security element for Voodoo Mobile and the recovery vehicle for disabled tracked vehicles.

Mortar—A tube-launched, indirect fire weapon, capable of immense destruction, it comes in a variety of sizes, some small enough for a man to carry, others so large they must be vehicle mounted.

Mosque—The Muslim place of worship, equivalent of a Christian church or a Jewish synagogue.

MSR—Acronym for Main Supply Route, it refers to a main road used by U.S. forces for transport of logistics.

MSR Michigan—A four-lane urban boulevard that travels from Fallujah through Ramadi, and on to points west.

MSR Mobile—Known by the Iraqi name, Highway 10, it is the main east-west thoroughfare across Iraq. It extends from Kuwait to Jordan, and is similar in construction to a U.S. interstate highway.

Mujahedeen—Arabic for holy warrior.

Mutarjem—Arabic for "interpreter."

Muzzle—The end of a gun barrel where the bullet comes out.

Muzzle flash—The flash of light that can be seen when a weapon is fired.

Narcan—Brand name for a medication known by the generic name naloxone. It is an antidote for narcotic overdose.

Nasotracheal intubation—A medical technique in which a small cuffed tube is inserted through the nose, past the vocal cords into the trachea. The cuff is inflated via a very small air tube to which a syringe is attached. The technique is useful when the patient's jaw cannot be opened for an oral approach—such as in a seizing patient or a patient with a cervical spinal injury—but the patient's condition does not require an immediate surgical airway.

NCO—Noncommissioned officer, a senior enlisted soldier, beginning with the rank of corporal, who provides leadership and is often considered the backbone of the army.

Night-vision equipment—Light amplifying system that enables the user to see in low-light situations.

Night Wrench—The M-88 recovery vehicle and night-shift crew assigned to OP

4, then later to Trooper Gate, Night Wrench was the security element for Night Voodoo.

Ogden Gate—the Southeastern gate to our FOB, it led to Route Michigan and the Tameem district of Ramadi.

OODA—Acronym for observe, orient, decide, act. It is the process by which we find a target, face toward them, decide if they are a threat, and then act accordingly.

OP 1—A U.S. observation post located about five miles west of the Euphrates, on a low hilltop overlooking a vast expanse of MSR Mobile (Highway 10). OP 1 was staffed by three-man teams from B Troop, 104th Cavalry, in an up-armored humvee with a crew-served weapon on the roof. The hilltop provided a sheltered area behind it where the roving patrols could take breaks safely, concealed from the traffic passing by on the MSR.

OP 2—A U.S. observation post located atop the first overpass west of the Euphrates, above MSR Mobile (Highway 10). OP 2 was staffed by three-man teams from B Troop, 104th Cavalry, in an up-armored humvee with a crew-served weapon on the roof. To the northwest, OP 2 overlooked Sheik Achmed Abood's compound and the village beyond it; to the northeast, OP 2 overlooked an Iraqi Highway Patrol Station; to the southeast OP 2 overlooked several houses and a popular market known as the "fruit stand." Al Quaida, and local insurgents would frequently observe OP 2 and take video from the fruit stand. Video of the entire Battle of OP 2 was taken from this vantage point and aired on Al Jazeera, the Middle-Eastern news organization. Following the Battle of OP 2, U.S. forces closed the fruit stand.

OP 3—A U.S. observation post located in the median atop High Water Bridge, and directly above OP Thumper, it was staffed by an M1A2 Main Battle Tank from B Troop 104th Cav, equipped with a 120mm main gun, as well as .50-caliber and .30-caliber machine guns.

OP 4—A U.S. observation post located atop the first highway overpass east of the Euphrates River on Route Mobile (Highway 10), it was staffed by an M-1A2 Main Battle Tank from Charlie Company equipped with a 120 mm main gun, as well as .50-caliber and .30-caliber machine guns. The overpass was closed to civilian traffic, but carried Route Pacer over Route Mobile. Route Pacer ran south across a bridge into downtown Ramadi and then north to the farmlands and rural villages known collectively as Jazeera.

OP 5—A U.S. observation post located on the second highway overpass over MSR Mobile (Highway 10) east of the Euphrates River, it was staffed by an M-1A2 Main Battle Tank from Charlie Company equipped with a 120 mm main gun, as well as .50-caliber and .30-caliber machine guns. The overpass was closed to civilian traffic. To the south were agricultural lands and Route Duster; to the north were more agricultural lands and the rural villages known as Jazeera.

OP Thumper—A U.S. observation post located on the western shore of the Euphrates River, directly beneath High Water Bridge and alongside Low Water Bridge, it was a built-up position, manned by an entire squad from HHC 172's Mortar Platoon. Typically there was one 113 armored personnel carrier and two armored humvees at this position. There were several fighting positions on the perimeter of OP Thumper, equipped with various crew-served weapons, including .50-cal and 240B.

Paramedic—A civilian level of pre-hospital emergency medical provider, the paramedic completes approximately two to three thousand hours of training, including the advanced trauma skills practiced by the Army medic, but also subjects such as advanced cardiac life support.

Parish—An area or group of people typically served by one priest or small group of priests. In the Continental United States, a parish is usually one or more towns that share one church facility, and one priest. In the military, the parish is not always clearly defined, and it may include soldiers from several units who worship together.

PEC 2—An infrared laser sight mounted on the standard M-16 assault rifle, it projects an infrared beam of light visible only through night-vision equipment. It has two options, a pinpoint beam and a floodlight.

PFC—Private first class (rank).

Physician's assistant (PA) —A graduate of a two-year accelerated program of instruction covering advanced anatomy and physiology, pathophysiology, and surgery. The PA is authorized to practice medicine under the supervision of a physician. In some jurisdictions, the MD must be on site, whereas in other jurisdictions, including the military, the physician may provide only general supervision, and is often located at a location remote from the PA.

Platoon—A group of soldiers, usually comprising three to four squads, an infantry platoon is thirty to sixty soldiers, while an armor platoon is two to three tank crews, each consisting of three to four soldiers. The platoon is led by a lieutenant, with a senior noncommissioned officer next in command.

Pneumothorax—Air in the chest cavity, commonly known as a collapsed lung.

Post Traumatic Stress Disorder (PTSD)—A psychological disorder experienced by many returning combat veterans, it is characterized by nightmares, flashbacks, depression and in extreme cases, psychosis.

Quick Reaction Force (QRF) —A military force that maintains a higher than normal state of readiness, prepared to respond rapidly to unexpected emergencies.

Quif—Arabic for "stop."

Ramadi—A city of approximately 500,000 people in the Great Western Desert of Iraq, it is the capital of the Al Anbar Province. Established as a trading post at the intersection of the Euphrates River and key trading routes to Jordan and Syria.

Recovery Section—A specialized military unit that retrieves disabled vehicles from the battlefield. Recovery vehicles include tracked vechicles (M-88) that can tow tanks and other armored vehicles and wheeled vehicles (five-ton wrecker, HMMT wrecker, LMTV wrecker, etc.) that are used to tow wheeled vehicles.

RN—Acronym for registered nurse, the RN is a licensed professional nurse, who, having graduated from an accredited school of nursing (typically either two or four years in length), has passed a standardized licensing examination.

Rocket Propelled Grenade (RPG)—A shoulder-fired weapon capable of destroying an armored vehicle. Plentiful and cheap, it is not very accurate.

Route Jones—A four-lane boulevard which cuts across Tameem, separating the residential area on one side from the industrial area and Al Anbar University on the other.

Route Mobile—A four-lane divided highway very much like a U.S. interstate. Also known by the Iraqi name, Highway 10, this route extends from Kuwait, through Baghdad, past Fallujah and Ramadi and on to Jordan and Syria. Our FOB's main entrance poured out onto Route Mobile and was known as Trooper Gate.

Rovers—Short for roving patrols, typically performed using two humvee gun trucks with six to ten troops.

RPG—Acronym for rocket propelled grenade.

Rushasha—Arabic for "machine gun."

SAW—An acronym for Squad Automatic Weapon, also known as the M-249, it is a 5.56 mm, caliber fully automatic light machine gun that can be belt fed or magazine fed. It is light and maneuverable, and can be shoulder-fired or used with a bipod. It is considerably lighter than its predecessor, the M60, more accurate, and can fire faster.

SFC—Sergeant First Class (rank).

Sheik—The tribal leader of a family clan in Iraq. With different forms of government coming and going over the last century, the sheiks were often the only consistent leadership. The sheiks are often very powerful, controlling most of the politics and commerce in their areas.

Shiite—The second largest denomination of Islam. The dominant faith in Iran and south-eastern Iraq.

Shrapnel—Pieces of debris, often metal, that fly through the air at a high rate of speed following an explosion.

Shukran—Arabic word for "thank you."

Small arms—A general description typically used to describe weapons that can be hand carried and hand fired.

Squad—A small team, generally eight to ten soldiers, it is the smallest unit of organization, and is typically led by a noncommissioned officer.

SPC—Specialist (rank).

SSG—Staff sergeant (rank).

Steady-state operations section—Term used to describe the combined treatment and evacuation sections.

Sunni—The largest denomination of Islam.

Support Platoon—Part of HHC, tasked with delivering support and supplies.

SWA hut—An acronym for a type of hastily constructed 8 x 8 plywood shack known as a "South West Asia" hut, it is used throughout the Iraq theatre of operations as temporary housing. SWA huts typically have at least minimal electrical service and air conditioning, both typically powered by generators.

Tameem District—A section of Ramadi that lies west of the Euphrates River, it is the hotbed of the insurgency. It was once military housing for Saddam's Republican Guard. Many of these soldiers simply went home when we invaded in 2003. They formed the backbone of the insurgency.

Task force—A temporary military unit organized around a task. The task force usually comprises smaller subordinate units brought together for a special purpose.

Task Force Saber—A task force primarily comprising HHC and C Company, 1st Battalion, of the 172nd Armor and A Company, 3rd Battalion, of the 172nd Infantry, Task Force Saber deployed to Ramadi Iraq from June 2005 until June 2006. Other units assigned to 1/172nd included B Company, 109th Infantry, Pennsylvania National Guard, Delta Company, 149th Infantry, Kentucky National Guard, a platoon from the 876th Engineer Battalion, Rhode Island National Guard, and two companies from the Iraqi Army. There were over nine hundred men assigned to Task Force Saber at its peak, and it was responsible for combat operations, counterinsurgency operations, and training the Iraqi Army.

TC—Acronym for track commander, it is also used to refer to the vehicle commander in a wheeled vehicle.

TOC—Acronym for Tactical Operations Center, it is the nerve center of the battalion.

Tourniquet—A constricting band, wrapped tightly around an arm or leg to stop bleeding by cutting off all blood supply to the affected area. It can be made from a variety of field-expedient materials. In our case, we used regular ratcheted cargo straps from a hardware store cut to length. They were donated by a volunteer fire company in rural Western Pennsylvania.

Track—A tracked armored vehicle.

Trauma—An injury. In common usage, trauma usually refers to significant injury to multiple organ systems in the body.

Triage—a french term, meaning to "sort." Used in medical circles to describe the process of sorting casualties and deciding which to care for first (immediate), who can wait (delayed), and who is beyond hope (expectant)

Trooper Gate—The main entrance to FOB Ramadi. It is located just a short distance from the Euphrates River on MSR Mobile. There is heavy security at this entrance, provided by the Utah Army National Guard's 2/222nd Field Artillery.

Trooper Record—The outermost defenses at Trooper geto, this position overlooked MSR Mobile.

Up-armored—A vehicle fitted with after-market armor, often improvised.

UXO—Acronym for unexploded ordinance.

VBIED—Acronym for vehicle borne improvised explosive device (a car bomb). It is pronounced Veebid, and describes a method of placing an explosive near our forces using a vehicle. VBIEDs can be parked and remotely detonated or can be driven into their target by a driver who then dies in the explosion (SVBIED or suicide VBIED)

VCP—Acronym for vehicle control point, it can refer to a semipermanent checkpoint or a hastily constructed portable checkpoint, sometimes referred to as a "snap VCP."

Voodoo Mobile—The M-113 ambulance and day-shift crew stationed at OP 4, later moved to Trooper Gate. Night Voodoo refers to the same 113 ambulance with the night-shift crew.

Voodoo Platoon—The 1/172nd armor medical platoon.

Wheen—Arabic for "where."

INDEX